Horatio Greenough: An American Sculptor's Drawings

DISTRIBUTED BY UNIVERSITY PRESS OF NEW ENGLAND

HANOVER AND LONDON

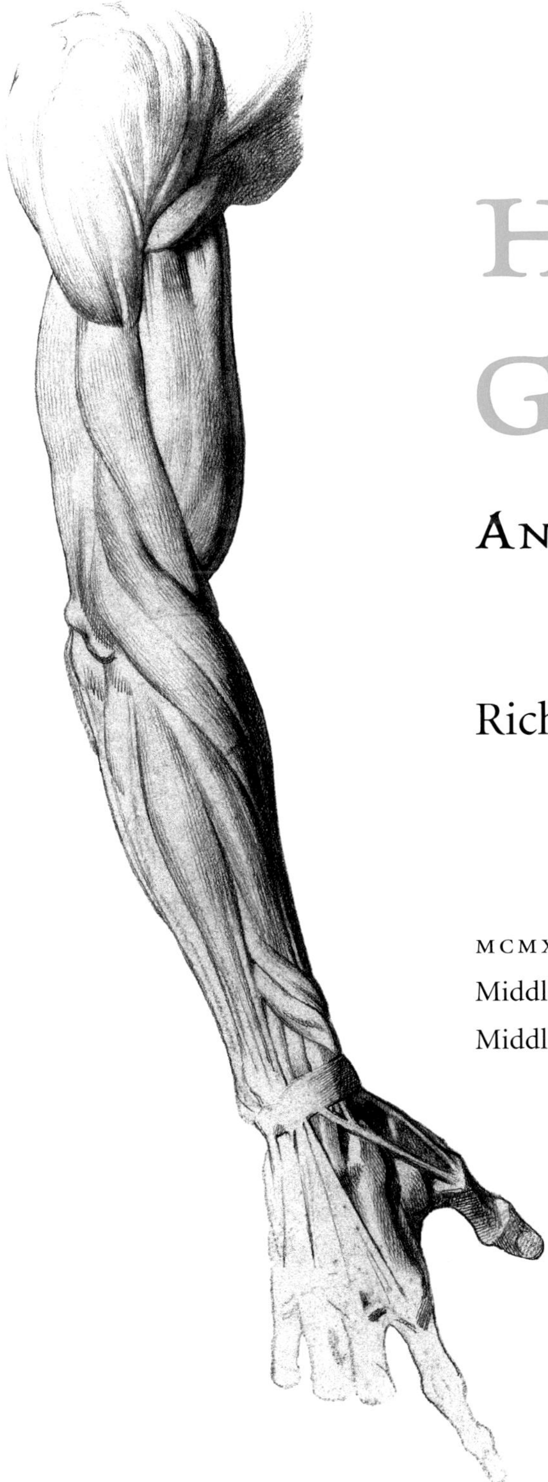

HORATIO GREENOUGH

An American Sculptor's Drawings

Richard H. Saunders

MCMXCIX
Middlebury College Museum of Art
Middlebury, Vermont

This catalogue accompanies the exhibition *Horatio Greenough: An American Sculptor's Drawings* on view at the Middlebury College Museum of Art, 14 September–12 December 1999.

Published by the Middlebury College Museum of Art
Middlebury, Vermont.

Library of Congress
Catalog Card Number 99-29965
ISBN 1-928825-00-1 (paperbound)

Drawings photography by Ken Burris
Edited by Fronia W. Simpson
Indexed by Norma Roberts

Printed by The Stinehour Press
Design by Christopher Kuntze

Distributed by University Press of New England, Hanover and London

Front cover: Study for *George Washington* (detail), c. 1834–35, cat. 54.
Back cover: Unknown, possibly John Adams Whipple, *Horatio Greenough*, 1852, cat. 66.
Title page: Musculature of the arm and hand, after a cast, 1832, cat. 10.

DEDICATED TO

George R. Rinhart

Contents

Foreword and Acknowledgments

Were it not for the indefatigable nature of Nathalia Wright, Horatio Greenough's biographer, the art-historical world would very likely be without most of the drawings and at least one of the sculptures that make up this study. Louis Pasteur once wrote, "In the fields of observation, chance favors only the mind that is prepared." No scholar was more prepared and determined to track down every lead, no matter how seemingly tangential, to ferret out the image of Horatio Greenough that we have today.

Wright first became interested in Greenough while studying at Yale in 1948–49, and during the succeeding decade her sleuthing and eventually her travels led her to contact numerous descendants of Horatio Greenough. Many of these elicited the polite but unhelpful replies familiar to many art historians. But when Wright contacted Mrs. Marguerite W. Horton of La Tour de Peilz, Switzerland, the granddaughter of Richard Greenough, Horatio's younger brother, she discovered a gold mine. There, in a rambling villa called Petit Sully, she found the long-forgotten, extensive correspondence, drawings, sculpture, and related memorabilia of the artist. Over the next three decades, during which Wright was able to purchase the Petit Sully collection, she continued to interpret and champion the sculptor and his writings.

In the last two decades other historians have added to our understanding of Greenough, while simultaneously the Petit Sully collection acquired by Wright has passed to George R. Rinhart, this nation's preeminent collector of photography. His interest in Greenough began with his wish to locate the daguerreotype of the sculptor owned by Wright and which is included in this exhibition. And once acquainted with the diversity of the Greenough collection, Rinhart quickly grasped its unique character and the need to keep it together.

For the past six years Rinhart has graciously permitted the Middlebury College Museum of Art (MCMA) to be the custodian of his collection. This has proved to be a wonderful opportunity for the museum and our students. Not only has the collection precipitated an earlier exhibition and seminar, it has allowed the museum to publish this volume and assemble the accompanying exhibition.

Projects such as this are always cooperative enterprises. I would like to express my profound gratitude to the many people who have helped in the research and organization of this exhibition and the accompanying catalogue.

I am particularly indebted to the considerable assistance received from Meredith Paige Davis, formerly registrar at the MCMA and currently a Ph.D. candidate at Columbia University. As my research assistant during the conceptional development of this exhibition and catalogue, she accomplished many logistical and research tasks, as well as visiting a number of collections to examine manuscripts, sculptures, and verify information. I would also like to acknowledge the contributions of two Middlebury College students, Shannon Detweiler and Melissa Knoll, both from the Class of 1995, who participated in my seminar "The Lure of Italy: Horatio Greenough and American Sculpture, 1800–1875." Research on this catalogue was significantly aided by funds provided for faculty research by Middlebury College.

Because of the fragile nature of marble sculpture, loan exhibitions of these objects require a tremendous amount of trust and goodwill. I would like especially to thank each of the lenders who recognized that this exhibition, the first time a retrospective of Greenough's work has ever been held, was worthy of their cooperation. I will be ever grateful for the enthusiastic support this project received from Jonathan L. Fairbanks, former Katharine Lane Weems Curator of American Decorative Arts and Sculpture, Museum of Fine Arts, Boston. At the United States Capitol I am also particularly grateful to Alan M. Hantman, Architect of the Capitol, and Barbara Wolanin, Curator of the Capitol, and members of the Joint Committee on the Library, Congress of the United States, who graciously permitted part of Greenough's sculpture *The Rescue* to be included in this exhibition. In conjunction with this request I would also like to thank United States Senator Patrick Leahy and Chuck Ross, State Director of the Office of Senator Patrick Leahy.

For their part in enabling loaned objects to come to Middlebury, I would like to thank individual staff members of the lending institutions: James Biddle, President, The Andalusia Foundation; Catharina Slautterback, Assistant Curator, and Michael Wentworth, Curator of the Gallery of Painting and Sculpture, Boston Athenæum; Kathrine Dibble, Supervisor of Research, Library Services, Boston Public Library; Louise Brownell, Chief Registrar, and Paul Rubenson, Associate Registrar, Maryland Historical Society; Kim Pashko, Assistant Registrar, Museum of Fine Arts, Boston; Michael J. Kutz, Assistant Archivist for Record Services, and James Zeender, Registrar, National Archives; George Gurney, Curator, and Elizabeth Broun, Director, National Museum of American Art; Gale Rawson, Registrar, Daniel Rosenfeld, The Edna S. Tuttleman Director of the Museum, and Lorena K. Sehgal, Associate Registrar, Pennsylvania Academy of the Fine Arts; Catrina Elia, Registrar, and Jon B. Zachman, Curator of General Collections, Valentine Museum.

Assembling an exhibition of this kind is a complex enterprise, which required the expertise of many people behind the scenes. At the MCMA I am especially grateful to Margaret Wallace, who coordinated the arrangements for the Rinhart Collection, as well as for each of the loaned objects, and myriad details related to the catalogue. Christine Friaoli worked diligently to see that all works in the Rinhart Collection were rematted. JoAnn Keeler, the MCMA office manager, kept everyone apprised of impending deadlines and admirably tracked the countless details that were an inevitable part of this project. Thanks also to Ken Burris, who took on the difficult task of photographing the drawings in the Rinhart Collection, and Erik Borg and Tad Merrick, who also assisted with aspects of photography. Special thanks are owed to Emmie Donadio, Associate Director of the MCMA, who shouldered many of my professional burdens during the extended period of time it took to write the manuscript. Ken Pohlman, our Exhibitions Designer and Preparator, deserves special recognition for making use of Greenough's own comments about the instrumental nature of pedestal colors, heights, and lighting angles to ensure that his work is exhibited to best advantage.

This project was also an opportunity for several of the drawings in the Rinhart Collection, as well as four Greenough sculptures, to be conserved and cleaned. Crucial to this effort have been Henry Lie, Director of the Straus Center for Conservation and Technical Studies at Harvard University, and Rebecca Johnston, Assistant Conservator of Paper, and Monica Berry, Associate Conservator of Objects, at the Williamstown Art Conservation Center.

I would also like to thank the following people who helped in a variety of ways: Will Brown, Thomas B. Brumbaugh, Lauretta Dimmick, Lydia Dufour, Stuart P. Feld, Jeffrey M. Flannery, Susan Greendyke, Jim Hatch, Thomas Johnson, Carlotta Owens, Elizabeth Saunders, Tiggy Sawbridge, John W. Sears, Jennifer Tolpa, and Mark Zurolo.

This publication also was the occasion to renew ties with past collaborators. Fronia W. Simpson has provided impeccable editing, and Christopher Kuntze has developed yet another remarkably elegant catalogue design, which has been exquisitely executed by The Stinehour Press.

Last, it is a great pleasure to see this catalogue and exhibition reach fruition, as they exemplify the real purpose of our museum. Not only have the faculty and students of Middlebury College had the opportunity to examine and help preserve these wonderful drawings, we have assisted in their interpretation and simultaneously added to our understanding of the changing nature of aesthetic taste in America.

Richard H. Saunders
Director

Lenders to the Exhibition

The Andalusia Foundation

The Boston Athenæum

The Boston Public Library

Maryland Historical Society

Museum of Fine Arts, Boston

National Archives and Records Administration

National Museum of American Art

Pennsylvania Academy of the Fine Arts

Private Collection

George R. Rinhart

The United States Capitol

Valentine Museum

Introduction

History has been particularly unkind to Horatio Greenough (1805–1852). Both his reputation and his sculpture have suffered at the hands of successive generations. Most of this abuse has consisted of varying degrees of neglect. Nineteenth-century American sculpture has never been especially fashionable with art historians or collectors, so in one sense Greenough has simply endured the sentence passed on many of his fellow artists.

But in Greenough's case the suffering has been far greater, in that his public works, such as his colossal full-length *George Washington* and his group sculpture *The Rescue* were initially placed on a higher societal pedestal and as a result had farther to fall. *The Rescue* suffered the ultimate humiliation, short of outright destruction, when it accidentally was dropped while being transported from one storage location to another in 1976 and broke into many pieces.

Greenough was never really able to reconcile the fact that he was not a "popular" artist. Because he spent most of his career in Italy, he was to some degree misled by the accolades and endorsements of his work he received from educated Europeans. His mistake was that he confused European and American sentiment. Only later in his career did he begin to rationalize his place in American art. At the relatively young age of thirty-nine, he very likely thought of his own predicament when he described the fate of Washington Allston, his friend and mentor. Greenough viewed Allston as an idealist, "and as the Ideal is a criticism of the Actual, he shared the fate of those who in whatever branch of culture, rise where the mass cannot follow."[1] Greenough's friends said as much of him.

Over the years historians have generally tipped their hats to Greenough as the first American sculptor to receive international recognition. But beyond this fact, attention has largely centered on the controversy generated by the popular displeasure with his statue of Washington. Because of these factors, it is not surprising that Greenough's drawings have received scant attention, aside from the insightful discussion of those that relate to his *George Washington*.[2]

Most people are not aware of the role drawings sometimes play in the creation of a sculptor's works. This is not all that surprising, in that few drawings by nineteenth-century American sculptors exist.[3] And Greenough's enthusiastic endorsement of drawing was not the norm for American sculptors.[4] But Greenough's case is unusual in other ways. As almost two hundred of his drawings survive, are highly diverse, and document almost the entire breadth of his career, they provide considerable insight about him. Not only do they reveal his skill as a draftsman, but combined with his substantial correspondence they document the workings of his mind and the crucial role drawing played in his fulfillment as an artist.

1. Horatio Greenough to Richard Dana, 23 September 1844. Every Greenough letter cited here is taken from Wright 1972, unless otherwise noted.
2. Fryd 1992, chapter 3.
3. For example, no sculptors are cited as draftsmen in Stebbins 1976.
4. Stebbins 1992, p. 70.

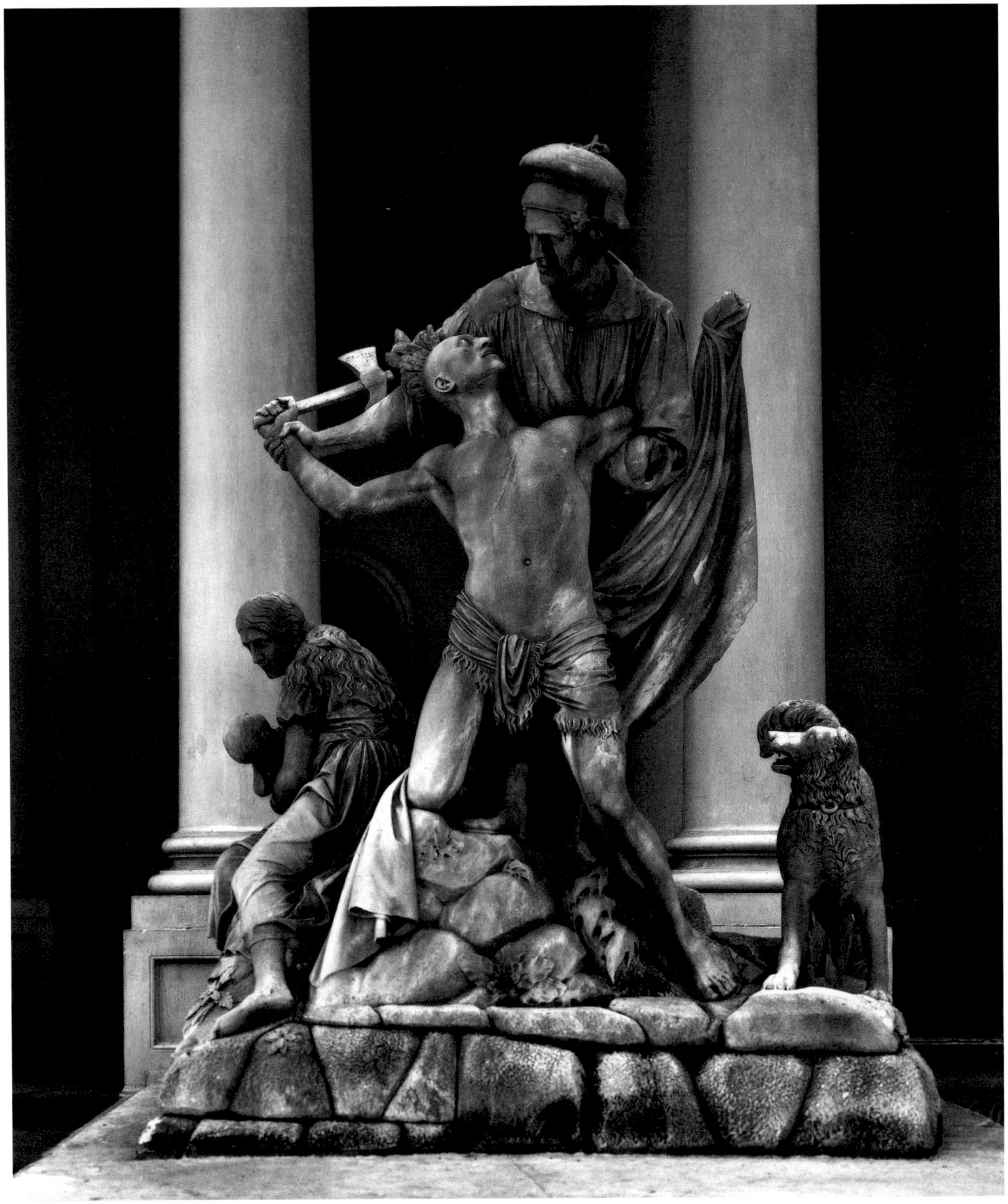

Fig. 2. Horatio Greenough, *The Rescue*, 1837–51. Marble, 144 × 122 inches. Photograph taken before 1920, showing the work in situ to the right on the staircase on the east facade of the U.S. Capitol. In storage since 1958. Courtesy of the Architect of the Capitol.

Horatio Greenough

AN ARTIST'S LIFE

"An American citizen, who has gone abroad to study a refined art, presents himself before his fellow-countrymen at disadvantage."[1] With these revealing words, Horatio Greenough began his collection of five essays, entitled *The Travels, Observations, and Experience of a Yankee Stonecutter*. Published in 1852, only four months before his premature death at the age of forty-seven, this slim volume serves in many ways as an apologia for a career that failed to achieve the national acclaim that so many of America's cultural elite expected.

Only a few months earlier, on his arrival at Washington, D.C., in November 1851, Greenough found himself before what should have been his greatest triumph: the colossal marble statue of George Washington (fig. 1), commissioned by the federal government for the Capitol rotunda. By then the much abused sculpture was resited, at Greenough's insistence, outdoors in the northeastern part of the Capitol grounds. In Washington he futilely awaited the arrival of *The Rescue* (fig. 2), the sculpture resulting from his second major

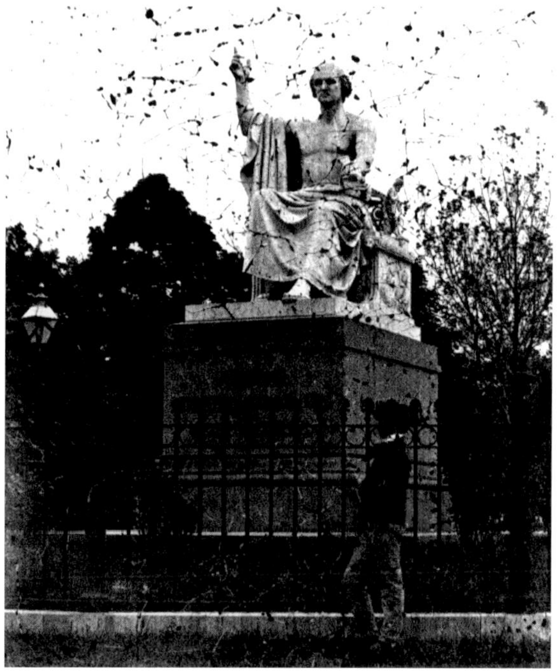

Fig. 1. Horatio Greenough, *George Washington*, 1832–41. Marble. Photograph by Mathew Brady, c. 1850–60, of the sculpture after placement outside the Capitol. Courtesy Meserve-Kunhardt Collection.

government commission. But its shipment from Italy was delayed. Greenough vainly hoped the latter work would rehabilitate his tarnished reputation and ignite a national appreciation of his work. But this did not happen, and Greenough's life came to a sudden and fitful end late that year, the culmination of a life plagued by behavior suggestive of manic depression.

Youth, Home Life, Education

Greenough was born in Boston on 6 September 1805. He was the fourth of eleven children, nine of whom lived to adulthood.[2] His father, David Greenough, was among Boston's first large-scale real estate developers. Properties in which he was involved included Colonnade Row (1810–14; fig. 3), on what is now Tremont Street, and Boston's first row of stone block buildings constructed on Brattle Street in 1818. Elizabeth Bender Greenough, the sculptor's mother, was known for her interests in gardening and poetry, of which she published a volume.

His father's fluctuating fortunes as a builder caused the Greenoughs to move several times during Horatio's youth, yet Horatio most likely thought of Colonnade Row as his home. His boyhood was nurturing and cultured, and his father, who was described as benevolent and practical,[3] seems to have heightened his son's awareness of architecture, architectural materials, and drawing. Greenough carved three small heads in wood, cast a pistol of lead, molded a lion in butter, and cut a head in plaster in imitation of a Roman coin.[4] He acknowledged that one source of his youthful desire to make sculpture was a marble statue of Phocion, which his father had placed on a mound in the family garden about 1816. More ambitious were his efforts to create a series of miniature busts in chalk and a full-length chalk figure of William Penn copied from an engraving.

About 1818, at age thirteen, he made a chalk copy of the bust of John Adams by John B. Binon (fl. Boston c. 1820; fig. 4), a French sculptor then living in Boston. This act precipitated several Bostonians' taking a particular interest in nurturing the young artist's abilities. Greenough's copy so impressed one unnamed gentleman that he took him to the Boston Athenæum and introduced him to William S. Shaw, the director, so that he might be given free entry to examine the collection of busts and engravings housed there. Subsequently, Horatio carved in alabaster or rock plaster of paris, and Solomon Willard,

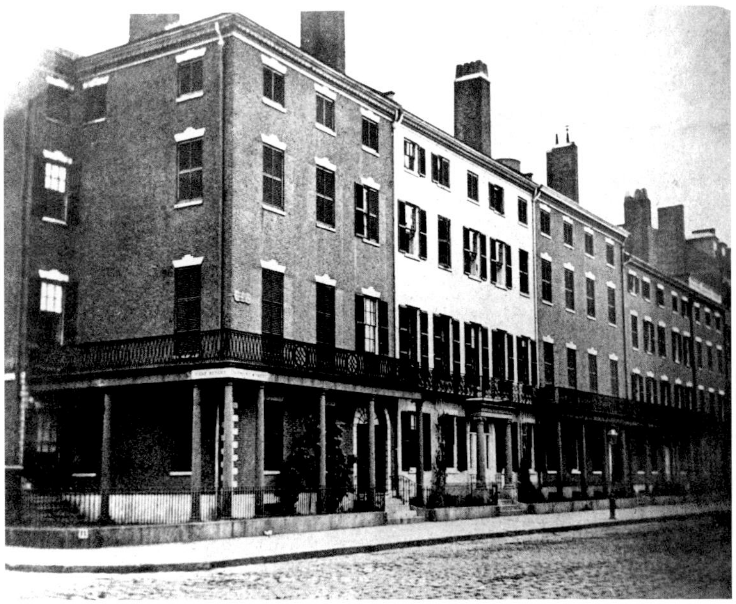

Fig. 3. *Colonnade Row, Boston,* looking from Number 1. Courtesy of The Bostonian Society/Old State House.

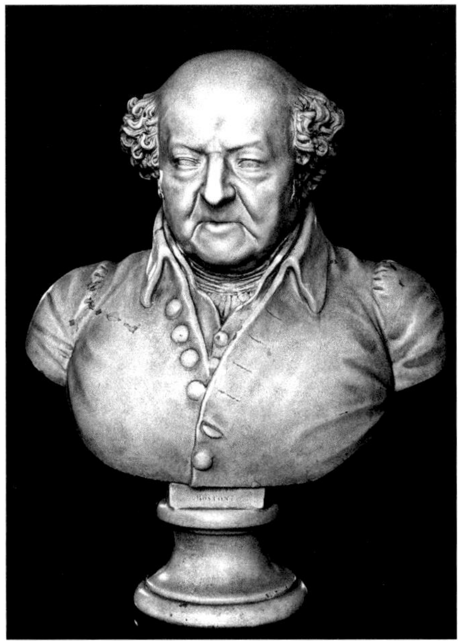

Fig. 4. John B. Binon, *John Adams,* 1819. Plaster, 25⅛ × 20¹⁄₁₆ × 10¾ inches. Courtesy of the Boston Athenæum.

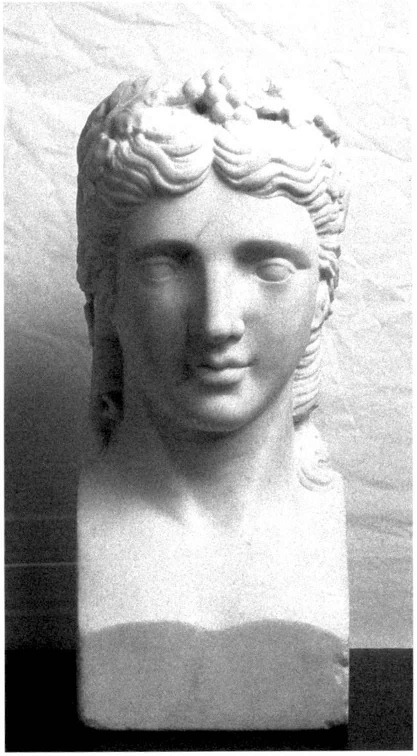

Fig. 5. Horatio Greenough, *Bacchus*, c. 1819. Marble, 12¼ × 5 × 4¾ inches. Courtesy of Brookgreen Gardens. Gift of Beatrice Gilman Proske.

the Boston architect, taught him the elements of clay modeling. Alpheus Cary, a Boston stonecutter, introduced him to marble carving, and the result was his earliest surviving work in this medium, a bust of Bacchus (fig. 5). Binon also became intrigued by this determined teen who made repeated visits to the older artist's studio.[5]

Despite Greenough's rapid progress, it is hardly surprising that his father insisted his son obtain a good general education. Given America's modest support for the arts, a career as an artist was fraught with uncertainty. In addition, the profession of carving was then largely devoted to the more perfunctory activities of carving gravestones, furniture, or ships' figureheads. At the time there were probably no more than a dozen artists in America trying to eke out careers as sculptors of figures in stone, and most of these were foreign-born followers of Antonio Canova (1757–1822) who settled in Washington, D.C., in anticipation of the extensive carving associated with completion of the nation's Capitol.[6] As a result, Horatio enrolled at Harvard in 1821.

In later life Greenough (like other alumni) disparaged his Harvard education. But it was here that he was exposed to a large body of literature devoted to rationalistic and utilitarian thought, which was so closely intertwined with the era's neoclassical artistic tastes.[7] Even more important, perhaps, was the combined influence of President John T. Kirkland, who encouraged foreign study, and four younger faculty—Edward Everett, George Ticknor, Joseph Cogswell, and George Bancroft, who had recently returned from Europe. Cogswell, Harvard's librarian, had returned with casts and drawings, some of which he loaned Greenough. Greenough later said of Cogswell that he, perhaps more than any other, helped to "fix his purpose."[8]

While at Harvard, Greenough also continued his own artistic pursuits, modeling busts of several contemporaries, of Washington from a Gilbert Stuart (1755–1828) portrait, and of Napoleon. One of his Harvard friends some years later remarked, "His taste for art was strong; the inspiration was upon him." His earliest surviving drawings are also from his days at Harvard: seven diminutive studies of animal skeletons copied from some of the engravings in William Cheselden's *Osteographia*, one of the books he borrowed from the Harvard library (cat. 1).[9]

It was during Greenough's junior year (1823–24) that he became a disciple of the painter Washington Allston (1779–1843). At the time Greenough was rooming with a fellow Harvard student, John Howard, in the Cambridge house of Edmund T. Dana, Allston's future brother-in-law. Allston, who by this time was Boston's most noted artist, customarily spent Saturday nights at the Danas, where he presided over a small circle with similar social and intellectual tastes. As later recounted to William Dunlap, the artist and historian, Greenough acknowledged that Allston "was to me a father"; he taught him "how to discriminate—how to think—how to feel."[10] Such a kinship was natural, as the worldly and accomplished painter represented much of that to which Greenough aspired. Allston had spent years in England, exhibited pictures in London at the Royal Academy and at the Salon in Paris, was the first artist of the young Republic to visit Italy, and had developed lasting friendships with Washington Irving and Samuel Taylor Coleridge.[11] Greenough, too, gravitated toward Allston's philosophical belief that the greatest art was an expression of the mind rather than an imitation of nature and that the European masters were the best teachers.[12]

Greenough's first effort to secure public patronage for one of his

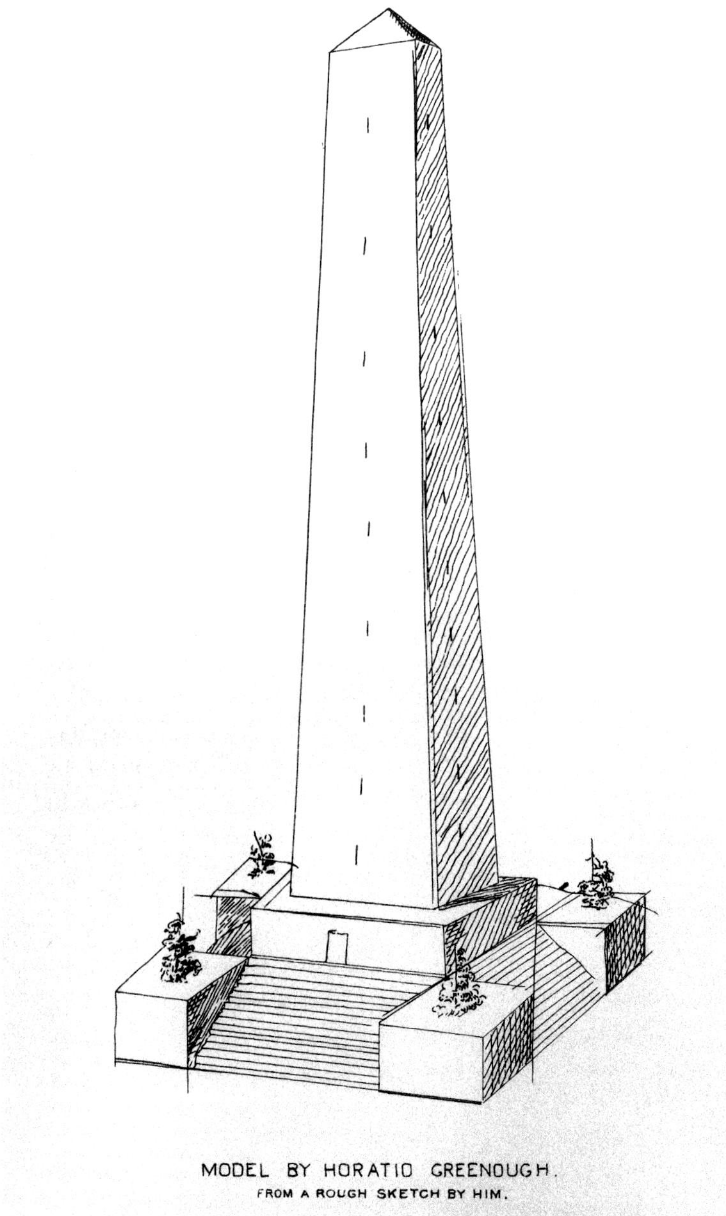

Fig. 6. *Bunker Hill Monument* proposal. Line drawing after Horatio Greenough. From George Washington Warren, *The History of the Bunker Hill Monument Association* (1877).

designs came in 1825, his senior year at Harvard. That year a public competition was held for the design of the Bunker Hill Monument. It was announced by the Bunker Hill Monument Association, which had been organized the preceding year and had originally sought subscriptions for a monument to be designed by Solomon Willard. Without providing explanation for their change in course, the association offered a $100 premium for the design of a 220-foot column to honor those Americans who had fought during the Revolutionary engagement held on Bunker and Breed's hills. Greenough submitted one of the approximately fifty proposals received by the 1 April deadline.

Greenough's proposal, which replaced the column with an obelisk and proposed four sculptural groups at the base (cat. 2), is substantial evidence of the young artist's considerable ambition and independent nature. A Board of Artists was appointed to act as contest judges (consisting of Allston, Ticknor, Gilbert Stuart, Laommi Baldwin, and Daniel Webster), and they selected Greenough's design over those by far better known contestants, including the architect Robert Mills and the surveyor John G. Hales. Political jockeying apparently influenced the outcome, and after the dust settled the association chose to erect a plainer version of Greenough's design. The result (fig. 6) was erected under Willard's supervision, and without any public credit to Greenough. In 1832 the sculptor lamented the absence of the plinth, which to his eyes "made the shaft start sheer from the dirt like a spear of asparagus."[13] Greenough had no way of knowing that this unsatisfactory venture into the arena of public monuments foretold future disappointments.

Travels

By the spring of his senior year at Harvard, Greenough was anxious to get on with his career as an artist and go to Europe. Because David Greenough was financially unable to support such travel, he obtained a loan for his son from a friend, the wealthy merchant Amos Lawrence.[14] Greenough received permission to leave college prior to commencement and departed for Europe in late April or early May 1825. Traveling by way of Gibraltar, Marseilles, Leghorn, Genoa, and Florence, he made his way to Rome.

Once in Rome, Greenough made the acquaintance of the young American painter Robert W. Weir (1803–1889), and shortly thereafter the two shared rooms. They first lived on the Pincian Hill, an area long popular with artists and travelers. Their house, on the Piazza Trinita dei Monte, was in Bramante's famous Tempietto and had been inhabited in the seventeenth century by Claude Lorrain (1600–1682). Situated nearby was the French Academy in the Villa Medici, where students could draw from nude models and study antique casts. Further down the Via Sistina was the apartment of the Dane Bertel Thorvaldsen (1770–1844), the most prominent sculptor in the contemporary arts community.

Greenough and Weir quickly established a routine to their days. The first part of the morning was spent at the French Academy, where they drew from antique casts. After breakfast they separated, and while Weir went to one gallery to copy pictures, Greenough went to

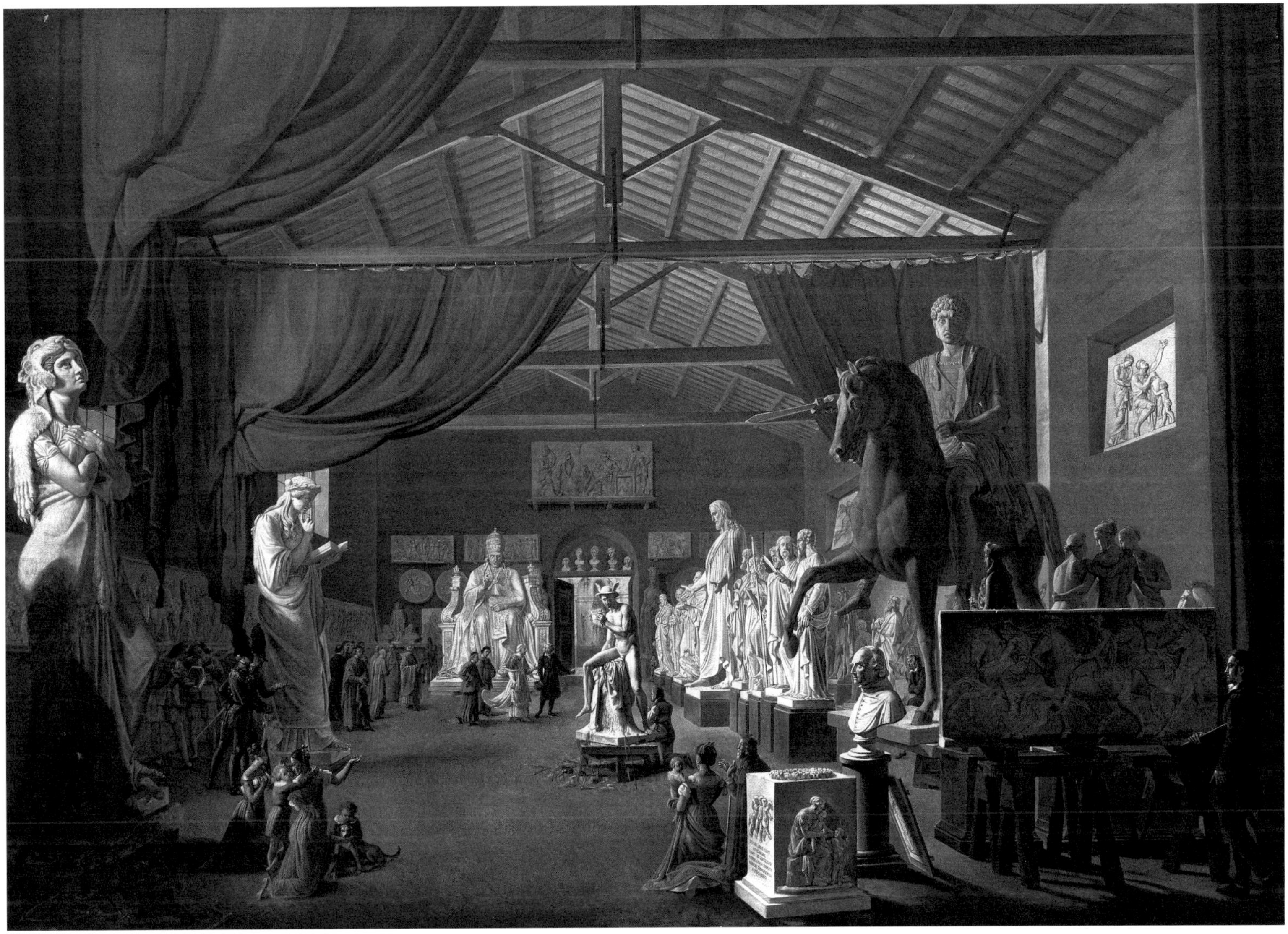

Fig. 7. H. D. C. Martens, *Pope Leo XII Visiting Thorvaldsen's Large Atelier at the Palazzo Barberini.* Oil on canvas. Courtesy of Statens Museum for Kunst, Copenhagen.

another to draw, or back to their rooms, which also served as their studio. After the galleries closed at three o'clock, they had lunch. In the late afternoon, Greenough worked on figures of his own composition. They dined at six and then retired to the Caffe Grecco, where they stayed until seven, when the life schools opened. They attended the English life school, where they drew for two hours. If there was sufficient moonlight, they then walked among the ruins of the Forum.[15] Much of what Greenough observed during this period is recorded in a small sketchbook he began in January 1826 (cat. 3).

Greenough had arrived in Rome with letters of introduction to the sculptor Thorvaldsen, whose studio provided a feast for his eyes (fig. 7). The Dane, perhaps more than any other artist, had a pronounced influence on him at this time. The young American was also impatient to model works that might be carved in marble. His first effort in this direction was a life-size *Dead Abel*, which does not survive. This was followed by a full-length *David*, which may have been modeled but never completed, as well as several busts, including one that was a self-portrait.[16]

Early signs of a lifelong battle Greenough had with periods of depression began to appear in Rome. Unsettled nights, during which he often rose to draw (cat. 8), were the first hints of a more deeply rooted malaise. To avoid the malarial season, during the summer of 1826 he left Rome for the Alban Hills. Although he continued to draw, the fact that he was alone may have accelerated a tendency toward depression. A bout of indigestion was followed by what was reportedly malaria. At one point the housekeeper at the inn where he was staying became so concerned that she contacted Weir, who came and cared for him.

When he recovered, Greenough was advised to take a change of air. He visited Naples but manifested signs of being mentally deranged. After initially being directed to an asylum at Aversa, the results of a second medical examination led the physician to conclude that Greenough's condition might be temporary. As a result, accompanied by Weir, he set out for America almost immediately and arrived in Boston on 23 May 1827.

America, 1827–28

This trip home was restorative in many ways. He stayed with his family, who were then living in Jamaica Plain, outside Boston, and spent his time drawing, modeling, reading, and writing. During this time he most likely saw several recent portraits of Washington and modeled a bust of Washington to take back with him to Italy (see cat. 49).[17]

Greenough also took the opportunity to seek possible commissions for sculptures to be completed in Italy. In this way he obtained his first commission, for a portrait of Josiah Quincy (fig. 8), Boston's mayor and later president of Harvard.[18] Toward the end of the year, Greenough decided to seek even greater visibility by going to Washington to model a bust of President John Quincy Adams. He took with him a letter of introduction from Quincy, along with letters from Allston to Samuel F. B. Morse (1791–1872) in New York and from Richard Dana to Gulian Verplanck, chairman of the Congressional Committee on Public Buildings.

On his way to Washington in February 1828 he stopped in New York, where he met Morse, William Dunlap (1766–1839), the painter Thomas Cole (1801–1848), and William Cullen Bryant, soon to be editor of the *Evening Post*. Morse, who was both a painter and president of the fledgling National Academy of Design, proved to be of considerable assistance to Greenough. In May of that year Greenough was

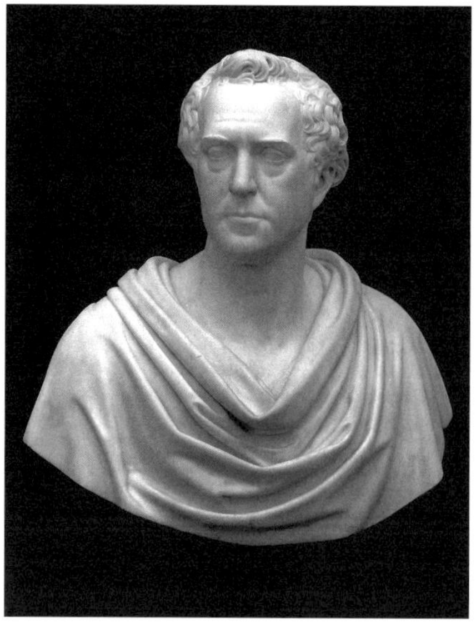

Fig. 8. Horatio Greenough, *Josiah Quincy*. Marble, H. 24½ inches. Courtesy of the National Portrait Gallery, Smithsonian Institution.

elected an honorary member of the academy and granted the (largely honorary) title Professor of Sculpture.

After a brief stop in Philadelphia, where he met Thomas Sully (1783–1872), Greenough arrived in Washington, where he found rooms with the portrait painter Charles Bird King (1785–1862). Successful in his efforts to obtain permission to sculpt President Adams (cat. 16), Greenough was also granted permission by the president to sculpt a portrait of his aged father, the ex-president John Adams. While in Washington he obtained a sitting with Chief Justice John Marshall, who ordered a plaster of the sculpture for display at his home in Richmond, Virginia.[19]

Greenough's hopes that his presence in Washington might lead to a public commission, however, went unrealized. Most of the sculptural decoration on the Capitol had either been arranged for or completed by a group of foreign craftsmen, led by the Italian Luigi Persico (1791–1860). Greenough joined the chorus of critics who dismissed these sculptures as the work of "a dozen dunderheads."[20] The year of Greenough's visit, Enrico Causici (active in America 1822–32), one of the visiting Italian artists, petitioned for appropriation to permit him to complete the two sculptural reliefs on which he was at work (fig. 9). This brought the retort from one senator that "a Yankee sailor with a jack-knife and a shingle, would carve images that would be better imitators of humanity."[21] Greenough's frustration with the situation was tempered by the realization that an artist of his skills would surely succeed in the face of such modestly talented competition. While in Washington, Greenough met with Persico and Charles Bulfinch (1763–1844), architect of the Capitol and a fellow Bostonian.

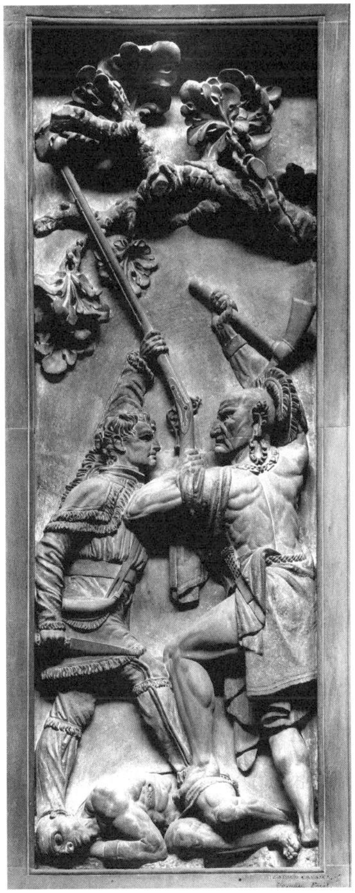

Fig. 9. Enrico Causici, *Conflict of Daniel Boone and the Indians*, 1826–27. Sandstone. U.S. Capitol Rotunda, above south door. Courtesy of the Architect of the Capitol.

Greenough's visit to Washington proved advantageous in other ways. There he met Robert Gilmor, Jr., a successful Baltimore merchant, who was among the foremost collectors of contemporary art. Gilmor visited Greenough's Washington studio, commissioned a bust of his wife, and invited him to his home to do the modeling. Greenough visited Gilmor in March, and the collector's satisfaction with the results led him to commission a statue, or group sculpture, to be executed in Italy of a subject to be determined later.[22] A few weeks later Greenough was back in Boston and set sail for Europe on 18 May.

Florence, 1828–36

By October 1828 Greenough was once again in Italy, but for a number of reasons he had decided to settle in Florence, which he described in a letter to Allston as "the most inspiring place in the world."[23] His reasons for relocating his studio were largely practical: Florence was only seventy-five miles from Carrara, where the finest marble was quarried; the climate was more healthful; and Greenough regarded the art collections as unparalleled. Before going to Florence, however, he first spent a few months in Carrara, where he came in contact with native stone carvers.

Greenough was also attracted to Florence by the favorable political climate. During the late 1820s and 1830s, the city, in part because of the liberal government of Austrian Grand Duke Leopold II, became a magnet for European artists, writers, intellectuals, and political exiles. Among them were Marquese Gino Capponi, who became a historian and statesman, the Swiss litterateur Gian Pietro Vieusseux, the dramatist G. B. Niccolini, the poet Giuseppe Giusti, various relatives of Napoleon I, and the sculptor Lorenzo Bartolini (1777–1850).[24]

In addition to this new environment, Greenough, who had just reached his twenty-third birthday, manifested a new level of maturity, confidence, and independent thought. Most indicative of this was his newfound admiration for Bartolini, Master of Sculpture at the Royal Academy in Florence, whose work he now saw "with an eye altogether different from that of 3 years since which I visited him for the first time."[25] Bartolini's sculpture of a young boy treading grapes,

L'Ammostatore (see fig. 24), which Greenough drew at Carrara, was singled out for particular praise. In so doing, Greenough was admitting to a newfound appreciation of more naturalistic and observed subjects, which in some ways was a repudiation of the cool, detached classicism which was then in fashion.[26]

Greenough was so enthralled with the prospect of learning from Bartolini, whom he asked to be his "instructor in drawing and modeling," that he was offered an apartment in the Italian artist's commodious studio, where he remained for the winter months.[27] "The ground aim of my studies since my return to Italy," he wrote Richard Henry Dana, the essayist and poet, "has been the formation of a method both in drawing and modeling which shall enable me to pay in the future, my whole attention to form and expression without continual interruption."[28]

It was at Florence in 1828 that Greenough met James Fenimore Cooper, who was advised by the American consul to have the artist model his bust (cat. 18). Cooper's friendship and patronage had a momentous effect on Greenough's career, because it led to the commission of an idealized work, *The Chanting Cherubs* (now lost). The subject, which Greenough diagrammed in a letter to Cooper (fig. 10), was "a copy of a passage in a picture [*Madonna del Baldacchino*] of Raphael at the Pitti Palace representing two cherub boys chaunting."[29] The sculpture, which reached America by 1831, was the first work by Greenough to be publicly displayed.

The period from 1829 to 1831 brought a number of American artists to Florence. Rembrandt Peale (1778–1860) arrived in 1829 and during his visit painted a portrait of Greenough (National Portrait Gallery, Washington, D.C.), which he exhibited at the National Academy that September. Horatio's brother, John, who also sought to establish himself as an artist, arrived in 1830. John C. Gore, a Boston landscape painter, whose sister Louisa would marry the sculptor a few years later, arrived shortly thereafter. By 1831 the Bostonian Amasa Hewins arrived, and Greenough sketched Hewins's profile in his notebook. They were joined by John Gadsby Chapman (1808–1889), a Virginia painter who had particular admiration for Greenough and painted a portrait of the determined artist (fig. 11), showing hair combed across his forehead to conceal a receding hairline. In addition, both Cole and Morse were now in Florence and shared rooms with Greenough. Like some of his fellow artists, Cole, too, sketched Greenough's portrait (fig. 12).

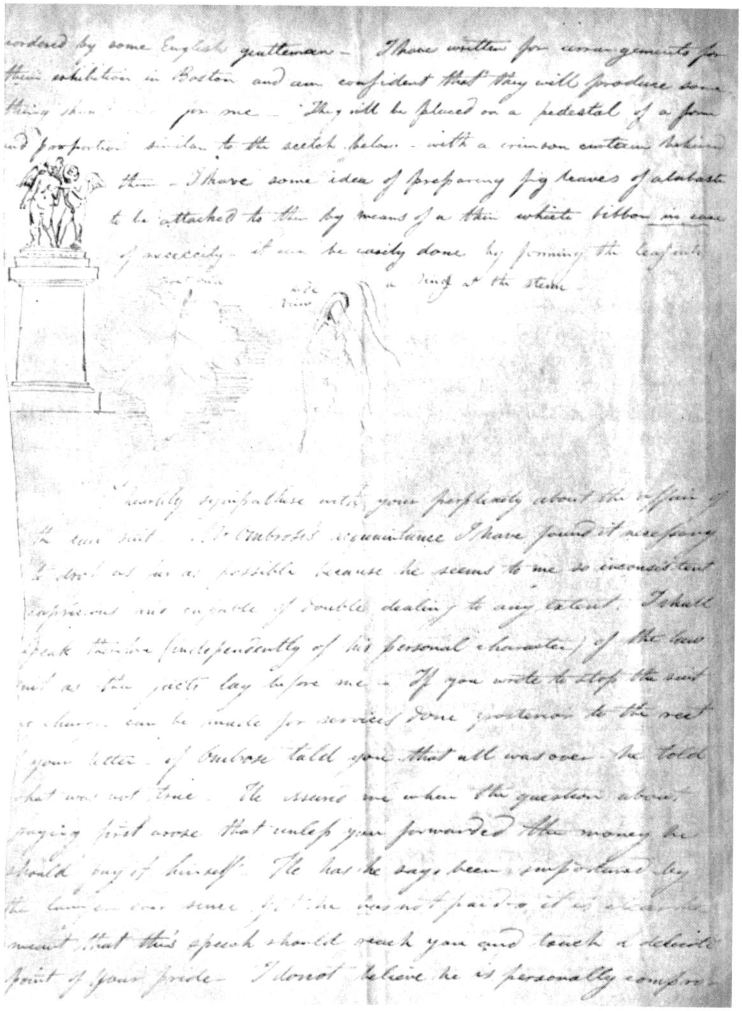

Fig. 10. Horatio Greenough, drawing of *The Chanting Cherubs* in a letter to James Fenimore Cooper, 20 December 1830. Courtesy of Nathalia Wright.

During these same years Greenough was occupied with a succession of sculptures. Busts from life included one for Cornelius Bradford, a friend of Cooper's then in Florence; ex-president Kirkland of Harvard, commissioned for presentation to the Boston Athenæum; Giulia Grisi, the young opera soprano, along with busts of Cole (fig. 13) and Morse (cat. 22). In addition, he received orders for two busts derived from the sculpture of Washington he had modeled in

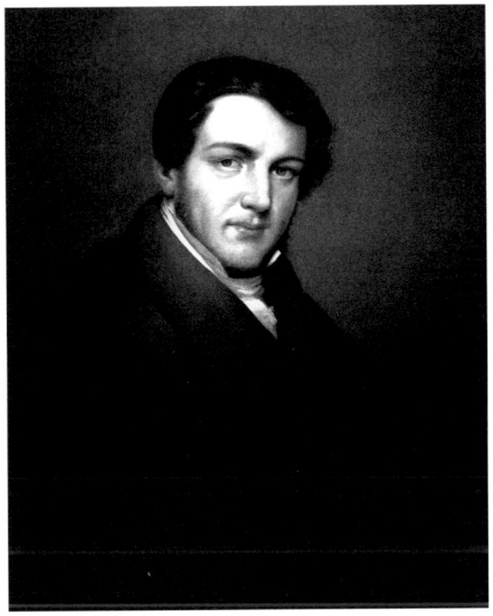

Fig. 11. John Gadsby Chapman, *Horatio Greenough*, 1831. Oil on canvas, 28¼ × 23½ inches. Courtesy of the Boston Athenæum.

Boston in 1827.[30] Figural work from life included a three-foot-high statue of the five-year-old Cornelia Grinnell (New Bedford Whaling Museum) and possibly a Newfoundland dog. Idealized work included a bust of Petrarch's Laura for a banker in Marseilles named Rogers.[31]

In the fall of 1831 Greenough hatched a plan to travel to Paris to model a bust of Lafayette (cat. 20). The thought appealed to him because Lafayette had an immense following in America. With Cooper's intervention, the plan succeeded and Greenough was absent from Florence for four months, returning in December 1831.

Greenough continued to cogitate over his efforts to secure the commission for a public monument to Washington and in March 1831 shared an illustration of his design in a letter to Cooper (see fig. 36). These musings led nowhere for the time being, however, and Greenough focused on completing a commission for Robert Gilmor. The subject, which had been left undetermined when first discussed in 1827, was the dead *Medora* (fig. 14) from Lord Byron's poem *The Corsair* (1814). Byron, who had resided in Florence and been sculpted by Thorvaldsen and Bartolini, was at the height of his popularity.[32] It was Greenough's first representation in marble of a life-size figure, his most ambitious undertaking to date, and his first female full-length statue. Once shipped to America, *Medora* became the second of

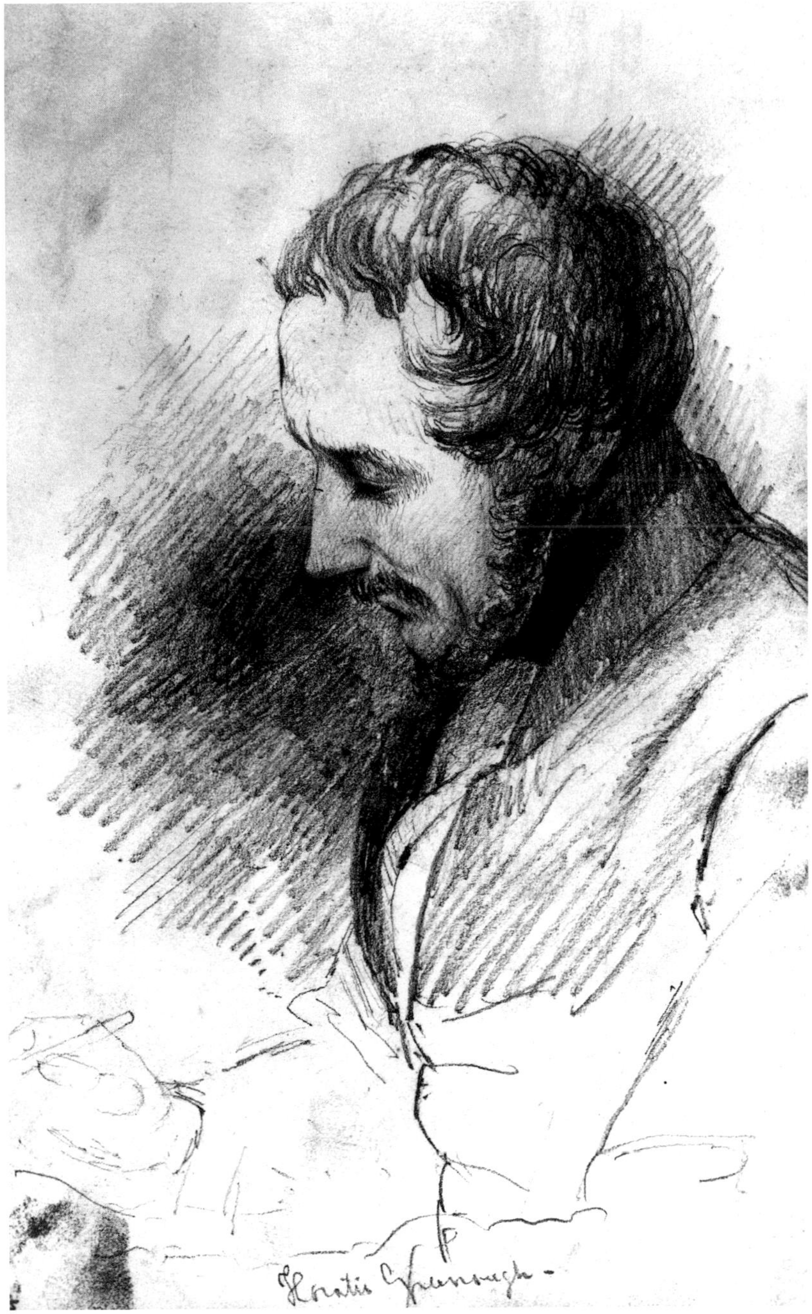

Fig. 12. Thomas Cole, *Horatio Greenough*, c. 1831–32. Graphite on paper. Courtesy of The Detroit Institute of Arts. Founders Society Purchase, William H. Murphy Fund.

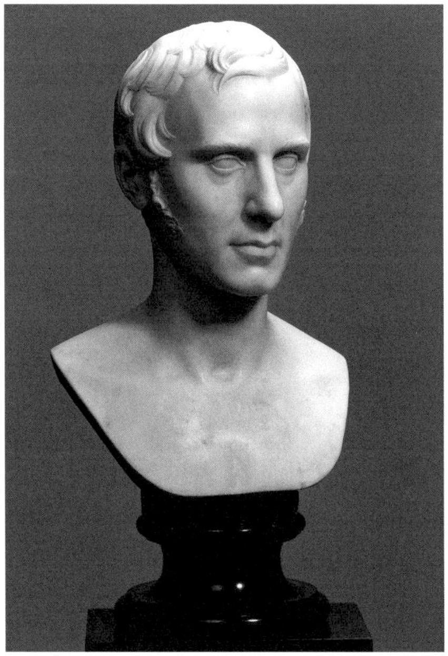

Fig. 13. Horatio Greenough, *Thomas Cole*, 1831. Marble, H. 17 inches. Wadsworth Atheneum, Hartford. Bequest of Florence Cole Vincent.

Greenough's works to be specially exhibited, as opposed to being shown in the annual exhibitions at the National Academy of Design or the Boston Athenæum.

In terms of activity, although not necessarily income, 1832 was a banner year for Greenough. Only twenty-seven, he began to have a regular stream of private commissions, the most notable of which were a marble bust of Lafayette (cat. 20), a marble bust of Washington for Commodore James Biddle of Philadelphia (cat. 49), and two small statues he titled *The Genius of Italy* (see cat. 44) and *The Genius of America.* In addition, Samuel Cabot of Boston commissioned a portrait of his eleven-year-old daughter Elizabeth and, more important, *The Ascension of a Child* (cat. 33), an idealized work similar in theme to *The Chanting Cherubs*, which depicts a child being guided to the spiritual realm by an angel. When completed, it became the third, and last, sculpture by Greenough to be specially exhibited in America.

All of these sculptural accomplishments, however, were but preamble to the long-awaited invitation from Congress to create a statue

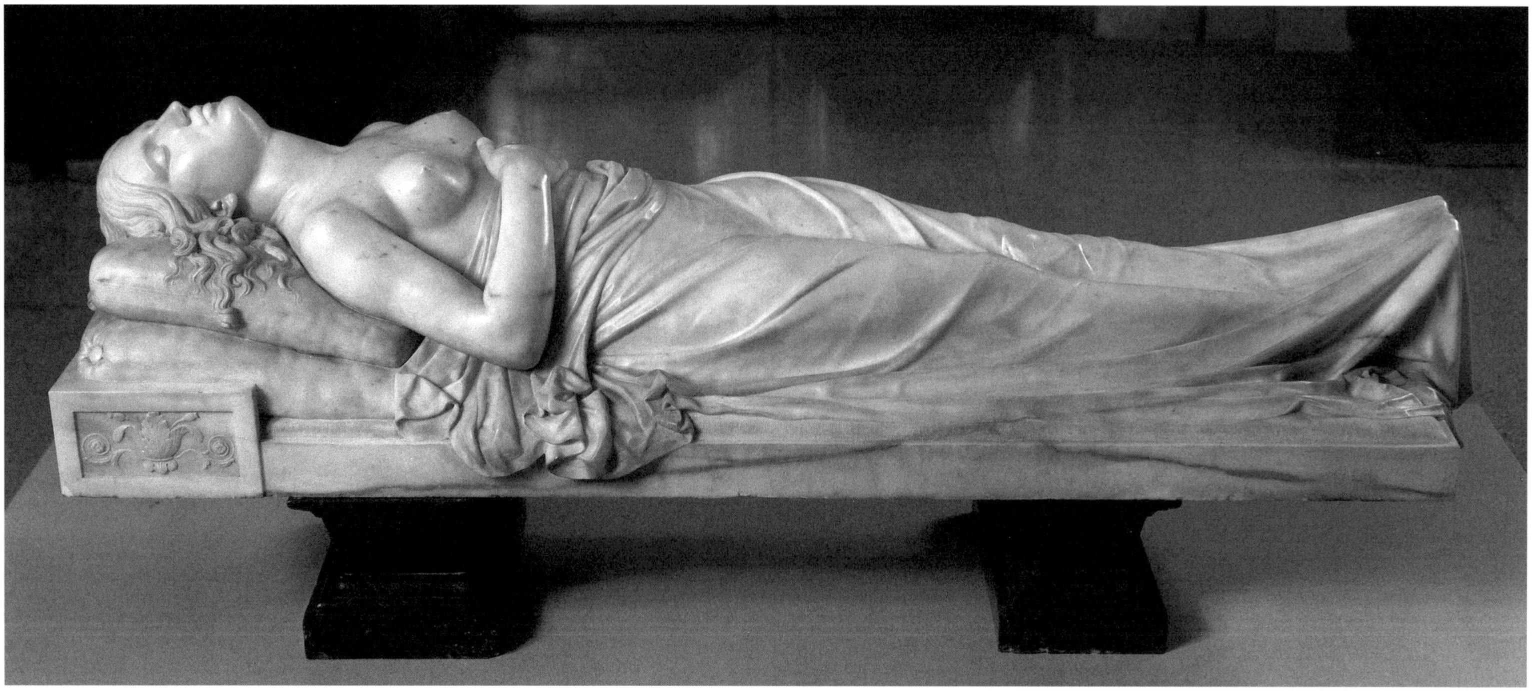

Fig. 14. Horatio Greenough, *Medora*, 1832. Marble, 14½ × 58 inches. Mayor and City Council of Baltimore, on extended loan to The Baltimore Museum of Art.

of Washington for permanent exhibition in the rotunda of the Capitol (see figs. 34, 35 and cats. 49–58). Its immediate effect, paradoxically enough, was to force Greenough to limit his other work precisely at the moment when he was increasingly sought after because of this recognition. It was not until the summer of 1833 that Greenough received his first payment toward the Washington commission.

In the time immediately prior to the federal commission, Greenough's correspondence hints at a belief that if his genius goes unrecognized in the future it will be because the "country remains as ignorant on that point as now."[33] In other words, if American society does not appreciate him, it is not from inadequacy on his part but rather a failure on the part of the country. Late in life Greenough may well have been thinking of his own predicament in describing a man of genius as one who seeks "responsibility." He tells you that "he is the right man for it" and views the harsh words of critics as a "reign of terror."[34] Such heightened expectation for himself undoubtedly made the humbling response to his colossal figure of Washington all the more difficult to accept and most likely contributed to his periodically depressed state.

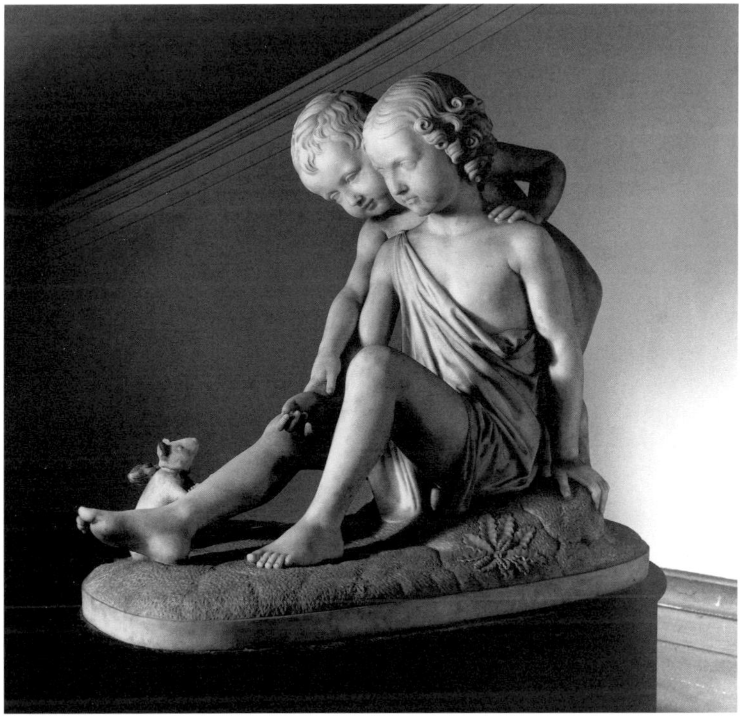

Fig. 15. Horatio Greenough, *Grace and Knyvet Winthrop Sears*, 1835–37. Marble, 29¼ × 34½ × 17¾ inches. Courtesy of the Massachusetts Historical Society.

By the fall of 1834, a year during which he took only four or five private commissions, he had at last secured a studio in which to set up his Washington statue. From then until the beginning of 1836 this project absorbed much of his attention. Although some of his friends tried to dissuade him from his plan to depict Washington as the Olympian Zeus, he would not be deterred. He wrote to Allston that Edward Everett, then a member of Congress from Massachusetts, "tells me he fears my plan will never do in our country," but he chose to ignore such advice.[35]

Greenough's notoriety brought a heightened demand for his work. In succession, Greenough completed portraits for members of the David Sears family of Boston, including his enchanting depiction of the Sears children playing with a pet squirrel (fig. 15), modeled a bust of William Cullen Bryant, executed an inventive design of two children playing battledore, designed to stand at either end of a room, and carved *Love Prisoner to Wisdom* (Museum of Fine Arts, Boston), a statue of Cupid chained to an owl.[36]

America, 1836

By early 1836 Greenough's *Washington* was cast in plaster. Since it took several months for a work of this size to dry and because Greenough felt a temporary degree of financial security, he took the opportunity to visit America. The pretext of the visit was to examine the Capitol rotunda and review plans for a pedestal for the statue. The real purpose, however, was to conduct some behind-the-scenes lobbying for the second of two sculptures the government intended to commission to flank the east staircase of the Capitol. In March he wrote his brother Henry that he had "plans of great moment, which depend partly on my getting there [to Washington] when Congress is sitting."[37]

In New York, on his way to Washington, Greenough made the acquaintance of Hiram Powers (1805–1873), a sculptor with aspirations similar to his own.[38] He then traveled to Boston, where his visit coincided with the death of his father on 27 July. By September he reported to Cooper that he was impatient to return to his "mud and his hammer" and that as a result of settling his father's affairs he was, for the immediate future, in a "very prosperous state."[39] On his return to Italy, he took with him his sister Louisa. The family hoped that a change of air would improve her health.

Florence, 1837–39

Horatio and his sister made their way to Florence via London and Paris. In London they visited their brother John and in Paris they encountered a number of Boston friends: the David Searses; Joseph Cogswell; Francis Calley Gray, a lawyer; and Joseph Russell, who was traveling with his stepdaughter Louisa Gore. Among them were two couples, the Nathan Appletons and the newlywed P. E. Thomases of Baltimore. Greenough modeled busts of both wives. Although the bust of Frances Appleton, once cut in marble, was considered a failure by her husband, that of Elizabeth Todhunter Thomas (cat. 23) was met with such approval that her husband commissioned a companion bust of himself (see fig. 25).

By January 1837 Greenough was once again in Florence, where his primary focus of attention was his statue of Washington. The following July Greenough learned that his efforts to secure the commission for the second sculptural group planned for the east steps of the Capitol had been successful. Greenough was aided in his cause by the two United States senators from South Carolina, William Campbell Preston and John C. Calhoun, who argued that "the talents of an accomplished citizen of our own country" should not be ignored.[40]

The appropriation bill passed by the Senate provided for one commission to go to Persico and the second to go to Greenough. Greenough was invited to submit a proposal for a pendant to Persico's plan to depict Columbus and the discovery of America (fig. 16). Greenough responded with two proposals. The one he clearly preferred was to "commemorate the dangers and difficulty of peopling our continent, and which shall also serve as a memorial of the Indian race, and an embodying of the Indian character."[41] This eventually became *The Rescue.*

Greenough's increased visibility during these years also precipitated larger numbers of visitors to his studio and a welcome influx of commissions for busts and ideal figures.[42] Soon after their arrival the Greenoughs were joined by some of their acquaintances from Paris. Among them were Joseph Russell and Louisa Gore, who was a good friend of Greenough's sister. By summer Greenough and Louisa were engaged; they were married on 14 October 1837.

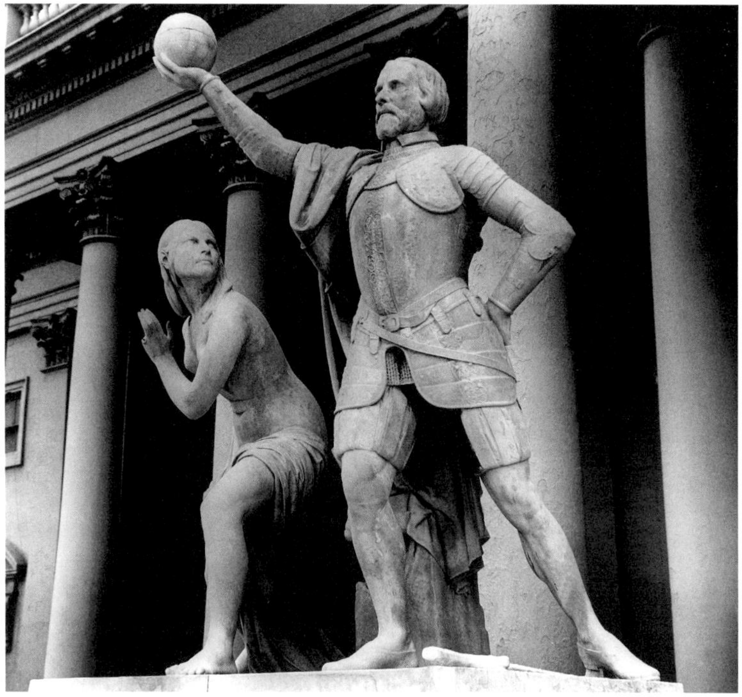

Fig. 16. Luigi Persico, *Discovery of America,* 1837–44. Marble, 191½ × 100 inches. Photograph showing the work in situ to the left of the staircase on the east facade of the U.S. Capitol. In storage since 1958. Courtesy of the Architect of the Capitol.

Louisa Gore, twenty-five at the time of her marriage, was the daughter of the wealthy Boston merchant John Gore and niece of Governor Christopher Gore. She had known Horatio for some years, as her brother John C. Gore had been a companion of the sculptor's in Florence in 1829–30. More important to Horatio, she was a woman of means. She inherited $50,000 on reaching her twenty-first birthday and had received an identical amount as a bequest from her mother the preceding year.[43]

Unfortunately, Greenough was unable to live within his means. His newly acquired wealth allowed him to indulge, at least momentarily, in a more lavish lifestyle, which meant his expenses greatly exceeded income. Decisions such as a move to the Casa Leblanc, in Via di Bardi, on a hill overlooking the Ponte alle Grazie and about two miles from his studio, were costly. In this setting the Greenoughs entertained constantly. Visitors in the winter of 1838–39 included Mr. and Mrs. Benjamin Daniel Greene of Boston. At the conclusion of one evening the Greenes were presented with a memento of their visit: a profile drawing of a standing greyhound (cat. 32), which the sculptor inscribed for them.

For all practical purposes the late 1830s were the pinnacle of Greenough's career. In fact, the sculptor described 1838 as his "most productive year."[44] Although only in his thirties, his professional and personal life were, for the moment, balanced and satisfying. A sense of this brief moment of supreme confidence is apparent in the portrait William J. Hubard painted of the sculptor in 1838–39 (cat. 65).

It was about this time that Greenough was at work on a remarkable statue, *Venus Victrix* (fig. 17), his first full-length female nude. The work was commissioned by John Lowell, a Boston lawyer and pamphleteer. As Lowell died before the work was sent to him, he most likely never had time to reflect on the fact that this was the first sculpture of a female nude by an American artist. As with so many aspects of Greenough's life, the idea for this work inspired others who ultimately reaped the benefits that eluded him. While *Venus Victrix* was quietly exhibited without fanfare or controversy at the Boston Athenæum beginning in 1842, Powers's nude, *The Greek Slave*, catapulted him to an international status that ensured him success for the remainder of his career.

One sign of Greenough's belief that by the late 1830s he had reached the threshold of success was the fact that he had a calling card printed that was inscribed simply *Greenough*. The implication was that a first name was superfluous for someone so well known. To others it suggested more "the rank of 'Bonaparte' rather than an American sculptor."[45] Greenough's marriage, too, brought stability, and any immediate financial worries were momentarily eliminated.[46] In addition, the number of commissions he received were now greater than at any point in his career. Last, he had not yet suffered the personal indignation that resulted from the failure of the American public to appreciate fully his statue of Washington for the Capitol.

This period also proved to be one in which he became increasingly interested in the format of marble cut in low relief. Greenough had long admired such works by John Flaxman (1755–1826), the British sculptor, and Thorvaldsen. As he also believed this format to be particularly challenging, his decision to experiment with it probably reflects an increased confidence in his own abilities. In succession he modeled three bas-reliefs: *Judgment of Paris* for John Lowell of Boston, *The Angel Warning St. John* (fig. 18), and *Memorial to George*

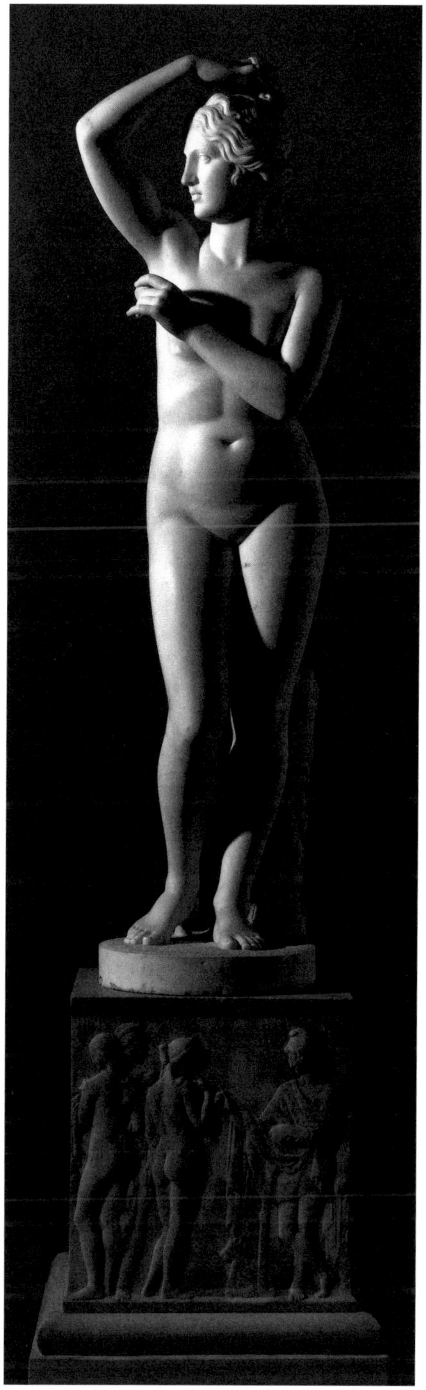

Fig. 17. Horatio Greenough, *Venus Victrix*, 1837–41. Marble, 57½ × 16⅛ × 18¾ inches; and *Judgment of Paris*. Marble, bas-relief set into base, 24⅝ × 21⅜ × 17 inches. Courtesy of the Boston Athenæum.

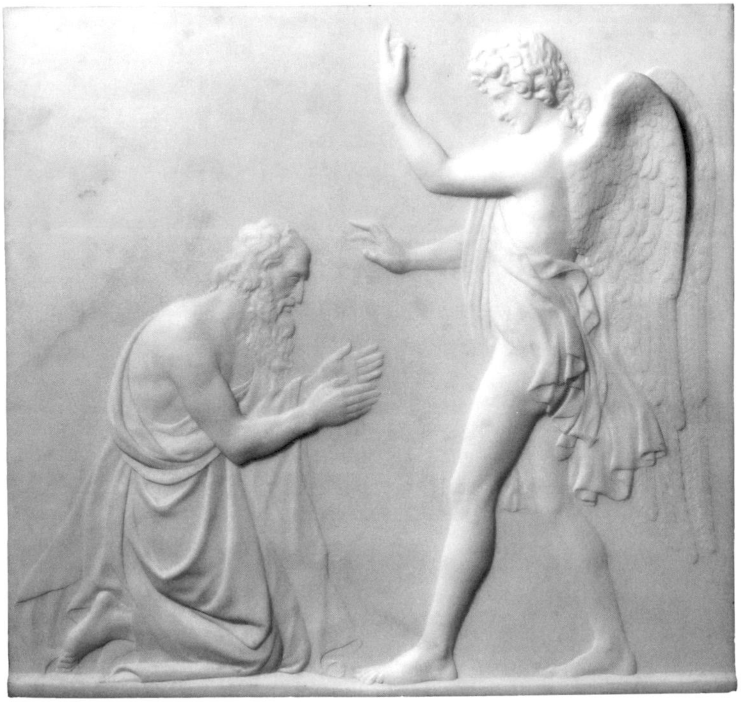

Fig. 18. Horatio Greenough, *The Angel Warning St. John*, c. 1838–41. Marble, 21½ × 23¼ × 24¼ inches. Yale University Art Gallery. Bequest of Edward E. Salisbury, B.A. 1832.

and Mary Gibbs. Also at this time Greenough resolved to include reliefs of Hercules Strangling the Serpent and Apollo in His Chariot on the chair for his figure of Washington.

Florence, 1839–42

When Greenough returned to Florence in 1836 he found that the weight of Washington's uplifted arm and drapery had bent the cast out of line. It took six months to correct this fault. Blocking out in marble was the next step, and this was done at Carrara by November 1837; Greenough visited several times to oversee the process. By March 1839 the statue was delivered to Greenough in Florence, and over the summer he employed as many as seven workmen on the ongoing finish work.[47]

Greenough had pronounced that the work would be ready to be shipped by October 1840. In February of that year he began to show the work publicly. By the following January he opened a studio-gallery in the city, in a space adjoining the church of San Giovannio dei Cavalieri in Via San Gallo (see fig. 22 in Chronology). Here, in January 1841, he showed his Washington by torchlight, and beginning the following month he announced in the local newspapers that it could be seen during the day as well.[48] On 8 June 1841 the statue left Leghorn for Washington, aboard the sloop *The Sea.*[49]

Public reaction to the work was divided. While a handful of articles were laudatory, the majority opinion was unfavorable. There was certainly respect for the sculpture's craftsmanship, but the primary lament was that Washington was not shown in the clothing of his day. All manner of indignation and witticism rained down on Greenough's creation. A piece in the New York *Herald* described Washington as having just risen from his coffin with his winding sheet about him. Henry Wise, a congressman, suggested the head be kept and the remainder be tossed in the Potomac.[50] Although Greenough anticipated a degree of public distaste for the sculpture, he seems to have reassured himself that those Americans with education and cultivated taste would recognize its merits.

Now that federal patronage and his marriage made Greenough financially secure, he decided to accept fewer private commissions and be more selective in their choice. In particular, he wanted to do fewer portraits and more ideal works, which would permit his creative energy to find an outlet. Busts he did complete were of his own choice, such as that of Marchese Gino Capponi, the historian. Portraits included that of Ada Reviczky (cat. 26), the two-year-old daughter of Count Adam Reviczky, a Polish political émigré in Florence, which allowed him to show the entire figure in a fanciful setting. Idealized work included his colossal bust of Lucifer (cat. 36), which he may well have done to indicate his ability on this scale.

The reduced pressure to generate income also meant that Greenough had more time to pursue other interests. He wrote a number of essays on topics such as the public monuments of London, decency in works of art, and the dress of Washington in sculpture. The latter two topics undoubtedly were intended as a defense of his statue for the Capitol. He also took time to significantly expand his library, acquire paintings and other works of art for his home, and, with his wife, be more active in Florentine social life.

In the spring of 1841 he moved across the Arno to the imposing seventeenth-century Palazzo Pucci in Via Pucci (fig. 19). There he

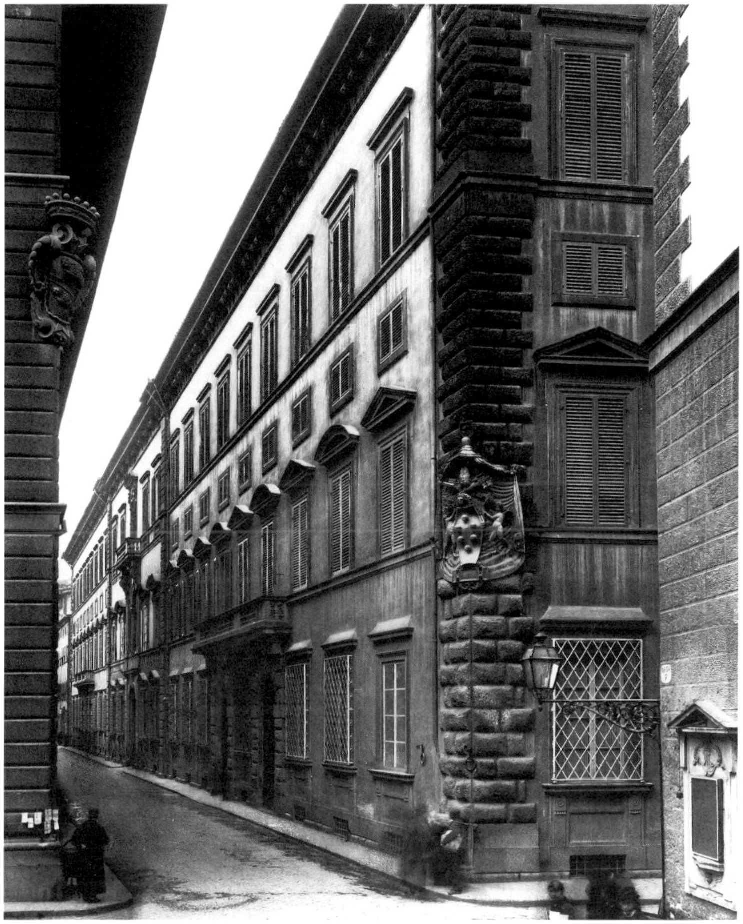

Fig. 19. Palazzo Pucci, Florence. Courtesy of Alinari.

rented the apartments of Marchese Felice Baciocchi, one of the two owners and a descendant of Napoleon's sister Eliza. Despite such outward manifestations of success, Greenough was beginning to be emotionally undone by the results of his federal commission. In the years following Greenough's submission of his design for the sculpture (cat. 53), mounting apprehension by members of Congress about the character of the work muted any possible welcome for it. This predicament may well have contributed to the government's tardy payments to the artist, as well as its failure to acknowledge the sculpture's arrival in Washington. Both situations disturbed him greatly.[51]

Adding to Greenough's deepening professional malaise was the poor state of his wife's health. By January 1842 she had experienced five consecutive miscarriages, and the Greenoughs remained childless. When her stepfather decided to return to America in the summer of 1842, Louisa went along to visit family. Despite the personal dislocation, Horatio undoubtedly valued the cathartic benefit such a trip might have for his wife.

America, 1842–43

During his wife's absence, Greenough traveled to France and England but by September had decided to join her in America. The trip provided him with the opportunity to arrange for a permanent pedestal for his Washington statue, and as a result, he spent five months in the capital. Greenough's mood during this visit was hostile; he was openly critical of the political scene and ambivalent about the urban landscape. His state of mind is reflected in his remarks brought on by the death of Allston that summer. He derisively remarked in a letter that America "has always acted toward her artists like a hen who has hatched ducklings—She cannot understand why they run to the water instead of thriving upon the dunghill—which only asks to be scratched in order to feed them all!"[52]

Another example of Greenough's being detached from American taste centered on the invitation from Robert M. Patterson, Master of the Mint at Philadelphia, to submit drawings for changes to American coinage. This he did, but the changes were considered such a radical departure from the existing designs that they were unusable.[53]

While in America Louisa received $12,000 from the sale of her share of the Gore property and thus replenished her financial resources.[54] By the middle of October she and Horatio were once again in Italy.

Florence and Graffenberg, 1843–46

Greenough was delighted to be back in Florence. In the succeeding months he was attentive to progress on *The Rescue* and was also at work on designs for an equestrian monument of Washington (cat. 58).

While the Greenoughs reestablished their Florentine routine after the return to Florence, it was disturbed by yet another miscarriage.[55] Presumably as a result of this event, they departed Florence in April 1844 for a spa-sanitorium in Graffenberg, Silesia (Austria), operated by Vincent Priessnitz. In the second half of the year they made another trip between Florence and Graffenberg and remained at the spa until the following spring. Despite bouts of poor health during the winter, the Greenoughs were rewarded on 11 May 1845 with a son they named Henry Saltonstall.[56]

By the time the Greenoughs set out for Florence it was July 1845 and Horatio had spent almost eighteen months away from his studio. His time, however, had not been inactive, as he had read and written a great deal. In particular, his wife's invalidism and her successful delivery of their son made him more reflective about spiritual matters. It also conceivably influenced his decision to sculpt a bust of Christ (cat. 37).

Risorgimento, 1847–51

The late 1840s were a time of turmoil in Tuscany, and throughout much of Europe, as various political constituencies sought to throw off the yoke of Austrian control and assert national identities. In Florence, citizens agitated for civic reform, and as a result Grand Duke Leopold II permitted the formation of the National or Civic Guards. To celebrate the forming of this organization in September 1847, a parade was held. Louisa helped to make a flag that Horatio carried through the streets. The Marchese Baciocchi put the courtyard of the Palazzo Pucci at the disposal of the Civic Guards, which they used for a military drill.[57] All of this activity and the Austrian suppression of the Italian attempt at independence in 1849, during which twenty thousand troops occupied the city, disturbed Greenough greatly, and he commented soon thereafter that the city "had lost much of its charm."[58]

On the business side of his life, Greenough modeled a number of sculptures and built a new studio. In August 1847 Greenough bought land at the intersection of Via San Francesco Poverino and Via San Caterina, on the newly laid-out Piazza Maria Antonia (now Piazza Independenza; fig. 20).[59] There he built himself a commodious studio. It was a marvel to visitors, such as the artists' biographer Henry T. Tuckerman, who observed: "All the rooms were on one floor, built with great strength and a fine ornamental stone work on the exterior, having in the center the cypher G. Attached to the structure was a beautiful garden: within was a spacious and admirably lighted exhibition-room—near by the sculptor's private studio, a large apartment

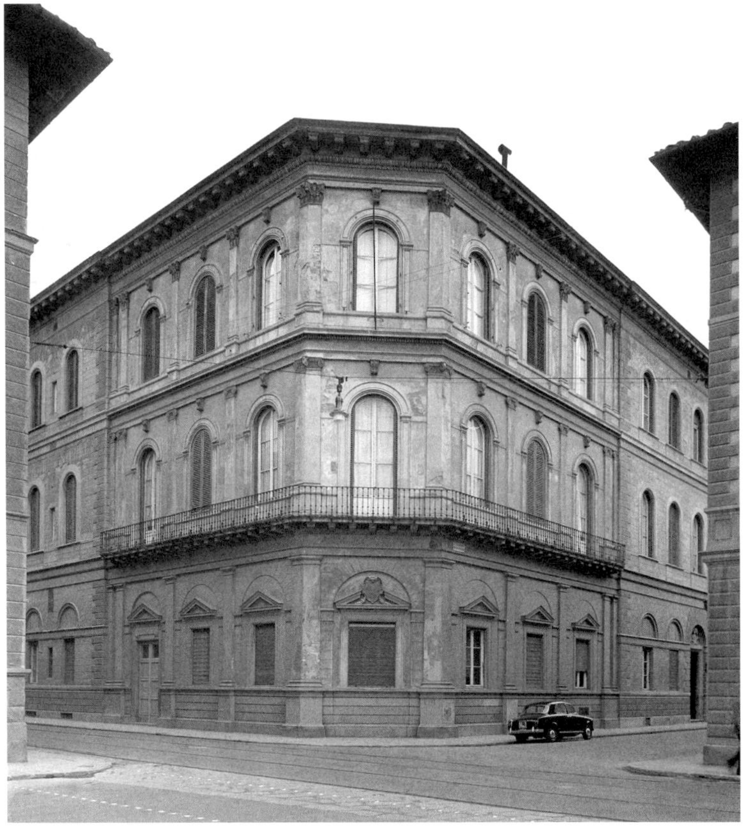

Fig. 20. Horatio Greenough's studio. Piazza Independenza, Florence. Courtesy of Nathalia Wright.

for the workmen, a gallery of plaster casts, a vestibule hung with pictures, a noble rotunda, leading by a short flight of steps to the garden, and a charming library."[60]

In addition to *The Rescue,* which occupied his attention during this period, Greenough devoted most of his time to ideal works. In May 1847 he modeled several bas-reliefs including two versions of *Castor and Pollux* (cat. 39), the most stunning of his surviving works in this format. For George Ticknor, who had loaned him money years earlier, he executed a relief depicting a dejected sculptor sitting before an unfinished work, while the dying lamp of inspiration is being refilled by an unseen hand (cat. 42). Other reliefs modeled about this time are *The Genius of Italy* (cat. 44) and *Bacchante and Faun* (cat. 46).[61] While it is not clear that either of these was carved in marble, the latter work indicates that he was capable of considerable animation and vigor in the difficult format.

In these last years in Florence, Greenough became increasingly concerned about the well-being of his family. After he and Louisa, as well as their son, Henry, fell sick in an epidemic of cholera, or spotted fever, the artist had increased misgivings about continuing to live in Florence. By the fall of 1849 the Greenoughs had moved to Villa Brichieri Colombi on the hill of Bellosguardo (see fig. 23 in Chronology) about a mile outside the Porta Romana. From their twenty-two-room house, not only were they removed from the congestion of Florence, but they could watch the sunset from their terrace.[62]

From his new quarters overlooking Florence, Greenough cogitated about his future. Issues of family health, Italian politics, and his own career as an expatriate artist induced him to consider returning permanently to America. In a letter to Joseph Cogswell in the fall of 1850, he lamented both his present predicament and his future: "partly on account of the complications of European politics and partly from the fear that my being so long out of sight will put me equally out of mind with the public of America."[63]

Despite these concerns, or because of them, Greenough decided by the spring of 1851 to return to America. Initially he thought the family might make this a short-term visit and return to Florence. But by the time he actually made shipping arrangements, his plan to stay in America was set. As a result, the list of studio works and personal belongings being shipped included six cases of books, six cases of marble busts, two cases of "plaster," one each of bas-reliefs, pictures, silver plate, and earthenware.[64] After spending part of the summer in Switzerland, the Greenoughs made their way to England, where they sailed from Liverpool for Boston on 4 October 1851.

America, 1851–52

Greenough's personal belief that he could right his now listing career became particularly evident on his return to America. His attentions vacillated between grandiose new projects, such as a colossal equestrian monument of Andrew Jackson and a complex memorial to Cooper (who had recently died), to a desire to oversee the installation of *The Rescue* on the east front of the Capitol. Business activity was punctuated by social events, which included meeting Henry Wadsworth Longfellow and a revealing correspondence with Ralph Waldo Emerson.[65]

Within a few weeks of arriving home, Greenough was on his way to Washington. There he waited for six weeks expecting the momentary arrival of *The Rescue.* The work was aptly named, as Greenough undoubtedly hoped it would rehabilitate his faltering reputation. Much to Greenough's disappointment, however, he learned that the work had not yet been shipped from Italy. But the hiatus proved productive in other ways, as Greenough took the occasion to write some, if not all, of the five essays that made up the pamphlet published as *Aesthetics at Washington.*

The essays decried the current state of artistic taste in our nation's capital. They also helped Greenough justify why his work, particularly the statue of Washington, failed to excite the passions of the American public. The sculptor chastised the prudishness and provinciality of American society regarding the issue of nudity and the public's failure to appreciate adequately such works as his *Chanting Cherubs.* He also implied that a lack of sophistication had led the citizenry to endorse Robert Mills's (1781–1855) misguided fusion of an Egyptian obelisk and Doric colonnade as the proposed Washington monument. In architecture, he both decried those "who would bend the Greek temple to every use" and dismissed the Gothic revival Smithsonian Institution as "that dark pile."[66] And just as he viewed his statue of Washington as a modern-day refinement of classical sculpture, he reserved his greatest praise for buildings like the Capitol, which embodied similar ideals in architecture.

In the spring of 1852 Greenough had one last opportunity to create a large public monument that might serve to raise his abilities in the eyes of public opinion. But this effort, an equestrian statue of Washington (cat. 58), which was to be carried out jointly with a second sculptor, Henry Kirke Brown (1814–1886), ended in a bitter contract dispute, and the commission fell to Brown alone.

With this most recent defeat, Greenough retreated to Newport, Rhode Island, where his family had gone for the summer. Although in the occasional letter he put a positive spin on his outlook on life, as when he remarked, "God is great and Newport is His abode," internal pressures continued to undermine his confidence. He had entirely given up the modeling of sculpture and increasingly sought other avenues for his abilities. His belief that he was being considered by "leading men of letters" in New York for a university professorship may have prompted a further shift toward lectures and writing.[67] Early in August he decided to publish a volume of essays, which he sent to G. P. Putnam, the New York publisher.[68]

By September it was clear that Greenough's return to America brought more problems than solutions. Henry T. Tuckerman later observed that the loss of Greenough's Tuscan "routine" and the relative tranquillity of his Italian existence were factors that permeated his mental decline in the fall of 1852. Although he took considerable enjoyment from corresponding with Emerson, who described him as "an extraordinary man, a man of sense, of virtue, and of rare elevation of thought and carriage," for all practical purposes his world was shrinking.[69]

On 4 December 1852 Greenough was taken in a strait jacket to McClean's Asylum in Somerville, Massachusetts, by his brother Henry. During the preceding days, while at home in Newport, Greenough had suffered an attack of "violent mania,"[70] which rendered him completely irrational. While signs of this manic depression had manifested themselves during the preceding weeks, the event that triggered the sculptor's tumble from rationality was most likely the realization that, in addition to a career in disarray, his financial situation was precarious. On 1 December he had asked Henry to procure a letter of credit for $2,000 to settle his account with his Florentine bankers. Also, earlier in the year he had hastily returned to Boston to avert a financial crisis in his wife's estate.[71]

On 21 November Greenough had attended a dinner at Tremont House in Boston hosted by Emerson for Arthur Clough, a visiting English poet. Also there were Hawthorne, Longfellow, Lowell, Theodore Parker, Charles Sumner, Samuel Ward, and Ellery Channing. On 24 November and again the following week he had given lectures on the subject "Art as Related to Life" in the Lecture Room of the New Music Hall on Winter Street. The events, which were poorly attended, realized only $14 in admission fees. Although none in attendance noticed, the patient records at McClean's document that his second lecture had consisted of a "curious *mixture of incomprehensibleness*."[72]

Greenough died on 18 December. The record of McClean's Asylum lists the cause of death as "brain fever." Cambridge Death Records give the cause of death as "nervous derangement." "Brain fever" is an obsolete euphemism for a fever of unknown origin. What remains unknown is whether the fever that precipitated Greenough's death was the cause of his irrational behavior in his last weeks, or whether the fever itself resulted from a neurological or other violent physiological disorder producing extremes of temperature.[73] His funeral, held three days later at his brother's, was conducted by the Reverend Dr. James Walker, president of Harvard. Interment was at Mount Auburn Cemetery, Cambridge. When Greenough's estate was settled, his assets were valued at $5,851.97, of which $5,830 was owed him by the federal government for *The Rescue*. The difference was largely composed of the pitiful income from his last two lectures. Even though Henry bore the cost of his brother's final hospital bill, when all the claims against the estate were entered, they exceeded his assets by almost $3,000.[74]

A SCULPTOR'S PLIGHT

"It takes a great deal of resolution to work through the elements in a foreign land, with one's milk-teeth unshed and little money."[75] So wrote Greenough to his brother a few years after establishing his studio in Florence. By this Greenough meant everything from the day-to-day issues involved in operating a studio and meeting expenses to the larger questions of finding patrons, being noticed, and worrying about competition.

Many of the professional decisions Greenough made during his career reflected a need to confront the practical aspects of being an artist in a society that placed a very low premium on the arts. Critical decisions such as where to live, how to find work, and how to gain publicity might mean the difference between success and failure. Leaving Massachusetts for Italy made sense for a great number of reasons. The country had a centuries-old heritage of carving, and there were large concentrations of antique, Renaissance, and modern masterpieces. Leading European sculptors, such as Thorvaldsen, Bartolini, and the Englishman John Gibson (1790–1866), resided there. Formal training, unavailable in America, could be had there as well.

The most obvious determinant for Greenough's remaining in Italy was the availability of Italian carvers. These craftsman, called boasters, were instrumental in the completion of nineteenth-century stone carving. The prevailing method of sculpting meant that the artist would model his subject in clay, as this was considered the creative part of the process.[76] This might be done directly from life or based on drawings. After applying the finishing touches, the sculptor turned the work over to assistants who produced a mold from which a plaster model was made. Using a system called "pointing," the plaster model then served as a guide for carving a marble block.[77] Crystalline white marble was prized because it lacked grain or impurities: "The clay was the life, plaster the death and marble, the Resurrection," Thorvaldsen had remarked to Emerson.[78] The marble was first roughed out using rasps and files, then finished and polished using fine sand or pumice stone. In Greenough's case, sculptures would be returned to him for applying the final surface. On at least one occasion, in the case of *The Chanting Cherubs*, he chose to carve the entire figure himself.[79]

For virtually his entire career, Greenough was beset by financial worry. Early on, Greenough lived frugally, on a few hundred dollars a year. In 1829, for example, he was paying $108 yearly for room and board and sharing living expenses with other artists.[80] For his first busts he received $100–150, and of this amount he received approximately two-thirds at the time it was modeled in clay, with the remainder paid on completion.[81] His decision in 1828 to relocate from Rome to Carrara and then Florence was conditioned by financial concerns. The cost of a boaster in Rome was $12–15 per bust, while in Carrara it was $6–7. Marble apparently cost about $80 per bust-sized block in Rome or Florence, but at Carrara he could get it for one-quarter that price. In addition, if the blocks were cut at Carrara, it was cheaper to replace them if flaws were found as the carving progressed. Even so, Greenough's profit margin was elusive. For example, crating and shipping *The Chanting Cherubs* to America cost $525, an enormous amount that dwarfed the $200 Greenough received for it.[82]

Debt was also Greenough's frequent companion. From the outset of his career, when his father borrowed money to send him to Italy, the sculptor was never far from a loan or a gift to ease his precarious financial existence. Dr. George Parkman, a prominent Boston physician who had shared his knowledge of anatomy with Greenough, also helped to underwrite Greenough's first Italian trip. In 1828 Gilmor interceded with a group of Boston merchants on Greenough's behalf. They in turn provided a loan of $1,000 toward Greenough's second Italian trip. During 1831–32 Cooper loaned Greenough 1,600 Francesconi (about $1,760). The previous year he received an anonymous gift of $1,200, which years later he learned came from his former Harvard professor, George Ticknor.[83] Early in 1832 Greenough unburdened himself in a letter to Morse: "Now when a man is poor very poor—stung by ambition—overwhelmed by obligations—encumbered with duties that tax him to the utmost—should he be capable in the midst of all this of finding a corner in his heavy heart wherein to enshrine an image of loveliness and purity which should be at once a blessing and scourge to him."[84]

Greenough's government commission for a statue of Washington lifted him into a different financial orbit. Congress allocated the enormous sum of $20,000 to the project. Nevertheless, Greenough's costs, which he outlined in detail, far exceeded this amount. Yet the work, at least in theory, relieved the day-to-day pressure of generating income from portrait busts. Although it took a number of years to complete, the Washington statue generated income equivalent to one to two hundred busts or ten to forty smaller ideal works.[85] It is little wonder, then, that Greenough considered this commission such a plum.

Greenough was also worried about the twin issues of patronage and publicity. Like any artist, Greenough sought ways to secure his financial situation and enhance his reputation. He realized that a few highly placed patrons might get his work seen and induce others to place commissions of their own. It was for this reason that in 1827 he sought to model portraits of Josiah Quincy and the presidents John Quincy Adams and John Adams. He had similar hopes for his busts of Cooper, Lafayette, and Morse.

Since ideal works meant higher prices and more prestige, it was crucial that Greenough have such works commissioned and seen. Patrons like Cooper and Gilmor were crucial to his larger plan. In particular, Cooper's willingness to purchase *The Chanting Cherubs* and then assist in the efforts to send the work on tour to Boston and New York meant that Greenough's sculptures could be seen by large numbers of people. For similar reasons, Greenough willingly sent works to the annual exhibits at the National Academy of Design and the Boston Athenæum.[86]

Greenough also spent considerable time cultivating those people who were placed in positions to lobby on his behalf. Such activity took different forms. Cooper, Bryant, and Dunlap wrote glowingly of Greenough, which served to enhance his reputation.[87] Patriarchal figures like Allston were also instrumental in enabling him to obtain the federal commission for the Washington statue.

And although Greenough lamented the fact he was abroad, being in Florence enabled him to entertain wealthy touring Americans. The vast majority of his private commissions for busts and ideal works were the results of such activity. Also, a visible and well-equipped studio helped to impress his many visitors. Greenough was at his best in such social situations, where his drawing abilities proved particularly useful; his interaction with potential clients was legendary. He certainly hoped that such visitors would regale their friends with their positive experiences and direct other patrons to him.

THE DRAWINGS

In his book *A Memorial of Horatio Greenough*, Henry T. Tuckerman nostalgically recalled his visits to the sculptor's studio during several months of 1833. There, beside a wood fire on winter evenings, among a few friends, the artist

> would often occupy himself with pen or crayon while thus enjoying a social hour; sometimes covering a sheet of paper with the remembered faces of the absent and the loved; and at others, making elaborate and carefully wrought designs for a basso-relievo or statue. He had studies enough for twenty years' use, partially sketched at the time of his death. A fine specimen of his facility and precision as a draughtsman is before me as I write—his parting gift when I left Florence.[88]

Greenough loved to draw. He did so over his entire professional career and for a wide variety of reasons. Approximately 185 independent drawings survive, along with numerous letters amplified by pictures. From the many references to drawings in his correspondence, it is clear that what survives is but a small fraction of his total output. In such activity he stands apart from other American sculptors of his generation: Hiram Powers, John Frazee (1790–1852), Thomas Crawford (1813?–1857), and Sholbal Clevenger (1812–1843). While drawings by some of these sculptors survive, none of them seemed to view drawing as a critical part of the artist experience.[89] European sculptors like Canova and Thorvaldsen, however, drew voraciously and well.[90]

Greenough's drawings range from the simplest scribbles and rudimentary *croquis* (sketches) to painstaking academic drawings and presentation works. His favorite media were graphite and charcoal or pen and ink on white or cream-colored paper. Greenough presumably began drawing in his youth, when his interest in carving started, but the earliest documented drawing is from his student days at Harvard (cat. 1). As he believed that there were times of day when a man has his best and most useful thoughts, he always carried with him a notebook, in which he made a rapid sketch of ideas that came to him.[91]

As a disciple of Allston, Greenough realized that European study was crucial to developing his skills. Allston is regarded as the most complete American draftsman of his time. His drawings range from quickly conceived compositional ideas to highly worked preparatory figure studies for paintings (fig. 21). It is likely that they made a significant impression on the younger artist. Eventually, Greenough's drawings' range of purpose rivaled that of Allston, although he never equaled his mentor in mastering technique. By the time Greenough reached Italy, he was well aware of the importance of drawing to the maturation of his artistic skills. Among the first things he did was make use of a leather-bound sketchbook (cat. 3) to compile drawings after casts, antique, Renaissance, and modern monuments, and from life. Over the next few years he devoted a significant proportion of his daily regimen to drawing from casts, making anatomical studies, drawing from models in life-drawing classes or hiring models to pose for him.

Greenough's drawings can be divided into two broad categories: those he kept and those he gave away. Among the former are drawings made initially, or exclusively, for his own use. His sketchbook, all of his student drawings, and many of the working drawings for com-

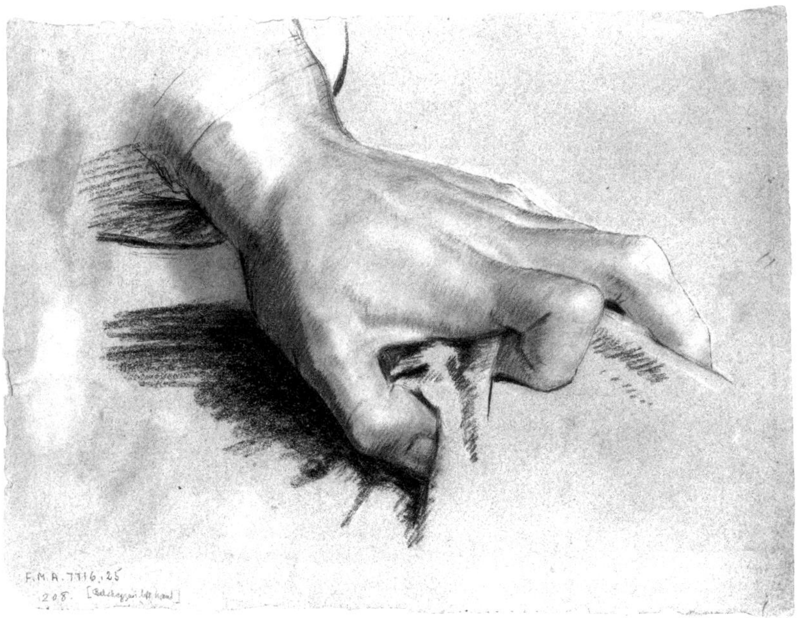

Fig. 21. Washington Allston, *Belshazzar's Left Hand*, c. 1821–28. Black chalk and white highlights on blue-gray paper, 9⅜ × 12½ inches. Fogg Art Museum, Harvard University, Art Museums. Loan from The Washington Allston Trust. © President and Fellows of Harvard College.

missioned work fall into this category. But from the very moment of his arrival in Europe, Greenough also used drawing as a way to communicate with or entertain friends. His letters are filled with caricatures and drawings of friends and illustrious figures. Among the over three hundred letters by Greenough to survive are many references to the enclosure of drawings with his correspondence. Such drawings served different purposes. He sent drawings to Allston or Morse, or his brother Henry, to indicate his current projects, the nature of his skills, or to seek critical reaction. He sent drawings to Gilmor, Cooper, Edward Salisbury, David Sears, and other patrons to indicate his proposed designs for compositions or to suggest possible works they might commission.[92]

In the case of his statue of Washington, he received a specific request from the government to furnish the Department of State from time to time with drawings of his design.[93] To accomplish this, he sent at least two drawings (and presumably others) to Edward Livingston, the Secretary of State (cat. 53).

Of the drawings Greenough kept, they, too, served different purposes. As a portraitist, he preferred to model sitters directly in clay. But as this was not always possible, drawings often served as his initial observations of sitters (cat. 21). Other portrait drawings were done simply to entertain or record friends, independent of any sculpture. Greenough realized that his gift for drawing provided him an easy and convenient means to provide visitors with mementos. Some of these were less than spontaneous, as when he noted in a letter to Cole that "the redoubtable Miss Douglas [Harriet Douglas] was here the other day and *impressed* me for a drawing."[94] On other occasions, however, he created elaborate presentation drawings to acknowledge friendship or patronage, as he did for Benjamin Greene in 1838 (cat. 32).

Complex or ambitious projects required many drawings. Some of these are hastily done and reflect his initial record of a specific idea. Others are details of larger projects, such as limbs of figures or single figures of multifigure commissions. Still other drawings suggest how a composition may have evolved over time, as he resolved the placement of a figure. It is not surprising that his two government commissions generated the greatest number of preparatory studies.

Some drawings also help to reveal Greenough's agitated mental state. For example, the great number of individual sheets covered with figures of different sizes, subjects, and in various states of finish—from scribbles to labored drawings—reflect his restless nature and hyperactivity (cat. 29). These drawings, perhaps more than any others in Greenough's oeuvre, document the great fertility of his mind and the way he used the medium as a vehicle to release vast quantities of nervous energy.

If Greenough had to single out a group of drawings for which he wished to be remembered, they would undoubtedly be those that document his various inventive compositions for ideal sculptures. For it was these ideal poetic images—drawn from literature or freely invented—that are the truest manifestation of his artistic vision.[95] Certainly, his correspondence is the most effusive when describing appealing subjects that have recently come to mind. These fresh, spontaneous drawings reveal the speed with which he is trying to capture a rush of imaginative images. One time he described a mailed drawing as his "first thoughts made after dinner with a cigar," while at another he cautioned the recipient "to look at this sketch merely as an expression of the general features of the composition & not as a sample of form or character."[96]

It is not surprising that Greenough continued to gain satisfaction from drawing even in the declining moments of his career. It was almost as though drawing became a recreational activity to relieve stress. Tuckerman, for example, visited Greenough in Newport during the fall of 1852 and found him "full of noble aims" and "kindled by the inspiration of nature and society."[97] During their last evening together, Greenough worked on a crayon head while the conversation moved from one subject to another.

What, then, does this array of drawings tell us about Greenough the artist? For one thing, they document that some American sculptors utilized the drawing medium extensively.[98] They also confirm that Greenough was a gifted draftsman, who had the ability to create drawings of tremendous sensitivity and deftness. The fact that so many of Greenough's drawings do not survive indicates that he rarely, if ever, thought about them as a means to document his abilities. As he never intended his drawings to be exhibited, he most likely would not have been surprised that subsequent generations ignored them.

The surviving drawings also make clear that to Greenough the medium was always a means to an end, never an end in itself. For this reason, the idea behind a drawing was frequently much more important than the detail or quality of finish of the graphic image. As a result, individually, the vast majority of his drawings do not rival those of the American artists remembered as the great draftsmen of the early nineteenth century: Allston, Cole, John Vanderlyn (1775–1852), and Rembrandt Peale.

Greenough's drawings, however, clearly establish their importance in understanding his working method. They also help to document a personality beset by conflicting tendencies. Such behavior convinced him that he could overcome competition from fellow sculptors and opposition from federal legislators and media pundits who misunderstood his work. Such a strategy, however, allowed no safety net when he failed. The very personality that spawned a limitless supply of ideas and supported a photographic memory were the benefits of an otherwise insidious mental condition. The drawings help to amplify the fact that hidden in the fruits of success were the seeds of his destruction.

Ironically, our assessment of Greenough recalls that of James Jackson Jarves written only a few years after the artist's death. Jarves adroitly observed that Greenough and Allston were very similar artists whose "execution was unequal to their conceptions." For Greenough, he noted, "we cannot point out any masterpiece, as showing an entirely satisfactory fulfillment of his own desires, but his whole career was an example in the right direction."[99] His story then is tragic, but one that we are, perhaps, better able to understand with the passage of time and a clearer appreciation of the drawings, which were such a crucial part of his artistic persona.

NOTES

1. Greenough 1958, p. 13.
2. Wright 1963a, p. 21.
3. Described by Wright 1963a, p. 20, as "practical"; by Horatio Greenough, to James Fenimore Cooper, 30 July 1836, as "honest and benevolent." Unless otherwised noted, all quotations from Greenough's letters are taken from Wright 1972.
4. Wright 1963a, p. 22.
5. Crane 1972, p. 23.
6. Craven 1984, pp. 64–66.
7. Important texts at Harvard during Greenough's years there were Hugh Blair's *Lectures on Rhetoric*, John Locke's *Essays*, William Paley's *Evidences of Christianity* and *Natural Theology*, Dugald Stewart's *Elements of the Philosophy of the Human Mind*, Joseph Butler's *Analogy* and the *Federalist*. See Wright 1963a, p. 27.
8. Quoted in Dunlap 1918, vol. 2, part 2, p. 421.
9. Wright 1963a, p. 29.
10. Quoted in Dunlap 1918, vol. 2, part 2, p. 421.
11. Gerdts and Stebbins 1979, p. 38.
12. Wright 1963a, p. 32.
13. Horatio Greenough to Samuel F. B. Morse, between 25 March and 23 April 1832.
14. Lawrence 1855, pp. 338–339.
15. Dunlap 1918, vol. 2, part 2, p. 392.
16. Horatio Greenough to Samuel F. B. Morse, 15 May 1828.
17. Wright 1963a, p. 48, and Richard H. Dana, Sr., to Gulian Verplanck, 2 April 1830. New-York Historical Society.
18. Horatio Greenough to Josiah Quincy, 4 September 1827.
19. Chief Justice Marshall to Joseph Story, 1, 26 May 1828. Massachusetts Historical Society.
20. Horatio Greenough to Washington Allston, 19, 20 September 1829.
21. Quoted in Neal 1943, pp. 38, 24.
22. Horatio Greenough to Robert Gilmor, Jr., 17 May 1828.
23. Horatio Greenough to Washington Allston, 10, 16, 17 October 1828.
24. Wright 1963a, pp. 64–65.
25. Horatio Greenough to Washington Allston, 10, 16, 17 October 1828.
26. Horatio Greenough to Washington Allston, 10, 16, 17 October 1828.
27. Wright 1963a, p. 61.
28. Horatio Greenough to Richard Henry Dana, 18 April 1829. Dana Collection, Massachusetts Historical Society. Quoted in Crane 1972, p. 39.
29. Horatio Greenough to Robert Gilmor, Jr., 25 February 1829.
30. Wright 1963a, p. 83.
31. Greenough 1887, Alfred Greenough to Henry Greenough, 1 April 1830.
32. Crane 1972, p. 55.
33. Horatio Greenough to Samuel F. B. Morse, 20 August 1832.
34. Tuckerman 1968, "Fragments," pp. 199–200.
35. Horatio Greenough to Washington Allston, 7 March 1835.
36. Wright 1963a, p.103.
37. Greenough 1887, Horatio Greenough to Henry Greenough, 19 March 1836.
38. Wunder 1991, vol. 1, p. 71.
39. Horatio Greenough to James Fenimore Cooper, 23 September 1836.
40. Fryd 1992, p. 90.
41. Horatio Greenough to John Forsyth, 1 July 1837.
42. Greenough 1887, Horatio Greenough to Henry Greenough, 16 June 1837.
43. Wright 1963a, p. 199.
44. Greenough 1887, Horatio Greenough to Henry Greenough, 2 January 1839.
45. Bronson 1928, vol. 3, pp. 408, 424.
46. Utilizing marriage to ease constant financial hardship was a route also taken by Thomas Crawford. Gale 1964, pp. 46–47, and Wunder 1991, vol. 1, p. 104.
47. Horatio Greenough to John Forsyth, 6 June 1837; Horatio Greenough to Aaron Vail, 26 June 1840; Horatio Greenough to James Fenimore Cooper, 15 December 1835, and Greenough 1887, Horatio Greenough to Henry Greenough, 18 March 1838.
48. Horatio Greenough to Gino Capponi, 8 January 1841; *Gazetta di Firenze*, 18 February 1841, and Florence *Giornale del Commercio*, 3 March 1841.
49. Wright 1963a, p. 140.
50. Wright 1963a, pp. 144–145.
51. Wright 1963a, pp. 221, 222.
52. Wright 1972, Horatio Greenough to Richard Henry Dana, 21 September 1843.
53. Horatio Greenough to Robert M. Patterson, 30 December 1842, and Chamberlain 1959.
54. Wright 1963a, p. 226.
55. Francis B. to Elizabeth B. Greenough, 21 May [1848]. See Wright 1963a, p. 349 n. 12.

56. Horatio Greenough to Hiram Powers, 13 May 1845.
57. Wright 1963a, p. 259.
58. Greenough 1887, Horatio Greenough to Henry Greenough, 13 August 1850.
59. Wright 1963a, p. 251.
60. Tuckerman 1967, p. 265.
61. Greenough 1887, Horatio Greenough to Henry Greenough, 22 October 1850.
62. Wright 1963a, p. 257.
63. Horatio Greenough to Joseph Cogswell, 26 September 1850.
64. Wright 1963a, p. 263. Works left behind in the studio included casts of Michelangelo's *Day* and *Night* and a bust of Richard Henry Wilde, lawyer, congressman, and poet.
65. See Metzger 1954.
66. Greenough 1958, p. 47.
67. Greenough 1887, Horatio Greenough to Henry Greenough, 20 May 1852.
68. *New York Evening Post*, 7 August 1852.
69. Emerson 1909–14, vol. 3, pp. 318–319.
70. Medical records at McClean's Asylum cited in Wright 1963a, p. 297.
71. Horatio Greenough to William Cullen Bryant, 5 February 1852.
72. Quoted in Wright 1963a, p. 297.
73. Crane 1972, pp. 132n, 133, and Wright 1963a, p. 298.
74. Suffolk County Registry of Probate (Boston), no. 38,180.
75. Greenough 1887, Horatio Greenough to Henry Greenough, 16 June 1835.
76. Craven 1984, p. 106.
77. "A pointing machine measures the depth from a given vertical, of, for example, the receding planes of the nose of a plaster cast and transfers the measurements to a hole drilled in the marble block. Scores of measured depths are thus transferred to the marble, until all that is left for the mason is to cut away the surplus stone." Murray and Murray 1963, s.v. "pointing machine."
78. Quoted in Brumbaugh 1971, p. 253.
79. Horatio Greenough to Robert Gilmor, 13 January 1832.
80. Wright 1963a, pp. 76, 93–94. In 1832 he shared quarters with his brother Henry; their rent was $3.00 a month and dinner cost $.25.
81. In 1830 Greenough received $100 for his busts of Cornelius Bradford and Joseph Grinnell's daughter. He received $150 for the bust of Mrs. Robert Gilmor, two-thirds paid on commencement; the remaining third was paid on completion.
82. Horatio Greenough to Washington Allston, 10, 16, 17 October 1828; Wright 1963a, pp. 58, 70.
83. Wright 1963a, pp. 29, 70, 77, and Horatio Greenough to Robert Gilmor, Jr., 17 May 1828.
84. Horatio Greenough to Samuel F. B. Morse, 5 January 1832.
85. These estimates are based on the fact that Greenough's fee for a bust was $100–150, while his ideal works ranged in cost from $200 (*The Chanting Cherubs*) to $2,000 (*Venus Victrix*, Boston Athenæum). Prices for other ideal works include $500 (*Medora*, The Baltimore Museum of Art); $600 (*The Angel Abdiel*, Yale University Art Gallery); $370 (*Mary Magdalen*, lost); $250 each (*The Genius of America* and *The Genius of Italy*, both lost).
86. From 1832 to 1852 Greenough exhibited 14 different sculptures at the Boston Athenæum. At the National Academy of Design in New York between 1832 and 1848 he exhibited 10 works. See Perkins and Gavin 1980, p. 67, and Cowdrey 1943, pp. 196–197.
87. James Fenimore Cooper to Andrew Jackson, 8 March 1832, quoted in Beard 1960–68, vol. 2, pp. 233–235; Bryant 1850, p. 236; and Dunlap 1918, vol. 2, part 2, pp. 412–426.
88. Tuckerman 1968, p. 25. The drawing given to Tuckerman was most likely the pen-and-ink sketch *Orestes Tormented by the Furies,* which was exhibited at the Boston Athenæum in 1836 (Perkins and Gavin 1980, p. 67).
89. Wunder 1991 makes little mention of drawings by Powers, although as a young adult he drew "hundreds of caricatures" (vol. 1, p. 45) and in 1834 drew a proposal for a fountain adjacent to the Capitol (p. 78). With the exception of one grand 1847 competition drawing for a monument to Washington in New York, surviving drawings by Frazee (Voss 1986) are of architectural subjects connected with his appointment as superintending architect for New York City's Custom House (pp. 43–45).
90. Campbell and Carlson 1993, pp. 272–279, 314–321. At least 1,800 drawings by Canova survive.
91. Memorandum by Mann S. Valentine II, conversation with Horatio Greenough, January 1852. Valentine Museum, Richmond, Virginia.
92. Greenough mentions that he is enclosing one or more drawings in at least 18 letters. The earliest example of this phenomenon is a letter of 1 August 1825 to his brother Henry, while the last is his of 3 September 1851, also to his brother Henry, in which he includes a proposal for a monument for Mr. Edmund (?) Dwight.
93. Edward Livingston to Horatio Greenough, 30 March 1833.
94. Horatio Greenough to Thomas Cole, 19 May 1832. According to Ms. Douglas's diary, Greenough drew heads of Washington and Lafayette in her sketchbook.
95. Headley 1991, p. 33.
96. Horatio Greenough to Robert Gilmor, Jr., 17 May 1828; Horatio Greenough to Edward Elbridge Salisbury, 3 January 1838.
97. Tuckerman 1968, p. 43.
98. Few drawings survive for either of the two other most notable American sculptors of Greenough's generation, Hiram Powers and Thomas Crawford.
99. Jarves 1960, pp. 261–262.

Chronology

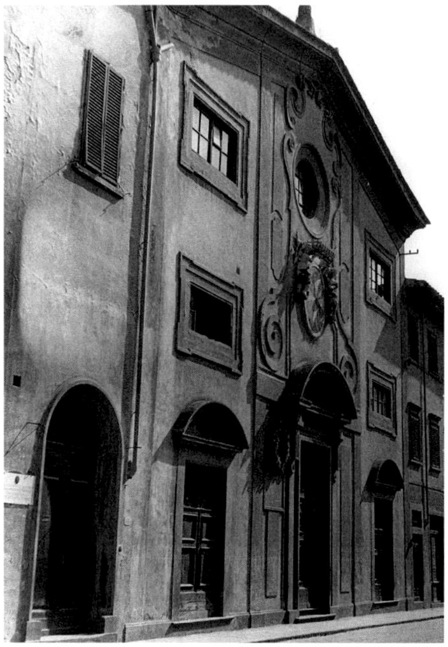

Fig. 22. School adjoining the church of San Giovannio dei Cavalieri, Via San Gallo, Florence. Here, in January 1841, Greenough first publicly exhibited his colossal figure of George Washington. Courtesy of Nathalia Wright.

1805 6 September, born in Boston

c. 1819 sculpts head of *Bacchus*, first work in marble

1821 enrolls at Harvard

1825 c. March, enters competition for design of Bunker Hill Monument
graduates from Harvard College
April or May, goes to Rome to study sculpture, arriving in the fall

1827 March, sails for Boston because of illness, arriving in May, accompanied by Robert W. Weir

1828 January–May, visits New York, Philadelphia, Washington, and Baltimore; shares Washington studio with Charles Bird King
May, sails for Italy
September–c. November, in Carrara
c. November, settles in Florence
December, begins study with Lorenzo Bartolini

1830 sculpts *The Chanting Cherubs*, first ideal work

1831 September–November, in Paris to model bust of Lafayette

1832 Commissioned by Congress to execute statue of Washington for rotunda of the Capitol
Moves to Via San Sebastiano

1834 August–September, in Paris to obtain cast of Houdon's bust of Washington

1836 May, sails for New York, arriving in June
June–July, in Washington to examine site for *Washington*
July–September, in Boston
September, with sister Louisa, sails for England
November–December, in London
December, goes to Paris

1837 January, goes from Paris to Florence
July, receives congressional commission for one of two sculptures to flank the east steps of the Capitol
14 October, marries Louisa Ingersoll Gore

1840 July, elected Professor of Sculpture at the Accademia di Belle Arti, Florence
September (?), publicly exhibits his statue of Washington in a room in the former monastery of the Cavalieri, adjoining the church of San Giovannio dei Cavalieri in Via San Gallo (fig. 22)

1841 June–September, in Paris
September, sails for New York
September–November, in Boston
November, goes to Washington

1843 January–July, arranges for removal of *Washington* to Capitol grounds
April, moves to Wilmington, Delaware
May–July, visits Philadelphia, Boston, and New York
July, sails for Liverpool
July, August, essays "Remarks on American Art" and "American Architecture" published in the *United States Magazine and Democratic Review*
July–September, in England
September–October, goes from London to Florence by way of Paris, Strasbourg, Munich, and Milan

1844 April, goes to Graffenberg, Silesia (Austria), for the water cure for his wife

1845 11 May, birth of son Henry (later Horatio) Saltonstall Greenough
September, returns to Florence

1846 May–September in Freiwaldau, Silesia

1848 Builds studio on Piazza Maria Antonia (now Independenza), Florence
25 July, birth of daughter Mary Louise (dies 1854)

1849 Moves to Villa Brichieri Colombi, on the hill of Bellosguardo (fig. 23)

1850 16 September, birth of daughter Charlotte, later Mrs. Hervoches Du Quilliou

1851 July, completes *The Rescue* and leaves Florence with family
July–August, in Switzerland
September, in England
October, sails for Boston
November, goes to Washington
December, *Aesthetics at Washington* published

1852 January, in Washington and New York
January–c. March, in Boston
April, establishes studio in Brooklyn
May, takes family to Newport, Rhode Island
c. 1 September, *The Travels, Observations, and Experience of a Yankee Stonecutter* published
September, in Washington
4 December, hospitalized
18 December, dies

NOTE: This chronology is derived largely from Wright 1972, pp. xxiii–xxiv.

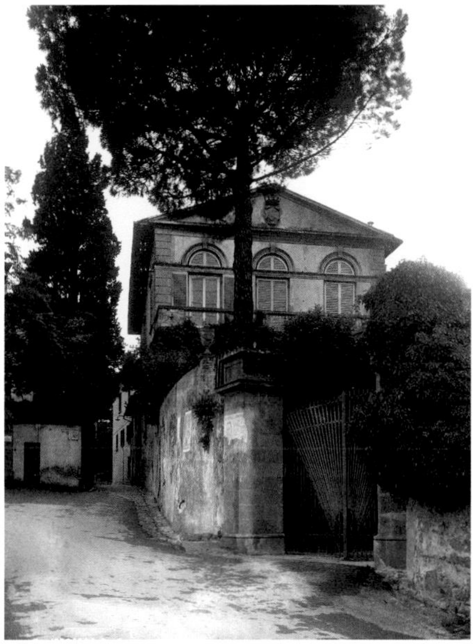

Fig. 23. Greenough's residence from 1849 to 1851. The Villa Brichieri Colombi, Bellosguardo. Courtesy of Nathalia Wright.

Catalogue of the Exhibition

Unless otherwise noted, all works in the catalogue of the exhibition are from the George R. Rinhart Collection.

The Student

1 Animal skeletons

c. 1821–25

Pen and ink, 8 × 10⅛ inches

93.8.010

This is believed to be Greenough's earliest surviving drawing. It was presumably done while he was a student at Harvard, during or after his sophomore year, when he began to study anatomy. The seven drawings of different birds and animals are miniature versions of illustrations he copied from William Cheselden's *Osteographia* (1733), then one of the standard reference works that depicted skeletal systems and a book that Greenough is documented as having borrowed from the Harvard College library.[1] The drawing corroborates stories of Greenough's insatiable curiosity about human and animal forms and his determination to train himself to comprehend and depict these physical structures. Such interests were encouraged by Dr. George Parkman, who is said to have lent him skeletons and books.[2]

As one might expect, an early drawing such as this exhibits a nervousness and lack of sophistication that Greenough outgrew with time.

1. Wright 1955, pp. 405–410.
2. Dunlap 1918, vol. 2, part 2, p. 415.

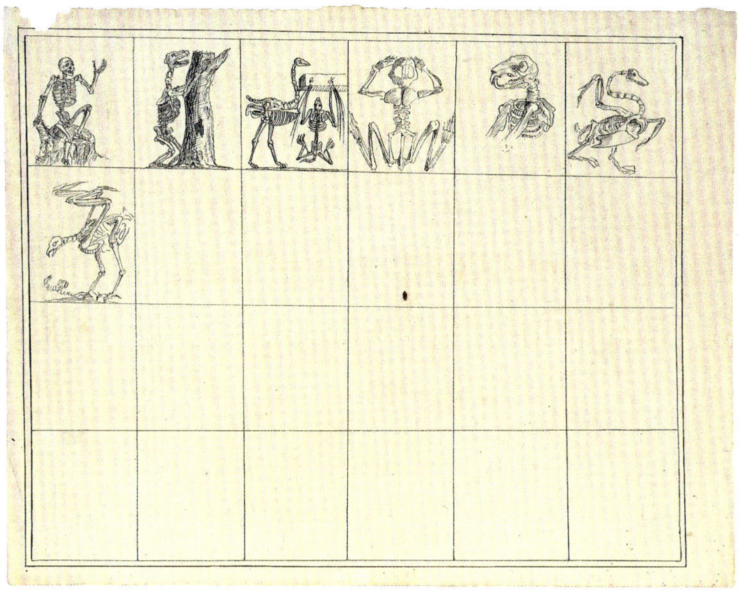

2A Henry Greenough (?), tracings after Horatio Greenough

Study for accessory statues to Bunker Hill Monument

c. 1825

Graphite and pen and ink on blue paper, 8¼ × 5¼ inches

Inscribed upper center: *"Western Corner. Subjection of the Colonies."*; center: *No. 1.*; bottom center: *No. 4.*; bottom right: *Unfinished sketch for Southern Corner/ Hg Gh*

93.8.033

2B Henry Greenough (?), tracings after Horatio Greenough

Study for accessory statues to Bunker Hill Monument

c. 1825

Graphite and pen and ink on blue paper, 8¼ × 5¼ inches

Inscribed upper center: *"Northern corner—. Resistance of the Colonies."*; center: *No. 2 / "Eastern Corner—. Discomfiture of the/British forces."*; bottom center: *No 3—*

93.8.032

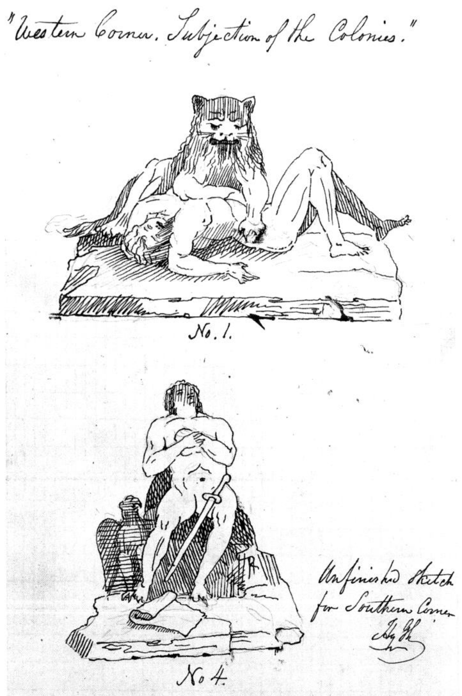

[2A]

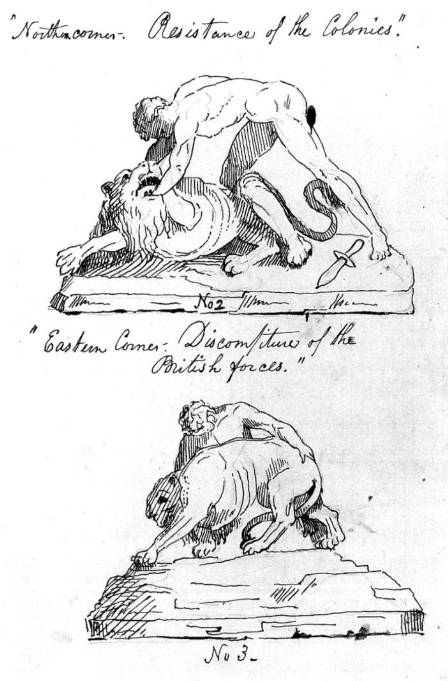

[2B]

These two drawings are actually tracings, presumably by Henry Greenough, Horatio's brother and sometime agent, of the four sculptural groups that Horatio proposed to anchor each corner of his obelisk design for the Bunker Hill Monument (see fig. 6).[1] In his proposal to the Bunker Hill Monument Association, which initiated the competition, Greenough explained that he chose the obelisk over the column "as the most purely monumental form of structure." He went on to explain that his proposal was for an obelisk one hundred feet high, the top of which would be reached by an interior circular staircase. He further explained that

> the entrance would be reached by ascending a flight of twenty steps—which are to be seen on each side of the lower base in the model—The four blocks at the angles are designed to receive four groups of monumental or allegorical sculpture—These are indicated by the pieces of clay seen on those parts of the model. But should any circumstance prevent or delay the erection of these, four large field pieces would form noble and appropriate ornaments.[2]

The sculptural groups depict a nude male figure being held down by a lion, then forcing the lion down, next seeming to embrace the lion, and last looking upward, his hands clasped, a sword resting on his leg, with an eagle and scroll on the ground before him. The first three drawings are titled *Subjection of the Colonies*, *Resistance of the Colonies*, and *Discomfiture of the British Forces*, while the fourth is untitled.

On 26 April 1825 the board met and recommended "that the premium of one hundred dollars be awarded to Mr. Horatio Greenough for the model and section of an obelisk," although they made it clear that they did not intend to construct the monument "precisely according to the model and plan of Mr. Greenough."[3]

Although the monument was not constructed with the sculptural elements he envisioned, aspects of the design did reappear later in his career: first, in 1831, as he planned a national monument to Washington (see fig. 36); and later as a precursor to his preliminary design for the sculpture commissioned for the east front of the Capitol (cat. 59).

1. Wright 1972, p. 4n, states that the tracings were "made by one of Henry Greenough's daughters," although a few years earlier (Wright 1963a, after p. 304) she observed that the inscriptions on the tracings were "in Henry Greenough's hand." The tracings of the drawing for the second group were illustrated in Swett 1864, p. 60.
2. Wright 1972, Greenough to the Bunker Hill Monument Association, [March?] 1825. Unless otherwise noted, all quotations from Greenough's letters are taken from Wright 1972.
3. Warren 1877, p. 158. Greenough estimated that a 220-foot-high version of his design would cost $57,956 to construct (Wright 1972, p. 5).

3 Roman sketchbook

c. 1826–28

Left page: nude male figure; right page: bust of Emperor Alexander I by Thorvaldsen

Leather-bound sketchbook, 7⅜ × 9 9/16 inches (page size)

Inscribed, right page: *Thorwalsen*

93.8.018

This sketchbook, which is a record of Greenough's drawing activity immediately on his arrival in Italy, is the only volume of drawings to survive from his career. It consists of forty-six pages, forty-three of which are covered on both sides, with sketches in pencil, ink, and occasionally a brown or yellow wash, along with a few inscriptions. The name *Horatio Greenough* appears on the inside of both covers but is not in his hand. Other writings in the book, however, including the inscriptions accompanying individual sketches, are in his hand. There are 169 sketches, of which approximately twenty appear unfinished.[1]

These sketches do not exhibit great skill or diversity. Their tentative and sometimes meticulous nature suggests a primary interest in recording what was before him, rather than the precise depiction of form that eighteenth-century anatomy books promoted. Nevertheless, the sketchbook provides a great deal of information about what Greenough saw, as well as his range of interests and priorities.

Approximately one-third of the drawings depict works by other artists; another third depict nudes, portraits from life, and original compositions; while the remaining third include a handful of landscapes, studies of foliage, a few fountains, horses, and anatomical casts. A number of the drawings done after other artists depict antique subjects, and of these a notable number are Hellenic Greek in

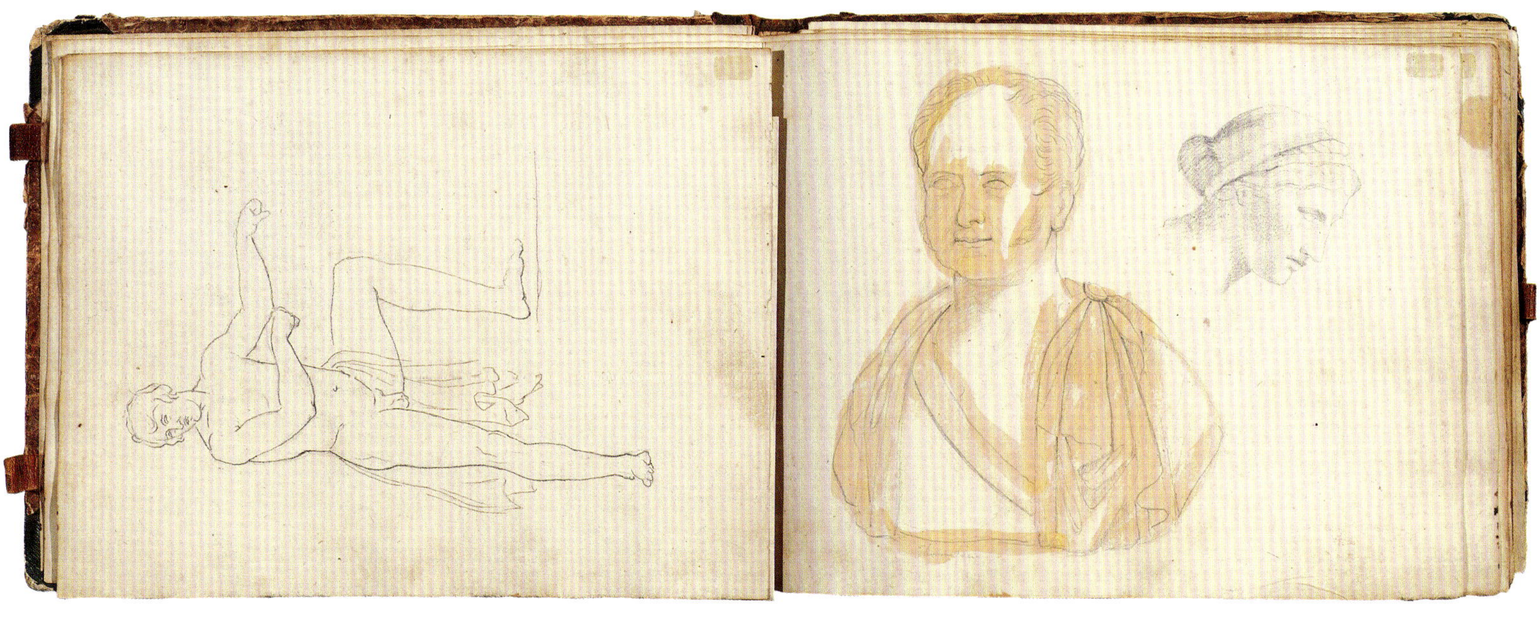

origin. These include five sketches of figures in the Parthenon frieze (see cat. 5) and several of athletes and young male deities: *Standing Discus Thrower*, *Hermes Belvedere* (both at the Vatican), *Borghese Mars*, and *Jason Hermes*.

Greenough was also attracted to the epic stories of ancient literature as depicted in sculptural form. These interests prompted sketches of Meleager and Achilles (at the Capitoline Museum), figures in Greek military dress, and, apparently, original compositions, such as Thetis appearing to Achilles from the water, as told early in the *Iliad*.

In his travels about Rome, Greenough also visited the Lateran Museum, where he sketched *Medea with the Daughters of Pelias*; the Villa Albani, where he sketched *Eurydice with Hermes and Orpheus*; and the Museum at Grotta Ferrata, near Rome, where he sketched a cast of the famous stele *Reading Youth*.

Second only to his interest in the antique was his interest in the Renaissance, and Michelangelo in particular. On the first two pages of this book are sketches of frescoes from the chapel of the Assumption in the church of the Trinita dei Monti, across the piazza from where Greenough rented rooms. These were decorated by Michelangelo's disciple Daniele da Volterra (1509–1566) and his pupils. He also sketched works by Michelangelo such as the *Madonna Taddei* as well as the *Christ* from the *Pietà* in St. Peter's and the *Risen Christ* in the church of Sta. Maria sopra Minerva.

In the margin, next to the latter sketch, which is dated 2 May 1826, Greenough disparaged the architectural setting in relation to the sculpture, which he lamented was "a true example of what is bad full of parts & without emphasis." This comment accentuates Greenough's particular interest in the bearing that architecture had on the presentation of sculpture, a concern that persisted throughout his career.

Among contemporary artists Greenough most admired Thorvaldsen during these years. This interest is reflected in sketches of *Alexander I*; *Mars and Amor*, the statue for the tomb of Count Wladimir Potocki, in Krakow; the group for the baptismal font in the castle church of Brahetolleborg; and the figures of a youth, a man, and a herdsman for the pediment of the cathedral in Copenhagen. Each of these was most likely sketched from casts in Thorvaldsen's studio, as the Dane customarily shipped his original casts to Carrara to be translated into marble, from where they were shipped directly to their final destinations.

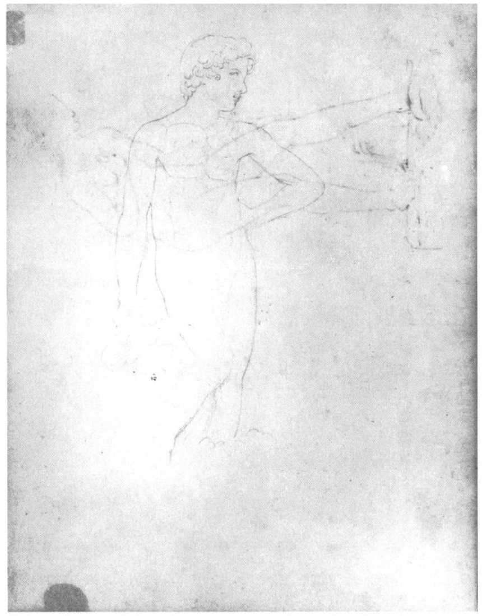

Fig. 24. Horatio Greenough, *L'Ammostatore* (The Grape Treader), from the Roman sketchbook, 1826–28. Graphite on paper, 9½ × 7¼ inches. George R. Rinhart Collection.

While virtually all the sketches were drawn prior to Greenough's departure from Rome in the spring of 1827, there do appear to be several exceptions. Two heads of George Washington (fol. 17r–v) were presumably made during Greenough's visit to Boston during the summer and fall of 1827, as one is a copy of Gilbert Stuart's Athenæum portrait of Washington (16r and 36v), exhibited at the first annual exhibition at the Boston Athenæum that year. The second (16v) may be a sketch after Raimondo Trentanove's (1792–1832) marble bust of Washington, which was given to the Athenæum in 1820.

In addition, Greenough drew a sketch after Lorenzo Bartolini's figure *L'Ammostatore*, or *The Grape Treader* (8v; fig. 24). He saw this work in the fall of 1828, at which time he told Allston in a letter that he "was much struck with the figure of a boy treading grapes which I saw at Carrara which was full of nature."[2]

1. This sketchbook is thoroughly discussed by Nathalia Wright (Wright 1963b), and much of what is cited here is from this source. Wright apparently purchased this sketchbook from the collector John Davis Hatch. At the time Hatch apparently retained at least one leaf from the sketchbook, that depicting a figure identified by Wright (1963b, p. 330) as a man copied after one of Thorvaldsen's figures for the pediment of the cathedral in Copenhagen. This work appeared on the art market in December 1998 (Wolf's Fine Arts Auctioneers, Cleveland, Ohio, 5 December 1998, lot 1007). This situation, and the fact that a number of the leaves of the sketchbook are detached from the binding, now makes it difficult to confirm the exact order of the drawings in the sketchbook.
2. Horatio Greenough to Washington Allston, 10, 16, 17 October 1828.

4 Landscape

c. 1826–28

Graphite and pen and ink, 8¼ × 10 inches

93.8.085

Aside from this single sheet and a second, which depicts Lake Nemi and Colonna Castle, the only other surviving landscape drawings by Greenough appear in his Roman sketchbook (cat. 3). This is hardly surprising, given that as a sculptor Greenough's focus was almost exclusively on the figure. This eloquent but rudimentary drawing, like those in the sketchbook (end leaf, 38r–v, 43r–v, 44v), is topographical in nature and entirely consistent with the English tradition of travel diary drawings.[1] Here Greenough sought to capture the essence of a particular view, in this case most likely the Alban Hills, near Rome, which he visited in the summer of 1826.[2] Unlike his friend Cole, whose drawings from nature are as diverse as Greenough's of the figure are, the sculptor's lack of specificity or detail perhaps reflects a degree of emotional detachment in the absence of a particular purpose in making the drawing.

1. New Haven 1977, cats. 13, 16, 19, 75, 104.
2. Wright 1963a, p. 45.

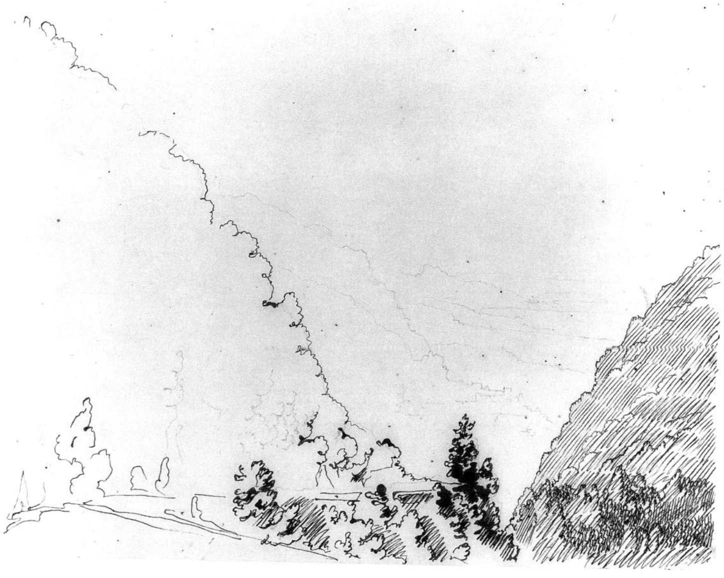

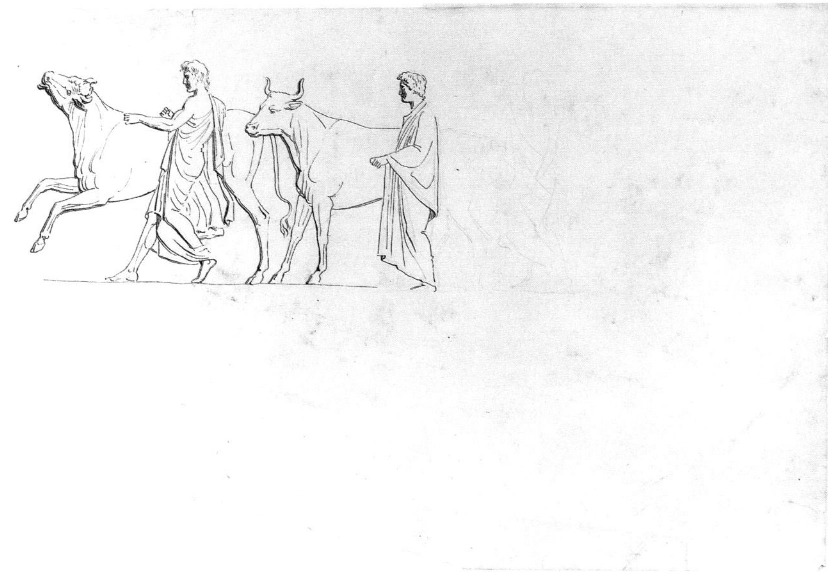

5 Two male figures accompanying cattle, after the Parthenon north frieze

c. 1826–32

Pen and ink over graphite, 8⅝ × 12 inches

93.8.016

Soon after arriving in Rome, Greenough's routine included morning visits to the French Academy, where he and his companion, the painter Robert W. Weir, drew from casts. The metopes, frieze, and pedimental sculptures from the Parthenon had by the eighteenth century achieved considerable acclaim. In 1808 Lord Elgin removed many of the surviving sculptures to London, including the north frieze. Eight years later, after lobbying efforts, including those of the British sculptors John Flaxman and Joseph Nollekens (1737–1823), they were acquired by the British Museum.

By the time Greenough was in Italy, casts made from the Parthenon sculptures had become part of the staple of models from which aspiring artists drew. This sheet is one of at least three drawings Greenough made from casts of sculpture from the Parthenon.[1]

This linear drawing was most likely made in Rome in 1826–28 but may have been done during the years immediately thereafter when Greenough was in Florence and still looking closely at antique monuments.

1. The two other drawings are part of Greenough's Roman sketchbook: 29r, horsemen from the west frieze; and 21r, a magistrate from the east frieze.

6 Head of Selene's team of horses, after a cast from the east pediment of the Parthenon

April 1832

Charcoal, 26 × 18 inches

Inscribed center left: *April. 1832.*

93.8.164

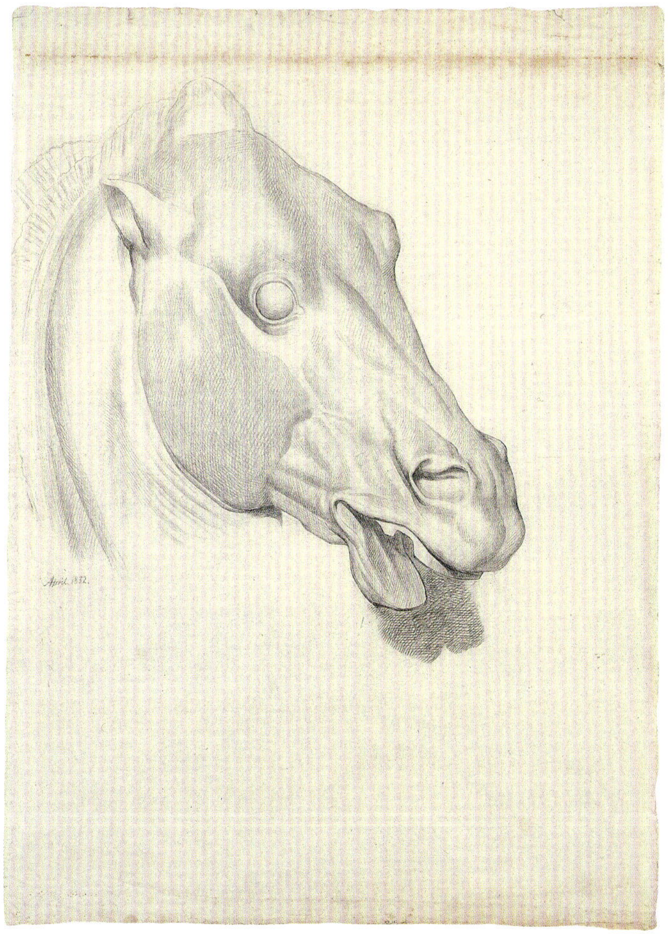

Among the most powerful and best-preserved carvings from the Partheon pediments is this horse's head. To reinforce its sense of monumentality, Greenough drew the head boldly, on a large sheet. Why he chose to date a drawing such as this is unclear, although its choice as a subject is consistent with his desire to create works on a large scale.

7 Multiple figure studies from classical sculptures and casts (?)

c. 1830–31

Graphite and pen and ink, 11⅝ × 17⅝ inches (double sheet)

93.8.053

8 Sea goddess, Neptune Fountain, Piazza della Signoria, Florence

29 June 1830

Graphite and pen and ink, 7¾ × 9 inches

Inscribed lower right: *June 29/1830—4 oclock AM/after a sleepless night*

93.8.049

In the period immediately after Greenough's return to Italy in 1828, his sense of confidence in his own ability was offset by fears of an uncertain future. Over the next several years, while he completed busts for clients such as Gilmor, Cooper, Quincy, and Adams, he became more and more obsessed with the idea of capturing a government commission, which would provide his best chance for national recognition. Despite his youth, he was haunted by the passage of time, lamenting in one letter that he had "Not one solid blow struck for a name—at an age when M. Angelo—had nearly finished his colossal David."[1] In addition, his financial resources were meager. In a letter to Allston in September 1829 he reported that he had only "200$ in pocket—of this 108 will be exhausted by board and lodging for the coming year."[2]

This drawing, done during the middle of a sleepless night, is ample evidence of Greenough's manic nature and debilitating insomnia. It is conceivable that Greenough visited the piazza that morning to

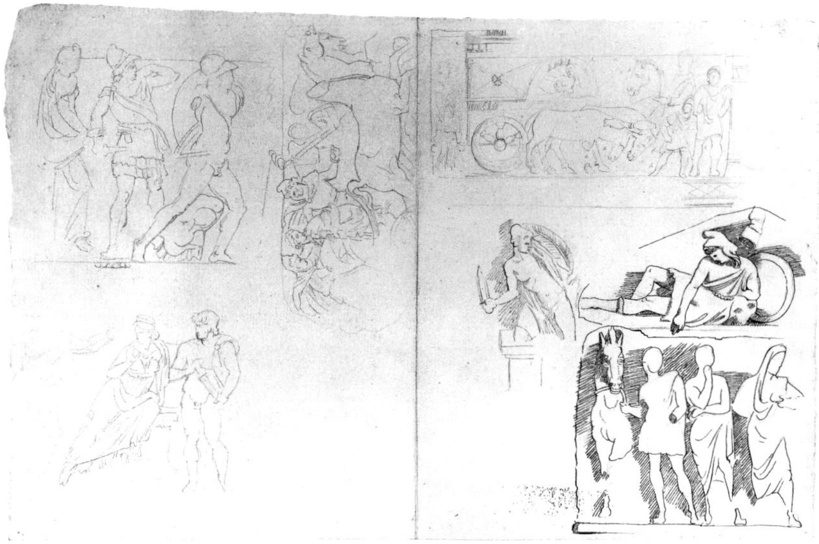

[7]

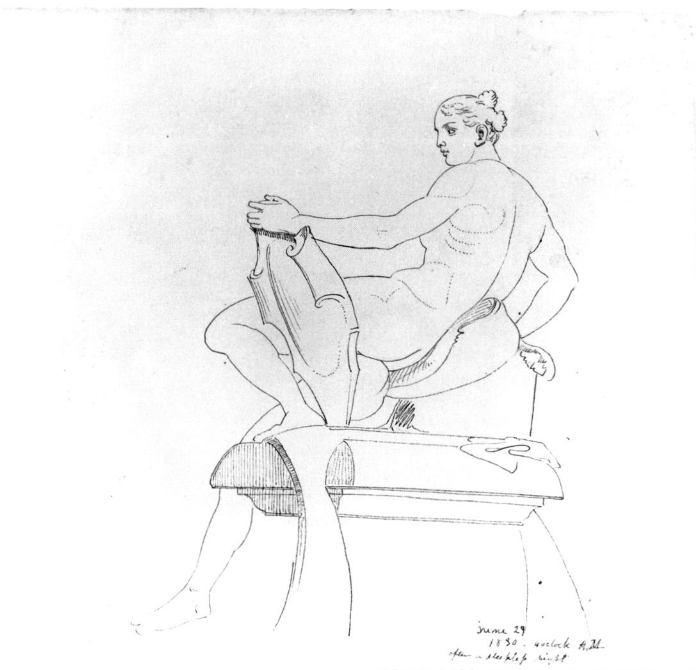

[8]

draw directly from the fountain, but more likely, given his remarkable visual memory, he simply drew this in his rooms. The subject is one of the sea goddesses who anchor the Neptune Fountain designed by Bartolommeo Ammanati (1511–1592). It was a logical choice for Greenough, as it was both a public monument and the work of an artist strongly influenced by Michelangelo, whom Greenough esteemed.

1. Horatio Greenough to Washington Allston, 17 November 1829.
2. Horatio Greenough to Washington Allston, 19, 20 September 1829.

9 Anatomical study of leg muscles and tendons

1832

Graphite, 27⅛ × 18¾ inches

Inscribed lower right: *Copied from a study at the Hospital of S. M. Nuova By Giuseppe Bezzuoli—1832—*

93.8.167

Ever since he was a student at Harvard, Greenough realized that a proper understanding of anatomy was crucial to his success as a sculptor. This interest intensified once he got to Italy, particularly after he received the federal government's commission for a statue of Washington. "On this occasion," he wrote to Cooper in May 1832:

> I've gone to the Hospital and, for the first time in my life, have dissected the dead subject—You know we generally learn anatomy by drawing the dissections of the surgeons—This dissection will hereafter be my constant study in the winter—In a couple of hours one sees more of the *why* of organization and form than in days of lecture reading or examining the living model. Its effect on one is most stirring—It seems as one follows the knife as if God himself were made visible and audible in the beauty strength and fitness of our frames.[1]

This sheet (also cats. 10, 11) was presumably drawn at the Arcispedale de Sta. Maria Nuova, where the city's medical college was housed. Giuseppe Bezzuoli (1784–1855) was a Florentine painter who worked in oil, watercolor, and fresco. His *Entry of Charles VIII into Florence* is now in the Academy of Fine Arts, Florence.[2]

1. Horatio Greenough to James Fenimore Cooper, 28 May 1832.
2. Wright 1972, p. 44n.

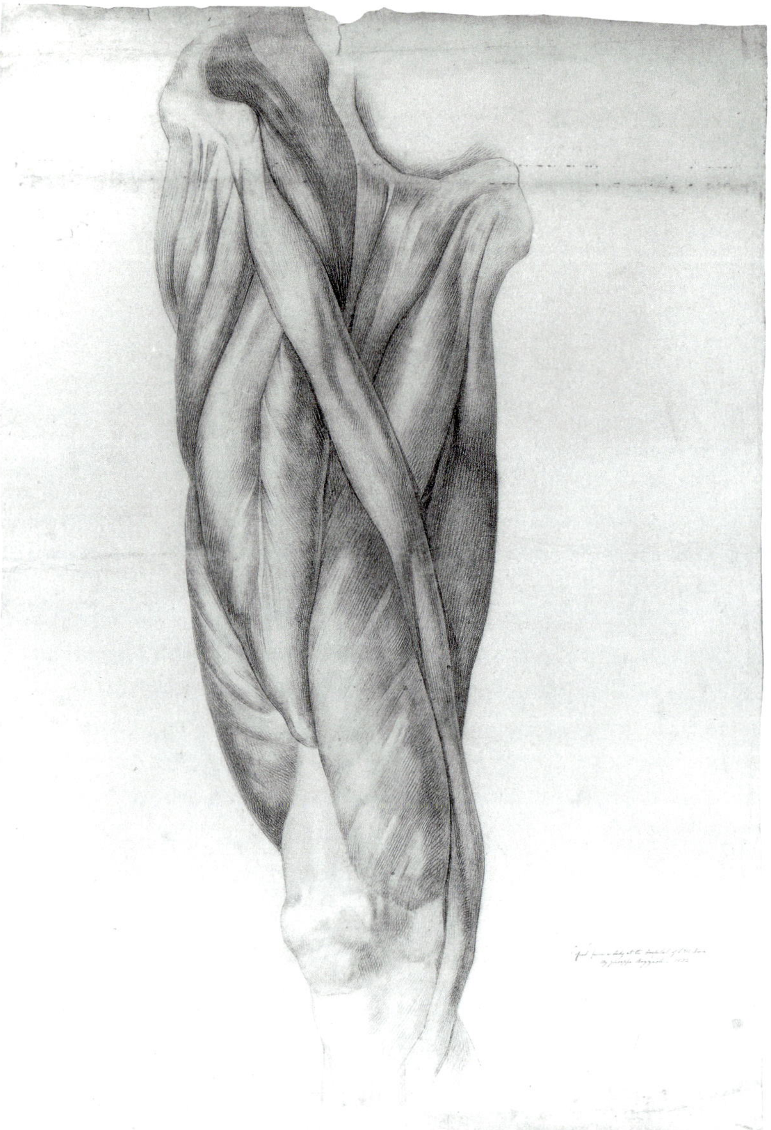

[9]

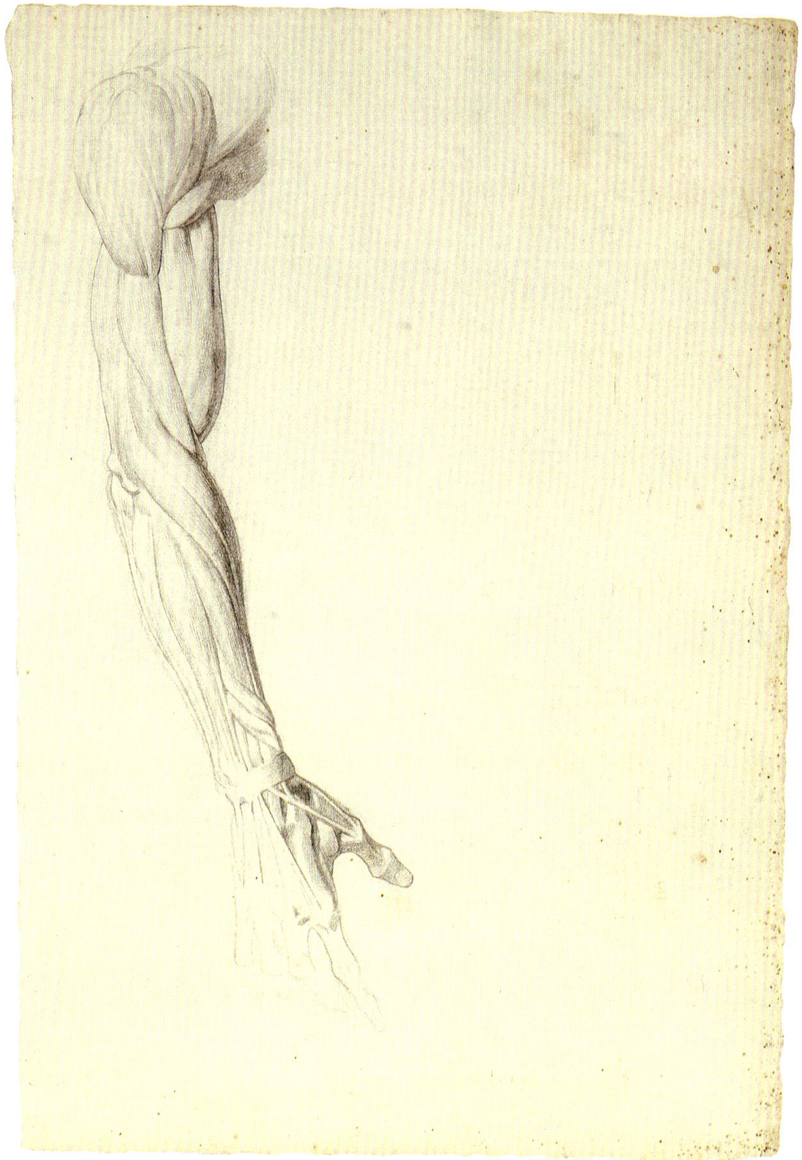

10 Musculature of the arm and hand, after a cast

1832

Graphite and black charcoal, 17½ × 11½ inches

93.8.064

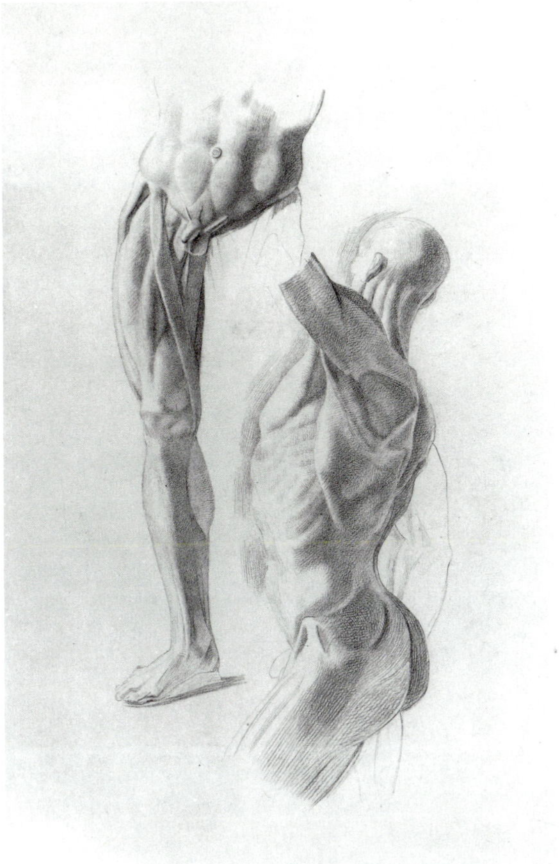

11 Musculature of leg and torso of a man, after a cast

c. 1832

Graphite and black charcoal, 15½ × 9⅞ inches

93.8.063

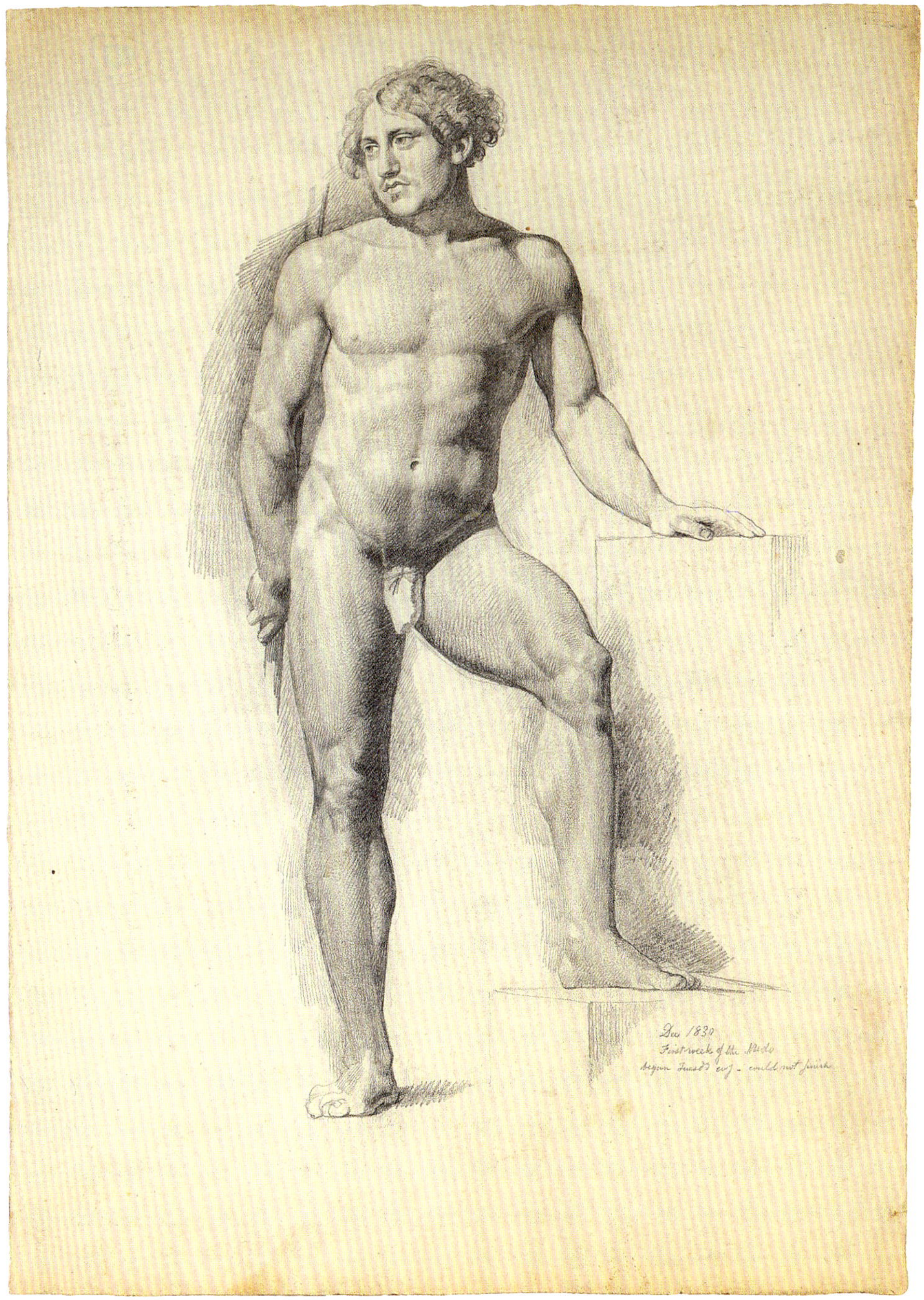

12 Standing male nude

December 1830

Graphite, 18 × 12½ inches

Inscribed lower right: *Dec 1830/First week of the Nudo/begun Tuesdy e vg—could not finish*

93.8.153

On his arrival at Rome in 1826 Greenough began drawing from life at the English school there. Such activity was renewed when Greenough later settled in Florence, but this is the only dated drawing to survive from his life-drawing classes. In a letter the preceding November to his friend Allston, Greenough underscored his belief in the crucial role drawing played for him:

> I copy what I see before me with tolerable readiness and accuracy—whatever the object be whether the naked drapery—hair or even animals and vegetables tis soon rendered by a hand schooled to obey an eye practiced in scanning geometrically its outline and dissecting its variety of surface from light to shade—This security of method I owe to the study of drawing—Twas drawing that taught me the necessity of scrupulous outline—twas drawing that taught me that the planes of a form are shaded in proportion to their obliquity to the source of light. The foundation of my system of modelling lies in this fact.[1]

This carefully observed and executed drawing of a muscular young male is clear evidence of Greenough's increasing abilities as a draftsman, and it is among his most fluent and subtle works. Here modeling and shadow are achieved through crosshatched and parallel lines while contours are carefully outlined and reworked.

Although Greenough by this point in his career was strongly under the influence of Thorvaldsen, finished and methodical life drawings such as this one are close in execution to the great number of painstaking examples executed by Canova.[2]

1. Horatio Greenough to Washington Allston, 17 November 1829.
2. See, for example, Canova's *Female Nude Seated on the Ground, Clutching Her Knee* and *Male Nude (Raised Fist)*, c. 1794–1801, in Campbell and Carlson 1993, pp. 272, 275.

13 Standing male nude

verso: Seated male nude

c. 1830

Graphite, 9⅜ × 6⅛ inches

93.8.050

Here the model has presumably struck the pose of an antique sculpture, a practice customary in life-drawing classes.

14 A left hand

verso: Standing classical figure holding a book; helmeted soldier

Graphite and charcoal on blue-gray paper, 9 × 11¾ inches

93.8.066

Despite the fact that the date of this drawing or the particular project with which it is associated is unknown, it is among Greenough's most confident and studied sheets. Possibly a rendering of his own hand, it possesses a sense of direct and subtle observation. Painstakingly shaded, the hand is particularly expressive. While each detail of human anatomy was important to the artist, Greenough realized that hands could be especially good conveyors of tension or calm and therefore required concentrated care. In addition, he has very successfully used the color of the paper for the highlights and to expand the drawing's value range.

Greenough's sculpture of *The Angel Warning St. John* (see fig. 18) depicts the kneeling St. John with his left hand raised in a position similar to that drawn here.

15 Right hand holding a rod

Pen and ink, 12 × 7¾ inches

93.8. 012

Some of Greenough's most attentive drawings were of hands. This drawing, of unknown date, relates to at least three others of hands holding rods, one of which is dated 1847.[1] Their significant number, similarity, and painstaking finish suggest that Greenough was particularly concerned about working out the way in which this right hand grasped a rod.

While several figures in his finished sculptures hold implements in their hands,[2] the closest sculptural parallel to this drawing is *The Genius of Italy* (cat. 44), modeled about 1850, in which a seated bearded figure, who personifies the Roman Catholic Church, clutches a shepherd's crook.

1. Horatio Greenough, *Right Hand Holding Short Rod*, pen and brown ink over graphite, 7$\frac{1}{16}$ × 10$\frac{15}{16}$ inches, inscribed: *H.G./Florence Dec. 47.* National Gallery of Art,

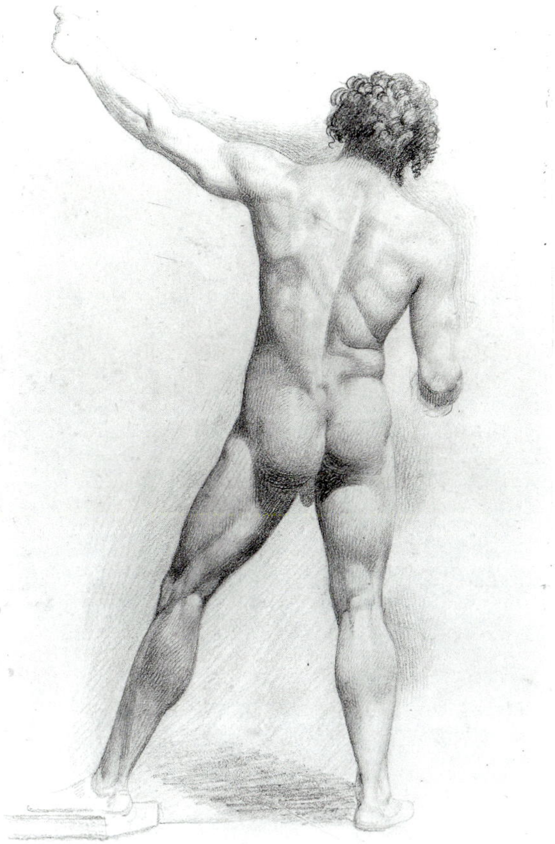

[13]

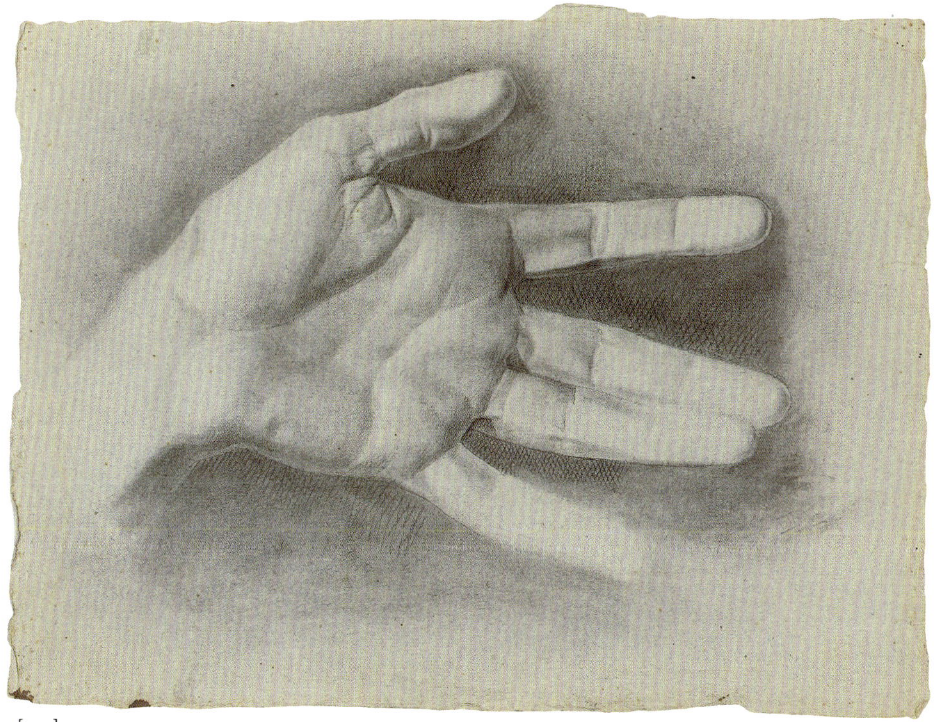

[14]

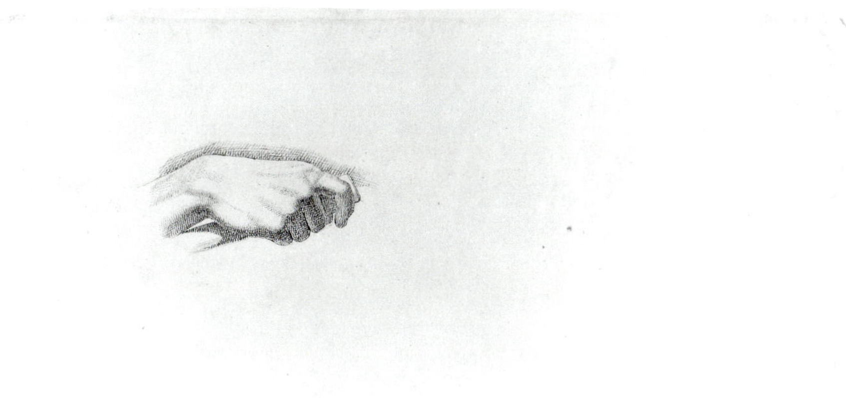

[15]

Washington, D.C., Department of Modern Prints and Drawings, John Davis Hatch Collection, 1979.20.49.
2. Greenough's *Angel Abdiel* (see fig. 30) grasps a short rod in his right hand, although there is considerably more tension in the hand.

16 *John Quincy Adams*

1828–29

Marble, 23¼ × 14 × 8½ inches

Signed, on shoulder, in Greek: Greenough made

Athenæum purchase from the artist, 1829. The Library of the Boston Athenæum

John Quincy Adams (1767–1848) was the son of Abigail Smith and John Adams, second president of the United States. Like his father, he pursued a lifelong career in the public arena. He served as congressman, minister to Russia, minister to the Court of St. James, and Secretary of State. He was elected sixth president of the United States in 1824.

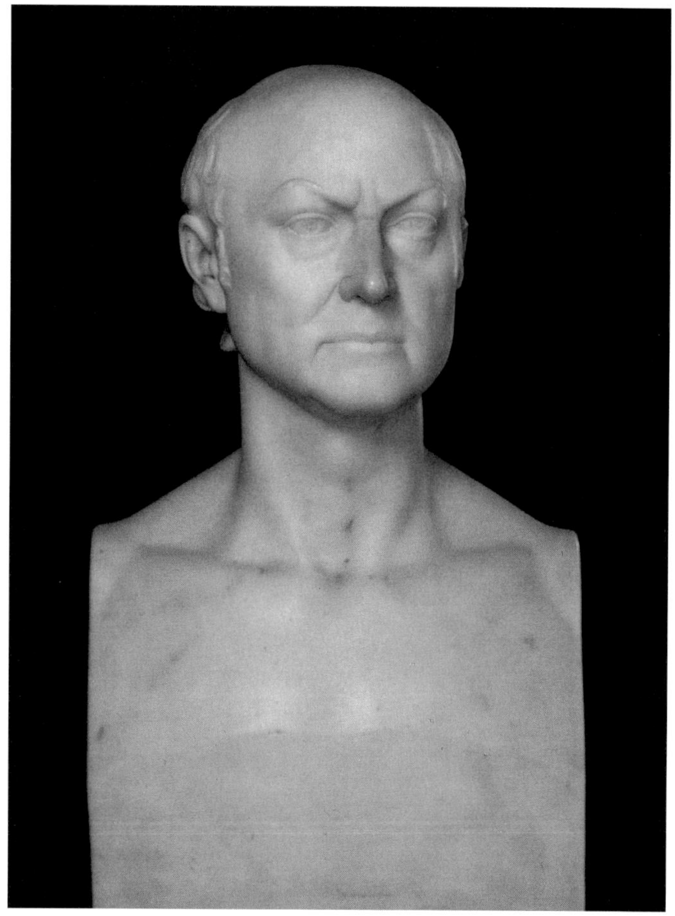

On 13 February 1828 Adams received a letter from his kinsman Josiah Quincy (see fig. 8) introducing Greenough "for the purposes of obtaining a portrait bust of the President of the United States."[1] Adams, who previously had been sculpted by Pietro Cardelli (d. 1822) and John Henry Isaac Browere (1790–1834), accommodated Greenough the following week at the Washington studio the sculptor rented from Charles Bird King.[2] Over the next five weeks Adams sat for Greenough on five occasions. Greenough wrote his brother:

> Mr. Adams give me his first sitting yesterday morning. A President is a man, you know, and so I put him in. He is much fallen away in flesh since Cardelli modelled him, and the character of his head is improved by it. His brow is unique. He gave me this morning nearly two hours. I think I have a likeness of him. . . . I shall not attempt (as Sully and others have done) to make him look cheerful. He does not and cannot. Gravity is natural to him, and a smile looks ill at home.[3]

Adams, who was notoriously critical of the portraits made of him, gave a rare unqualified approval, which Greenough shortly thereafter reported: "I have finished the head of the President, and shall probably cast it on Monday. He thinks well of it, and says he should not wish the head other than it is. 'It is a noble art,' he said, as he stood before the work on the last day."[4] As Greenough hoped, the successful modeling of this bust led the president to commission a subsequent bust of his father for the Adams family monument in the Stone Temple, or United First Parish Church, Quincy, Massachusetts.

The squared herm form with cropped shoulders, employed here, echoes the antique and accentuates a sense of solemnity and detached nobility, which Greenough undoubtedly deemed appropriate to the great distinction of the sitter. This copy was purchased by the Boston Athenæum for $200 in 1829.[5] Two other versions of the bust exist: one is the same size (New-York Historical Society) and the second is half-size (Museum of Fine Arts, Boston).

1. Adams Papers, Josiah Quincy to John Quincy Adams, 27 January 1828. Massachusetts Historical Society.
2. Oliver 1970, p. 149.
3. Greenough 1887, Horatio Greenough to Henry Greenough, 21 February 1828.
4. Ibid., Horatio Greenough to Henry Greenough, 8 March 1828.
5. Perkins and Gavin 1980, p. 34.

17 *John Quincy Adams*

c. 1828–29

Pen and ink, 8 × 6⅝ inches

Inscription lower center: *I do not say that it was a bid/but if it was it was a good one!/but it was not enough!!*

93.8.006

Small profile drawings, such as this, were Greenough's favorite format for depicting both friends and illustrious citizens. It seems unlikely that this drawing, which has the character of the quick sketches Greenough was known for making during his evening conversations with dinner companions, was made in preparation for the bust he sculpted of the president. More likely, it is a sketch from memory, as was the case with a drawing of Dr. John C. Warren (Rinhart Collection,

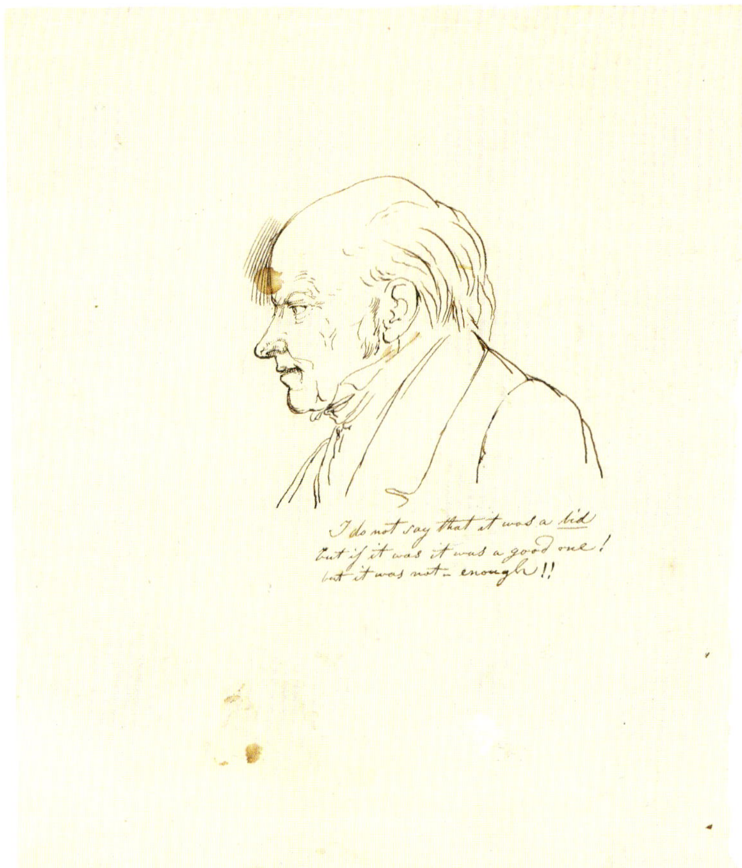

93.8.008), which Greenough inscribed, *from memory*.[1] Nevertheless, Greenough's sharp sense of observation and his ability to draw notable physical characteristics, such as Adams's long, angular nose, bald pate, and gaunt features, leave no doubt as to who is depicted.

The accompanying quotation is presumably taken from one of Adams's public addresses.

1. John Collins Warren was a Boston surgeon, author, and member of the faculty of the Harvard Medical School (1809–47). Greenough sculpted his bust (Harvard Medical School) and shipped it to the sitter in late 1838 or early 1839 (Horatio Greenough to John Collins Warren, 1 March 1839).

18 *James Fenimore Cooper*

1831

Marble, 24 × 12 × 6½ inches

Courtesy of the Trustees of the Boston Public Library

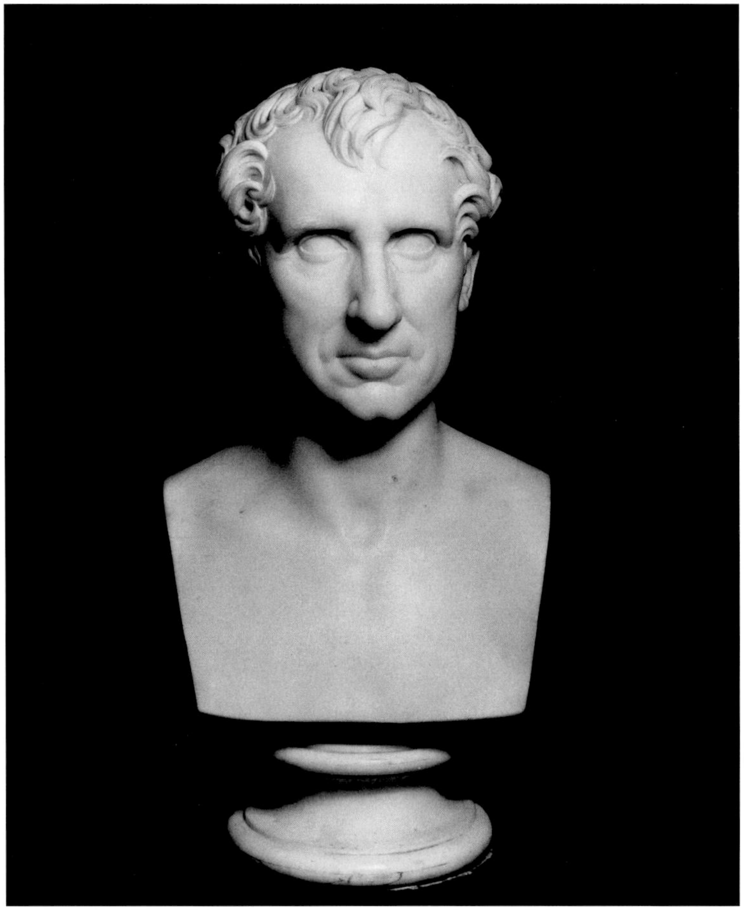

This bust of James Fenimore Cooper (1789–1851) is the result of a lengthy and fruitful relationship between the novelist and the sculptor. By October 1828, when Cooper and his family arrived in Florence, the author had already achieved considerable success for, among other writings, three of his novels in the series known as *The Leather-Stocking Tales*: *The Pioneers* (1823), *The Prairie* (1827), and *The Last of the Mohicans* (1827).

The two aesthetes were introduced by James Ombrosi, the first United States consul in Florence, who suggested that the writer have his bust made by the sculptor.[1] By February 1829 Greenough reported that he had "completed the model about a month since and have commenced the marble." Although the bust was not a commission, the idea of making a bust of a notable figure like Cooper was of considerable interest to Greenough: by association with the writer, the sculpture brought prestige to its maker. Also, it could be shown to potential patrons who might visit Greenough's studio. In April Greenough reported that the marble bust was done.[2]

This bust is actually the second Greenough made of Cooper. In October 1831 Greenough wrote that, while visiting the novelist in Paris, he had "remodelled the bust of Mr. Cooper on account of his remarkable change for the better in his appearance since I made his last portrait."[3] In December 1831 Cooper wrote imploring Greenough, "Dont *finish* my bust. I hope to give you some sittings for that part of the work."[4] This version was not cut in marble until 1832, when Greenough wrote Cooper: "Your bust is cutting from a block which seems a lump of virgin wax." He added, "I shall make the mouth from the old one if you conclude not to return here."[5] The original marble bust of Cooper, which depicted the writer with heavier features as the result of a considerable gain in weight, was later recut by Greenough for his bust of Samuel F. B. Morse (cat. 22).

This bust presumably remained in Greenough's Florence studio until his return to America. At some point, it was acquired by Charles Henry Parker, who was married to the sculptor's sister Charlotte Greenough, and in 1909 presented by their children to the library.[6]

1. Horatio Greenough to Robert Gilmor, Jr., 25 February 1829.
2. Horatio Greenough to Thomas Aspinwall, 1 April 1829.
3. Horatio Greenough to Robert Gilmor, Jr., 10 October 1831, and Horatio Greenough to Washington Allston, October 1831.
4. Beard 1960–68, vol. 2, p. 166, James Fenimore Cooper to Horatio Greenough, 24 December 1831.
5. Horatio Greenough to James Fenimore Cooper, 28 June 1832.
6. Wadlin 1911, p. 171.

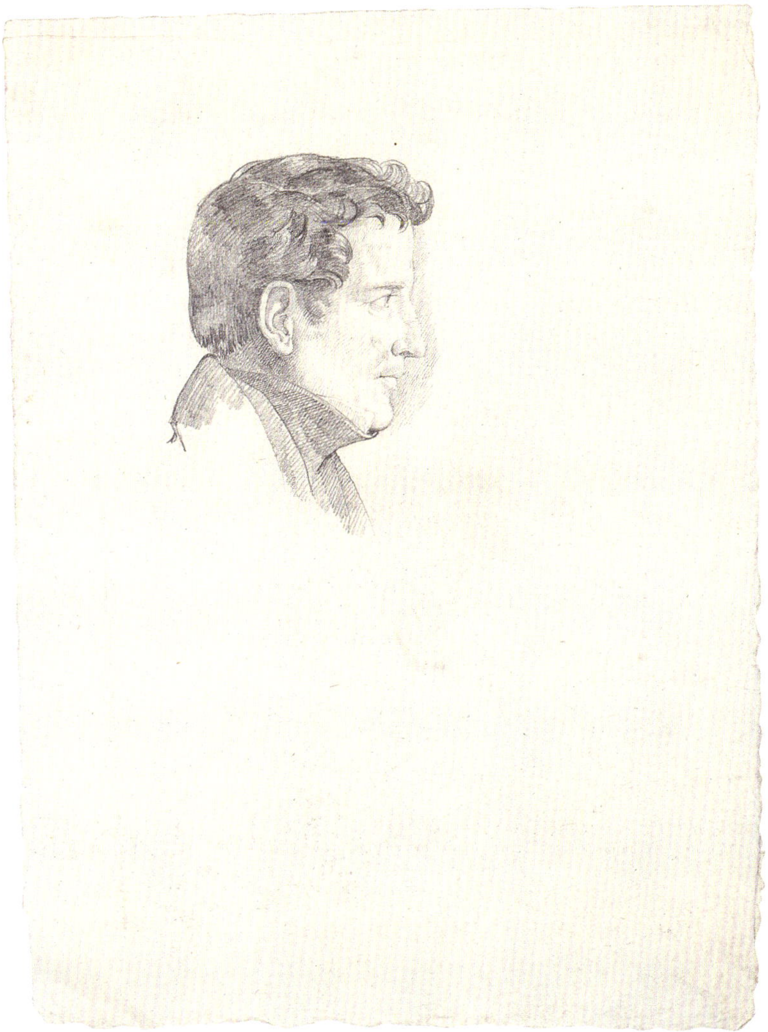

[19]

19 *James Fenimore Cooper*

c. 1828–31

Graphite, 9⅛ × 7⅞ inches

93.8.009

This diminutive profile drawing attests to Greenough's skills of observation. While the drawing may have been made as early as the fall of 1830 when the sculptor and writer met, its similarity to Greenough's drawing of Lafayette (cat. 21) suggests it may have been done in Paris the following year. With slight variation in pencil pressure, Greenough has effectively captured a sense of Cooper's tousled hair, his most distinguishing feature.

A few years earlier, Greenough described his increasing fondness for portraiture in a letter to Allston. "I have found it a difficult but a very interesting study—to seize the character of an individual—& then there is always so much beautiful & characteristic detail in a face that much of execution & form may be learned from modelling it."[1]

1. Horatio Greenough to Washington Allston, 9 May 1826.

20 *The Marquis de Lafayette*

1831–32

Marble, 25¾ × 23½ × 12¾ inches

Signed on back in monogram: *HG*

Courtesy of the Pennsylvania Academy of the Fine Arts, Philadelphia. Gift of Francis Kinloch

Universally admired as a soldier and statesman, Marie Joseph Paul Yves Roche Gilbert du Motier, marquis de Lafayette (1757–1834), was a natural choice by Greenough for a portrait bust. He was a hero of the American Revolution whose popularity was reaffirmed in 1824–25 when he made a triumphant tour of the United States. In wishing to do his portrait, Greenough joined a long list of both American and European artists who sought, and frequently obtained, audiences with the general for the purpose of making both painted and sculpted portraits. Greenough knew that in 1825 his friend Samuel F. B. Morse had succeeded in outmaneuvering the likes of Thomas Sully,

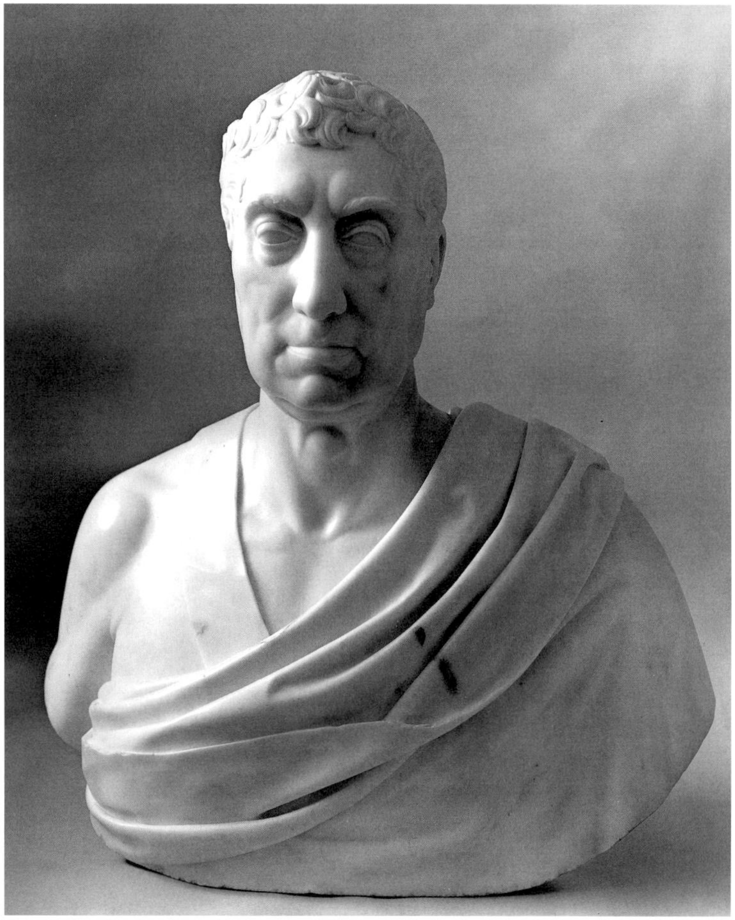

John Vanderlyn, and Rembrandt Peale, among others, to obtain the commission from the City of New York for a full-length painting of Lafayette (City of New York).[1]

On 6 December 1830 Greenough wrote Cooper inquiring whether the writer thought Lafayette would "give me sittings for his head if I were to make a jaunt to Paris?" He added, "His portrait would be worth a fortune to me hereafter," presumably meaning both the prestige associated with the occasion as well as the opportunity to make subsequent marble copies from the original plaster cast.[2] Cooper consented and later, in a long letter to William Dunlap, explained his role as "mediator" in the process and how "General Lafayette yielded at last to my importunities." He added:

> The fidelity of Greenough's bust may be proved by a single fact, to which I can personally testify. The head of Lafayette was very remarkable. The forward part of it, or the brows, the face, jaws, cheeks, and indeed all the features were massive and noble; while the portions behind seemed to be formed on an entirely different scale. His ears were the largest I remember ever to have seen, but they lay so flat to the head, and the portion of the head where these organs are placed, was so contracted in comparison with the face, that when one stood directly before the latter, at the distance of three or four feet, no part of them was to be seen. Greenough pointed out to me this peculiarity, in which I cannot be mistaken, for I think Mr. Morse can testify to the same thing. I caused the latter, who was often with us at the sittings, to observe it also. The bust of Greenough is true in this particular, which I think is the fact with no other, and you will readily understand how much such a distinguishing mark would effect the faithfulness of a resemblance. I cannot recall another head formed in this manner.[3]

Greenough gave the writer an enormous amount of credit for the successful results of his sittings. In a letter to Rembrandt Peale, he noted, "I have finished however and they say it's like him—thanks to Cooper who pinned the old gentleman to the chair one morning for two whole hours with stories and *bons mots*—I believe it was the saving of my bust—for I had become out of humour with it and you know how fatal that often proves."[4]

The resulting sculpture depicts Lafayette with his left shoulder draped and a strap, in the fashion of a Roman warrior, over the other. Greenough made no attempt to mask the sagging and creased flesh of the general's seventy-four-year-old face. Cooper made a point of contrasting Greenough's bust with that of the French sculptor Pierre-Jean David (1788–1856), carved two years earlier. On seeing both busts, Lafayette remarked that "one is a French bust, the other American." Cooper described David's idealized characterization, in which his skin is smooth rather than wrinkled, as "heroic and poetical" and particularly French. Greenough's "fidelity," or overt realism, he saw as typically American.

This replica was commissioned by Francis Kinloch, of Charleston, South Carolina, an artist friend who lived in Florence from 1832 until his death.[5] In the spring of 1832 Greenough wrote Morse that "My 'Lafayette' is boasted without a stain."[6] The bust was given to the Pennsylvania Academy of the Fine Arts in 1834.[7]

Another life-size version of the bust is owned by the Massachusetts State House, Boston. A half-life-size reduction was given by Mrs. Horatio Greenough to the Museum of Fine Arts, Boston.[8] Once back in

Florence, Greenough had Enrico Bandini make an engraving of the bust.[9]

1. Staiti 1989, p. 117. Morse and Cooper had been friends in New York, where they were members of the exclusive and influential Bread and Cheese Club.
2. Horatio Greenough to James Fenimore Cooper, 6 December 1830.
3. Quoted in Dunlap 1918, vol. 2, pp. 424–425.
4. Horatio Greenough to Rembrandt Peale, 8 November 1831.
5. Wright 1960 and Wright 1972, p. 113n.
6. Horatio Greenough to Samuel F. B. Morse, between 25 March and 23 April 1832. Wright misread the word stain as "strain."
7. James-Gadzinski and Cunningham 1997, p. 26.
8. Greenthal, Kozol, and Ramirez 1986, pp. 13–14.
9. Greenough reported to his brother Henry (Greenough 1887) on 3 September 1834 that he went to see the French painter Jean-Auguste-Dominique Ingres (1780–1867) and "carried a proof of the print they are making of my Lafayette, and had the pleasure of hearing it called 'very like, and in a *beau style*,' by a man who never flatters." There is a copy at Lafayette College, Easton, Pa.

21 *The Marquis de Lafayette*

1831

Graphite, 8 × 9¾ inches

93.8.115

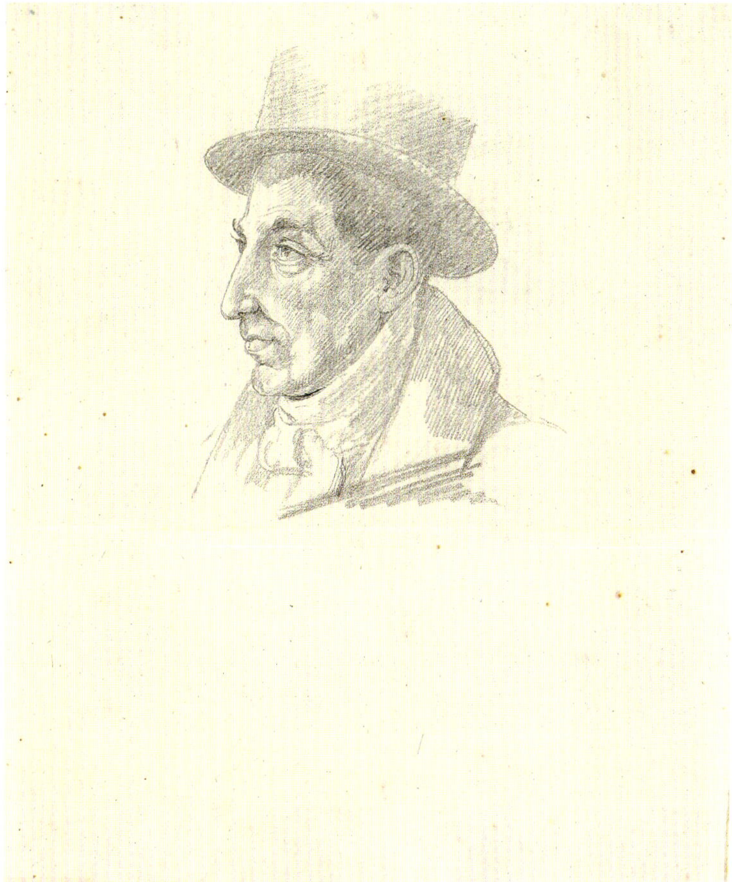

When Cooper first responded to Greenough's request to make arrangements for him to sculpt Lafayette, the writer indicated that Lafayette was much too busy and that "his sitting at present is out of the question." On reflection the general added, however, "how can I refuse an American sculptor."[1] Once in Paris, Greenough had to wait two weeks "to seize each pitiful quarter of an hour afforded by the pressure of General Lafayette's affairs."[2]

The bust was sculpted over six sittings, presumably at Lafayette's home at Lagrange, outside Paris. The first sitting took place on 13 October, and the following day Greenough excitedly wrote his brother that "Lafayette has been so much occupied with public duties, that although he had the best will in the world, he has not been able to sit until now. I had half an hour from him yesterday, and made a sketch which is recognized by everyone. Morse says it can never be more like him."[3]

This sketch, presumably one of a number Greenough made during his sittings, is unusual in that it depicts Lafayette wearing a coat and top hat. While this is the attire Lafayette is shown wearing in many other portraits of him, Greenough chose to abandon contemporary dress for the sculpture, as he did for all his sitters.

1. Beard 1960–68, vol. 2, pp. 44–46, James Fenimore Cooper to Horatio Greenough, 10 December 1830.
2. Horatio Greenough to Rembrandt Peale, 8 November 1831.
3. Greenough 1887, Horatio Greenough to Henry Greenough, 14 October 1831.

22 *Samuel F. B. Morse*

1831

Marble, 19½ × 12 × 8¾ inches

Inscribed on back: *1831*

National Museum of American Art, Smithsonian Institution.
Gift of Edward L. Morse

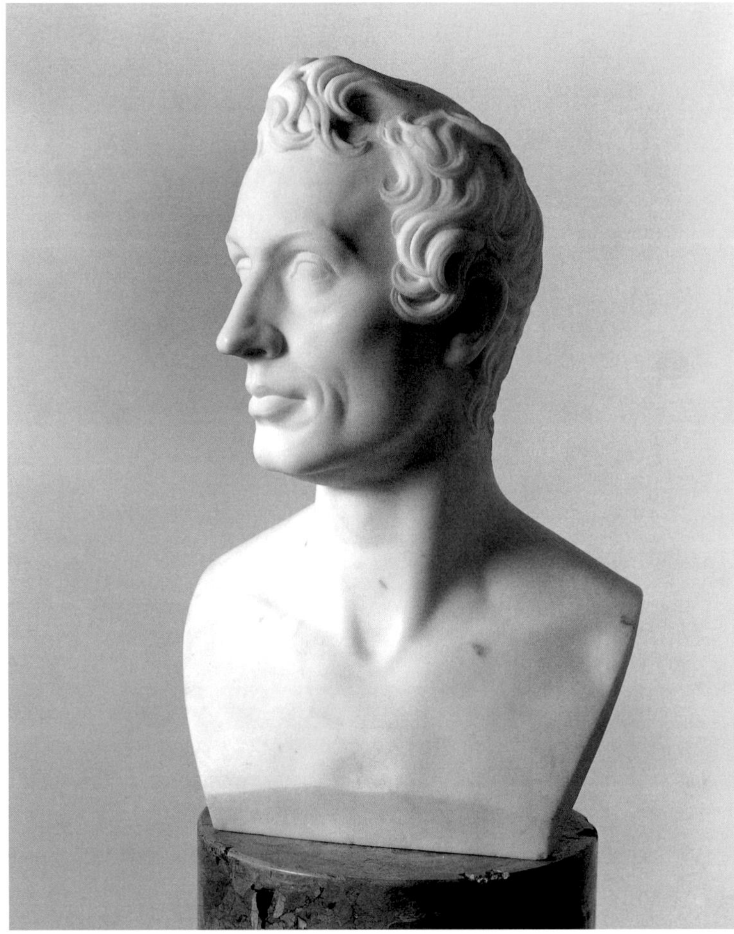

In March 1831 Morse, who was then on an extended trip to Europe (1829–32), made his way from Rome to Florence, where he took rooms on the Via Valfonda with Greenough, Cole, and the painter John Cranch (1807–1901).[1] Two months later, before Morse continued on his way to Bologna, Ferrara, and Venice, Greenough sculpted this portrait.[2] Although no drawings for this portrait survive, Greenough did draw a caricature of Morse sometime after October 1831, which he included on a page of figural sketches (cat. 29), with the inscription, *expects to be lathered.* In 1832 he also noted in a letter to Morse, "I have done your pen drawing likewise and only wait an opportunity to send it [to] you—It was done mainly in the winter evenings without models and is a failure in so many respects that I would burn it were there not in it a proof that I have not neglected your request."[3]

By December 1831 Cooper wrote Greenough to say, "Samuel [Morse] sayeth that you have converted my old bust into one of him. He is much tickled with the transformation, for I suppose he remembers that Minerva was knocked out of the head of Jupiter, by means of a hammer." He added that he thought Morse had some advantage in the prominence of his "side-locks," but that he supposed he had given the painter "a wig."[4] The portrait is among Greenough's best. The simplified herm format draws attention to Morse's strong features, such as his high peaked forehead and aquiline nose.

In March 1832 Greenough wrote Morse that "your bust and Cole's have both gone, directed to Mr. Morton."[5] John Ludlow Morton (1798–1871) was a portrait, historical, and landscape painter who served for many years as the first secretary of the National Academy of Design. Simultaneously, Greenough wrote Morton that, along with his bust of Cole (see fig. 13), he was sending him "the one of our good president." He added that "should these busts arrive in season for your exhibition may I beg you will find a good light for them?"[6] Morse's bust, along with that of Cole, was included in the spring exhibition at the National Academy of Design.

1. Wright 1963a, p. 80. The artists lived together at number 4488, where rooms cost about $6.00 per month.
2. Morse had earlier passed through Florence, in 1830, but there was probably insufficient time for Greenough to sculpt the painter's portrait.
3. Horatio Greenough to Samuel F. B. Morse, 3 June 1832.
4. Beard 1960–68, vol. 2, p. 167.
5. Horatio Greenough to Samuel F. B. Morse, 25 March and 23 April 1832.
6. Horatio Greenough to John Ludlow Morton, 27 March 1832.

23 *Elizabeth Todhunter Thomas*

1837
Marble, 26 × 19 × 11 inches
Signed on back: *HG 37*
Maryland Historical Society

By the 1830s the social circles of London and Paris had for some time been awash with Americans of status who reveled in a constant whirl of dinners, soirées, and balls that brought them together.[1] It was in just such settings that the engaging, witty, and urbane Greenough

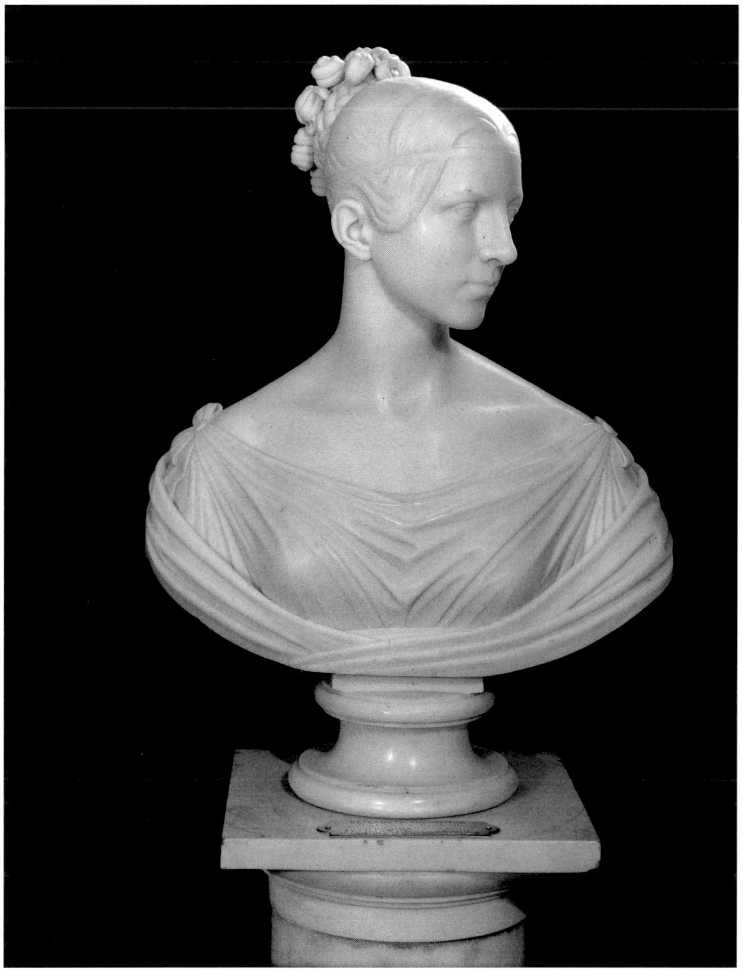

easily circulated and helped initiate some of the portrait commissions on which he depended for financial stability.

While in Paris in 1836 Greenough met Elizabeth Todhunter Thomas and her husband, Philip Evan Thomas (fig. 25).[2] The couple, who had married the preceding year, were touring Europe on their wedding trip. This was the second marriage for Philip Thomas, who had retired that year as president and director of the Baltimore and Ohio Railroad.[3] The busts were sculpted either in Paris during Greenough's six-week stay there or in Florence the following spring, when Greenough reported that he had done "a good deal of work," including a bust of "Mr. Thomas, of Baltimore."[4]

Greenough, like many American artists, had ambivalent feelings about making portraits. On the one hand, portraits such as this were essential to his career. Greenough, however, always saw them as a means to an end. Patrons like the Thomases, who initially commissioned portrait busts, might later become interested in an ideal work by him as well. This was certainly the pattern that had emerged with other patrons, such as Gilmor and Cooper. Greenough did not say much in his letters about the ongoing need to sculpt portraits, although occasionally one finds the passing reference to being "wearied with bust making."[5] By the mid-1830s the federal commission for a colossal figure of Washington to a great degree relieved him of this burden.

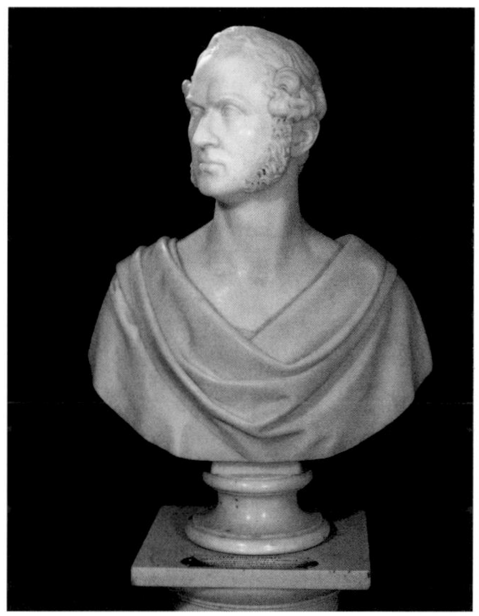

Fig. 25. Horatio Greenough, *Philip Evan Thomas*, c. 1836–37. Marble. Maryland Historical Society.

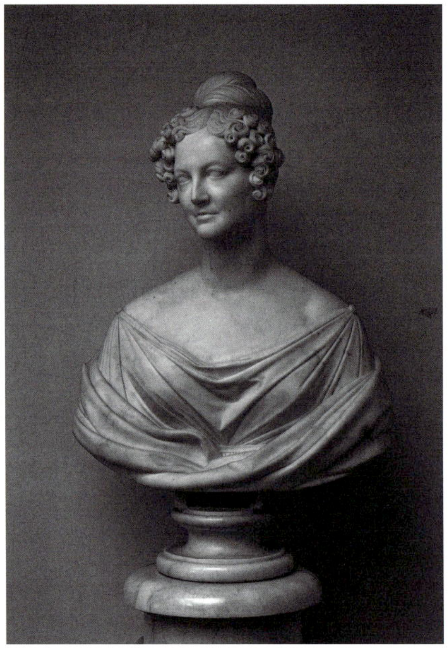

Fig. 26. Lorenzo Bartolini, *Bust of Anna McCurdy Hart Hull*, 1836–37. Marble, 27⅜ × 21⅛ × 13⅛ inches. Courtesy of the Boston Athenæum.

Elizabeth Todhunter Thomas is among Greenough's most satisfying female portraits. It also represents Greenough at his most confident. While it is an observed portrait, it also serves as Greenough's neoclassical vision of ideal feminine beauty. As such, it exhibits the strong influence of Bartolini (fig. 26), one of Greenough's mentors. Greenough has taken particular care with the sitter's refined features and stylish, smooth hair. It is symmetrically parted and held tight to her head by a fillet, or headband. Pulled back and braided, it is drawn up on the top of her head in the severe fashion popular with her generation.

Together with its pendant, these two busts form the most delicate and elegant pair of Greenough portraits to survive. Because they were designed to be seen together, Mrs. Thomas's head is turned slightly to the right, while that of her husband is turned in the opposite direction. When the portrait was finished, another of Greenough's social circle thought the "pretty" lady not comparable to the bust itself.[6]

1. Cooper 1993, p. 37.
2. Wright 1963a, p. 195.
3. DAB 1964, vol. 9, pp. 442–443.
4. Greenough 1887, Horatio Greenough to Henry Greenough, 16 June 1837.
5. Horatio Greenough to James Fenimore Cooper, 21 June 1831.
6. Wright 1963a, p. 196.

24 Portrait study of a woman

c. 1845–50

Graphite, 7½ × 7⅛ inches

93.8.159

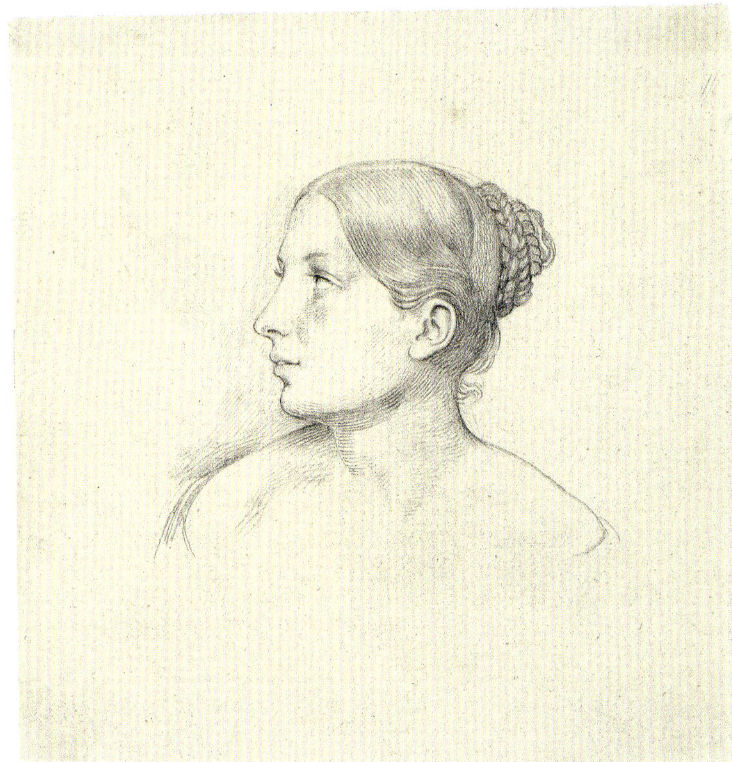

This delicate pencil drawing bears a marked similarity to the portrait of Elizabeth Todhunter Thomas (cat. 23). Whether or not it was done in preparation for a portrait, it seems likely that this is a drawing made in preparation for a clay model. It is also the type of drawing Greenough might have done to convince a potential sitter of his abilities.[1]

1. Nathalia Wright's notations on the mat for this drawing indicate she believed this could possibly be a portrait of Frances Boott Greenough, wife of Henry Greenough, Horatio's brother. Greenough did sculpt a bust of Frances (Wright 1963a, p. 204), but because it does not survive and no known portraits of her are now known, this identification cannot be confirmed.

25 Portrait study of a man

1831

Graphite, 4¾ × 3⅞ inches

Inscribed and dated lower left: *1831—*; lower right: *Ho. Gh.*

93.8.030

From the overt frontality of this drawing and the fact that Greenough took time to sign and date it, this sheet most likely portrays someone for whom Greenough cared a great deal. Circumstantial evidence suggests that it may be a portrait of Greenough's brother Henry, who was the sculptor's closest living relative.[1] This said, there are no identified portraits of him to which it can be compared.

The sculptor's great affection for his brother is evident in their extensive correspondence over twenty-seven years (1825–52), which was published in 1887.[2] Soon after Henry arrived in Florence in February 1830 the sculptor wrote Cooper that he was "intoxicated" by his arrival.[3] Henry remained in Florence until the summer of 1833.

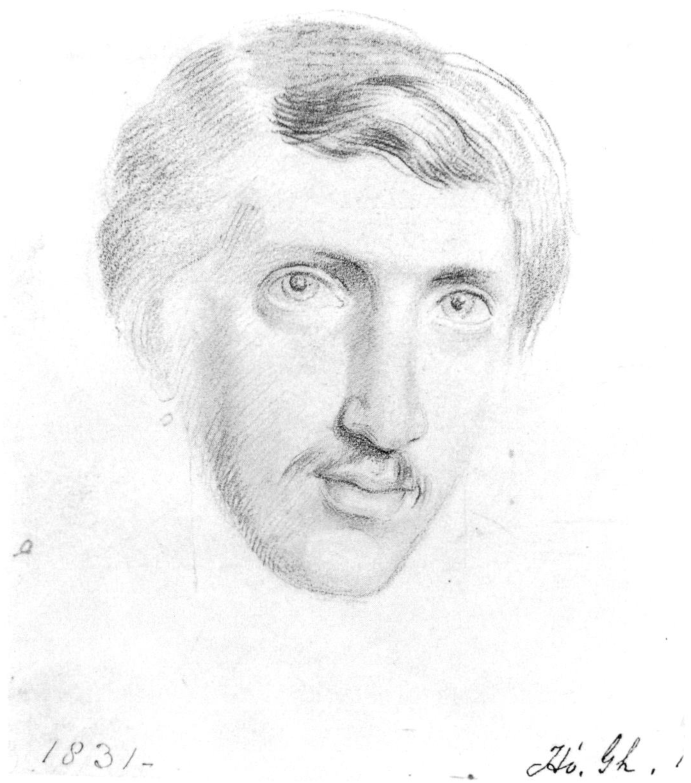

1. Nathalia Wright made notations on the drawing's mount indicating that she believed it might represent Henry Greenough.
2. Greenough 1887.
3. Horatio Greenough to James Fenimore Cooper, 5 March 1830.

26 *Ada Reviczky*

c. 1840

Pen and ink, 6⅛ × 4⅛ inches

93.8.105

This sheet preserves the only surviving drawings for Greenough's full-length statue of Ada Reviczky (b. 1838), the two-year-old daughter of Count Adam Reviczky von Reviczky. The elder Reviczky was a native of Hungary and its Lord High Chancellor until 1836, when he became Austrian minister to Tuscany.[1] In July 1840 Greenough noted in a letter that he had already modeled the figure for this work.[2]

Greenough was extremely pleased with this sculpture, which has been lost from view for decades and is only reidentified here (fig. 27). The sculpture was complete by early 1841, at which time Greenough wrote his brother:

> I wish you could see my statue of the daughter of the Austrian minister. It stands in the centre of their salon, in a fine light. I believe I have described the action to you formerly. The pedestal is of dark purple, oriental marble, with gold letters raised, to tell the name and age of the child. I am now making a bust of the mother, who is very beautiful.[3]

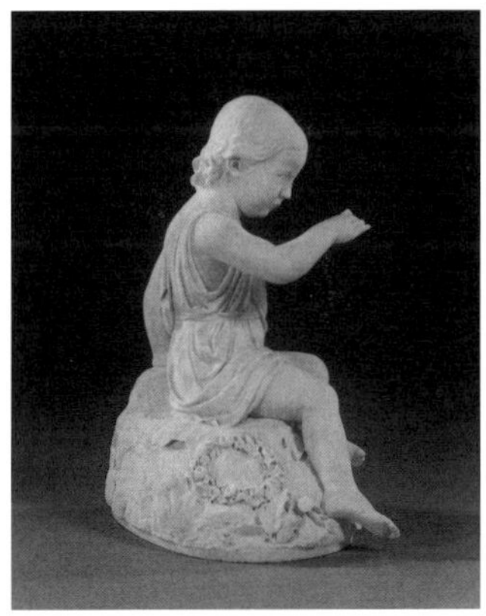

Fig. 27. Horatio Greenough, *Ada Reviczky*, c. 1840. Marble, H. 27 inches. Private Collection.

The sculpture depicts the child seated on a mound with her right arm extended to allow a butterfly to alight on her fingers. At one side is a wreath of flowers, and at the other a lizard creeps toward her.

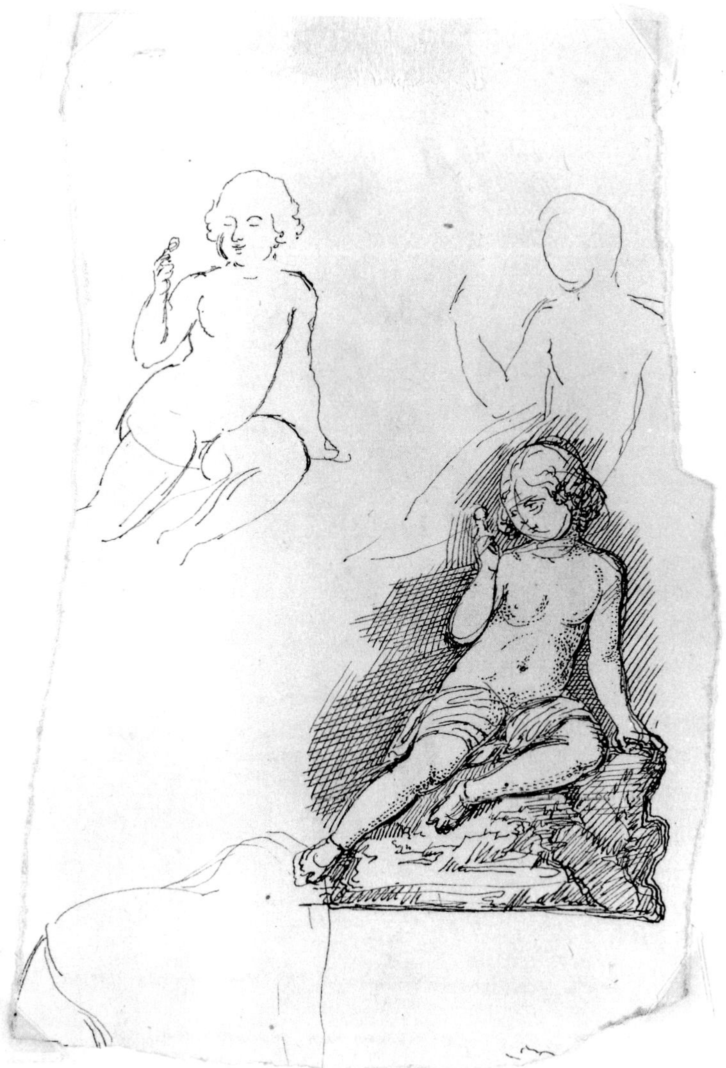

Beginning with his *Chanting Cherubs*, Greenough had a number of opportunities to create full-length statues of children. He was very comfortable in this format and here has adapted the ancient statue *Hercules with a Serpent* (fig. 28), by replacing the reptile with an insect. While the drawing shows the figure wrapped in a drape at the waist, for the sculpture Greenough has dressed the child in a toga to make it acceptable to nineteenth-century eyes.

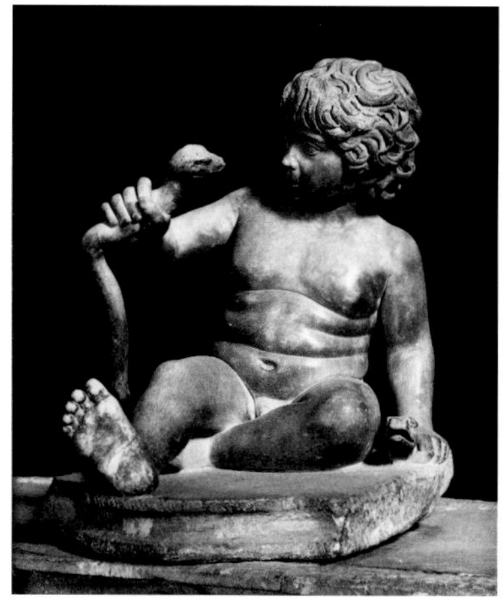

Fig. 28. *Hercules with a Serpent.* Marble. Capitoline Museum, Rome. Courtesy of the Archive of the Negativo Archivo fotografico dei Musei Capitolini.

Although the subject appears mawkish to late-twentieth-century eyes, audiences in Greenough's day were generous with their praise. Edward Everett described it "as among the most charming creations of Mr. Greenough's chisel," and a Florentine critic noted the symbolism of the insect as the emblem of Psyche in classical mythology and in Dante of the evolution of the human spirit.[4]

1. Wright 1972, p. 212n.
2. Horatio Greenough to Charles Sumner, 12 July 1840. "I have lately been much gratified by an order from the Countess Reviczky wife of the Austrian Minister here to make a full length portrait of her daughter. It is already modelled."
3. Greenough 1887, Horatio Greenough to Henry Greenough, 15 May 1841.
4. Tuckerman 1967, p. 259, and Wright 1963a, p. 215.

27 Female profile

c. 1845–50

Graphite and charcoal, 17⅛ × 11⅛ inches

93.8.161

Although this drawing recalls the considerable number of profile drawings produced as finished portraits by artists earlier in the century,[1] it most likely played a specialized role for Greenough. In Greenough's effort to properly grasp anatomy, profile drawings served as useful complements to the three-quarter views that he was apt to draw more casually. Here, because of the particular attention given to

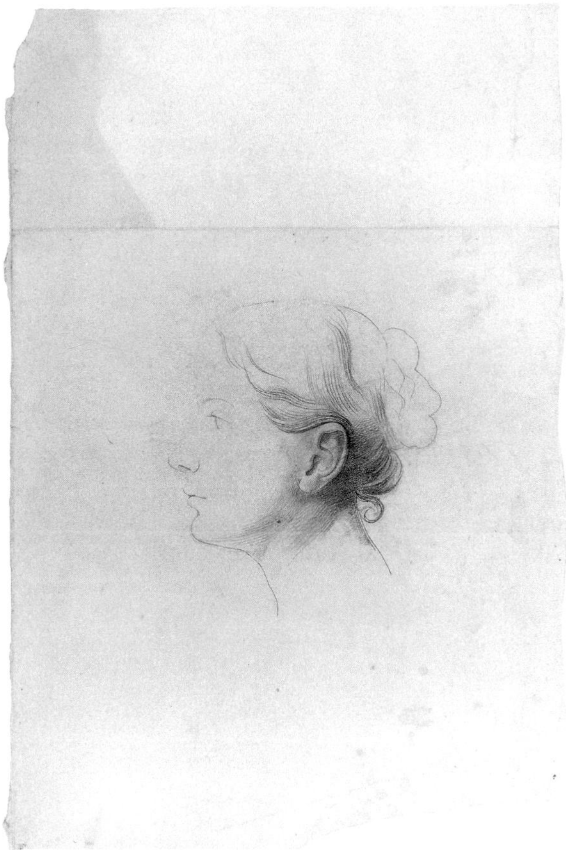

the ear and nape of the neck, this drawing may well have been used as reference when modeling a clay bust.

1. See Sadik and Pfister 1980, p. 9, and Stebbins 1976, pp. 45–47.

28 *Arno*

1839

Marble, 25¼ × 51½ × 22½ inches

Museum of Fine Arts, Boston. Arthur Tracy Cabot Fund

This sculpture, named for the river that flows through Florence, depicts the greyhound that was Greenough's constant companion after the sculptor purchased him in 1835. In January of that year he wrote his brother, "I have at this moment a fine, tall, milk-white greyhound frolicking about me. He puts his forepaws on my shoulders as I stand erect. His nose is pink, and his ears look like rose-leaves. Everybody is enamoured of him. I gave five dollars for him, and have already received fifty-five dollars' worth of pleasure."[1] As early as 1830 Greenough had a dog as a companion, when his brother Alfred sent him a Newfoundland at his request to be used as a model.[2]

Greenough became particularly fond of his greyhound, and he sketched it frequently. In an 1836 letter he joked that while away he would send Arno a letter.[3] The following year he wrote Henry that he was waiting to hear from a Mr. Whitwell, "about the model of the dog,"[4] which is presumably a reference to this sculpture.

Greenough's selection of the greyhound as a subject is in and of itself a subtle classical allusion. The greyhound is an ancient and noble breed that guarded the tombs of the pharaohs and was used in hunting. As a subject in both painting and sculpture, the breed has a long and distinguished history traceable from the fourth century B.C.[5] The most obvious precedent for Greenough was the work of Joseph Gott (1785–1860), an English-born sculptor who lived in Rome from 1824 until his death. Gott developed a reputation as an *animalier*, and Greenough was undoubtedly familiar with *Greyhound with Her Two Puppies Suckling* (Wadsworth Atheneum, Hartford) or similar works.

Greenough's visitors found his affection for Arno notable. William J. Hubard made Arno, along with a second greyhound, an integral

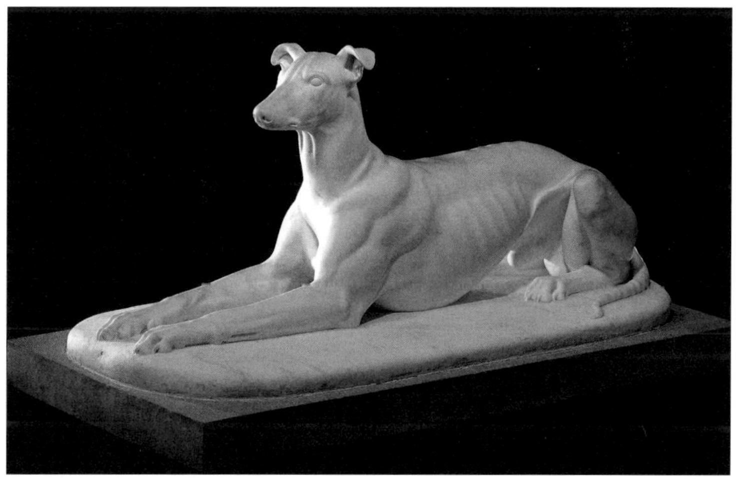

part of his 1839 portrait of the sculptor (cat. 65). Tuckerman remarked that during the walks he took with the sculptor they were "usually accompanied by a remarkably fine English greyhound, a great pet of Greenough's called Arno, whose intelligent gambols always amused him; this favorite dog lived to a green old age, and his marble effigy, in an attitude peculiar to him from the chisel of his master, now ornaments the library of the Hon. Edward Everett."[6]

Everett, too, took note of Greenough's dog when he visited the sculptor. In 1842 he wrote that the dog's portrait was then owned by Peter Chardon Brooks of Medford, Massachusetts, and he added, the "noble animal, Arno, destined no doubt to share in marble the immortality of his owner the artist, has recovered from the effect of a sad accident which befell him the past winter [1841], by which one of his legs was fractured."[7]

When *Arno* first arrived in America it was owned by William Sturgis, a Boston lawyer. In 1840 Sturgis lent it to an exhibit at the Boston Athenæum, where it was seen along with five other works by Greenough.[8] By 1852 the sculpture was acquired by Everett who sought Greenough's advice on how best to place it in his library.[9]

1. Greenough 1887, Horatio Greenough to Henry Greenough, 18 January 1835.
2. Greenough 1887, Alfred Greenough to Henry Greenough, 30 August 1830.
3. Horatio Greenough to Richard Henry Wilde, 18, 19 August 1836.
4. Greenough 1887, Horatio Greenough to Henry Greenough, 18 August 1837.
5. Cooper 1993, p. 63, and Vermeule 1975, p. 981.
6. Tuckerman 1968, p. 25.
7. Everett 1842, p. 6.
8. Perkins and Gavin 1980, p. 67.
9. Wright 1963a, p. 274, and "Diary of Edward Everett for 1852," 21 February 1852, Massachusetts Historical Society: "Mr Horatio Greenough called to consult about the position of the Arno in the new library."

29 Greyhound and multiple figure studies

c. 1838–39

Pen and ink, 15⅞ × 9¾ inches (double sheet)

93.8.038

Perhaps more than any other sheet of sketches, this page epitomizes Greenough's delight with the medium of drawing. To him, a blank sheet of paper was an invitation to release the thoughts of a fertile mind as well as to capture observations of what was around him. Repeatedly turning the sheet ninety degrees, he quickly filled up every available space with a veritable patchwork of faces and figures.

The centerpiece of this sheet is a greyhound, presumably Greenough's beloved Arno. It is one of at least six drawings that depict Arno, or a second greyhound the sculptor acquired by 1839.[1] This sheet has mistakenly been dated 1831 because the drawings appear on what was originally a page used for correspondence. The paragraph beginning with the word *Nature* is from an unidentified letter, but the second paragraph is from a letter to Washington Allston dated October 1831.[2] Because of this, Nathalia Wright assumed that the drawings on the sheet were made at the same time and that the sculptor therefore also owned a greyhound by this date. The issue was further confused by a second author who misread a letter of 1830 in which Greenough's brother Alfred noted sending the sculptor a Newfoundland dog.[3] This led to the mistaken belief that when Greenough purchased Arno in 1835 he was buying a second greyhound, although he did not acquire a second greyhound until 1839, when Hubard included two of them in his portrait of the sculptor.

It seems most likely, however, that this drawing was made about 1838 when Greenough dated another drawing of a greyhound (cat. 32). That sheet, like this one, is dominated by the figure of a standing greyhound but also includes several portrait profiles.

To the left of Arno's head, on this drawing, are two profiles. The one to the left, next to which is inscribed, *expects to be lathered*, depicts Samuel Morse. The profile immediately to the right is of Luigi Persico. This is confirmed by an identified frontal view of Persico that appears as a complement to another drawing of a greyhound (cat. 32). The fact that Persico appears on two drawings from the period 1838–39 makes sense, for it was at this moment that Greenough signed the contract for *The Rescue* (cats. 58–62), which was intended to be a pendant to Persico's sculpture *The Discovery of America*.

1. In addition to the four drawings illustrated here (cats. 29–32), two drawings of greyhounds are in the collection of the Philadelphia Free Library. One of these depicts a virtually identical standing greyhound seen in profile.
2. Horatio Greenough to Washington Allston, October 1831. It is conceivable that Greenough drew the human ear at this time, since he had been asked by Allston to try to locate a cast of an ear for him.
3. Crane 1972, p. 87, misread the letter from Alfred Greenough to Henry Greenough, 30 August 1830.

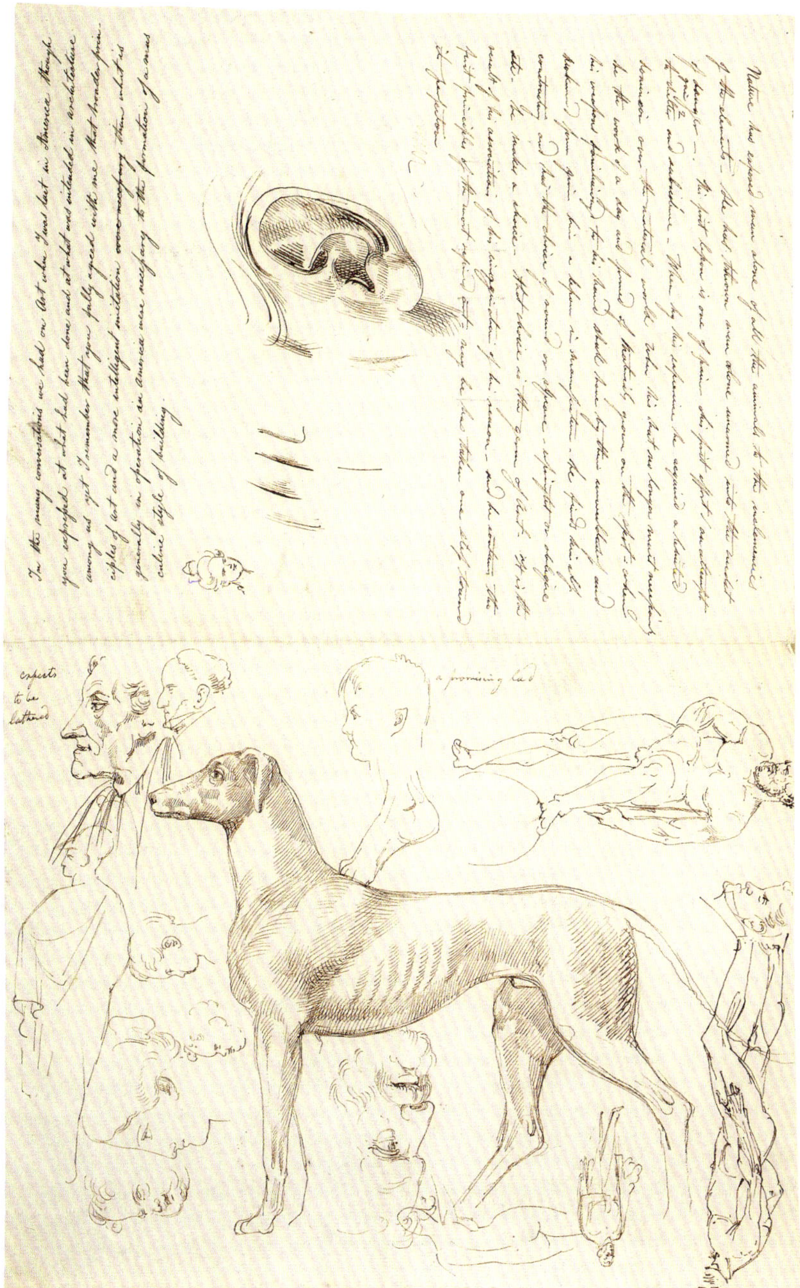

[29]

30 Study for *Arno*

verso: Four studies of heads, dying patient, and study of a hand

c. 1835–38

Pen and ink, 7½ × 9⅜ inches

93.8.077

Of the three views of a greyhound depicted here, the uppermost drawing closely resembles the pose of the finished *Arno*. As in the sculpture, the drawing shows a dog with taut body and alert ears. While the sculpture suggests that the cause of the alertness may be his master's whistle, the drawing indicates it is actually the presence of a mouse that has stirred him.

31 Multiple drawings of greyhounds in motion; head of a man

c. 1835–39

Pen and ink, 11¾ × 7 inches

93.8.078

32 Study of a greyhound, with portraits of Hiram Powers and Luigi Persico

1838

Pen and brown ink, over graphite on paper, 8⅞ × 12¼ inches

Signed, dated, and inscribed at lower right: *To BD Greene/from Hor Greenough/28th Xber '38;* on the back at upper left of original mount, before removal, behind portrait at upper right, now mounted on back of frame: *Persico*; at upper right of original mount, before removal, behind portrait at upper left, now mounted on back of frame: *Powers*

Private Collection

Although Greenough's correspondence documents his fondness for presenting drawings to friends, this stunning and important work is the only thoroughly documented example now known. The drawing, which depicts a standing greyhound flanked by portraits of Powers and Persico, may have begun its life as a proposal for a bas-relief of

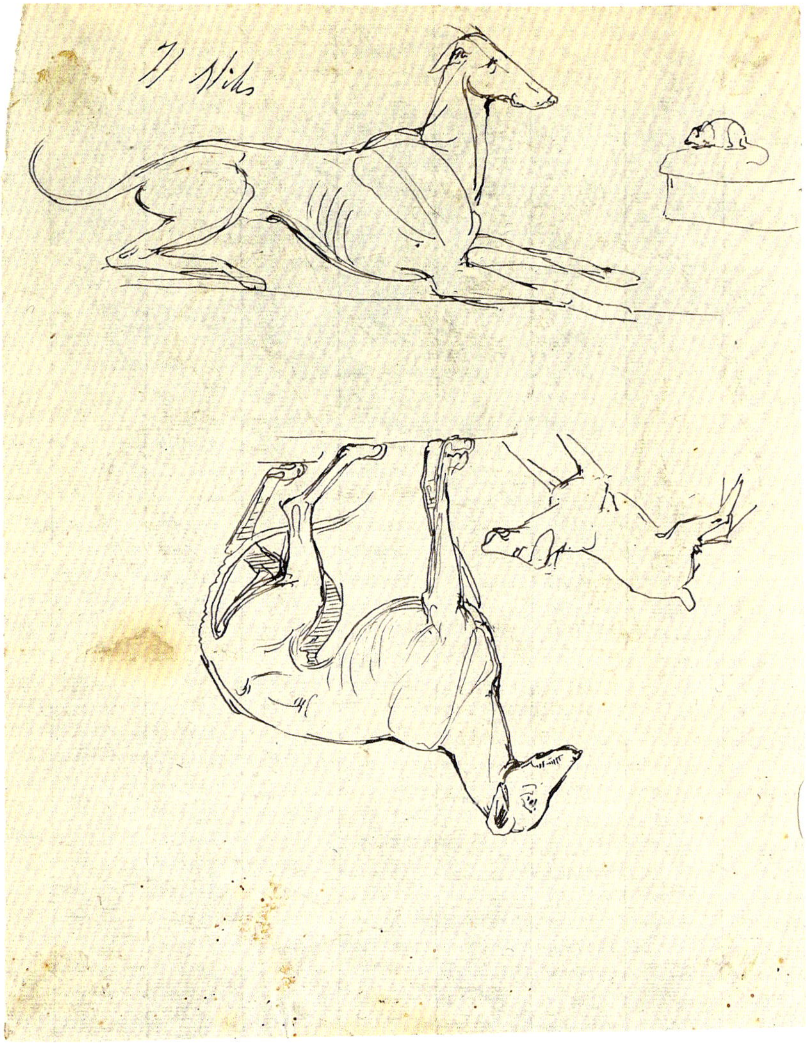

[30]

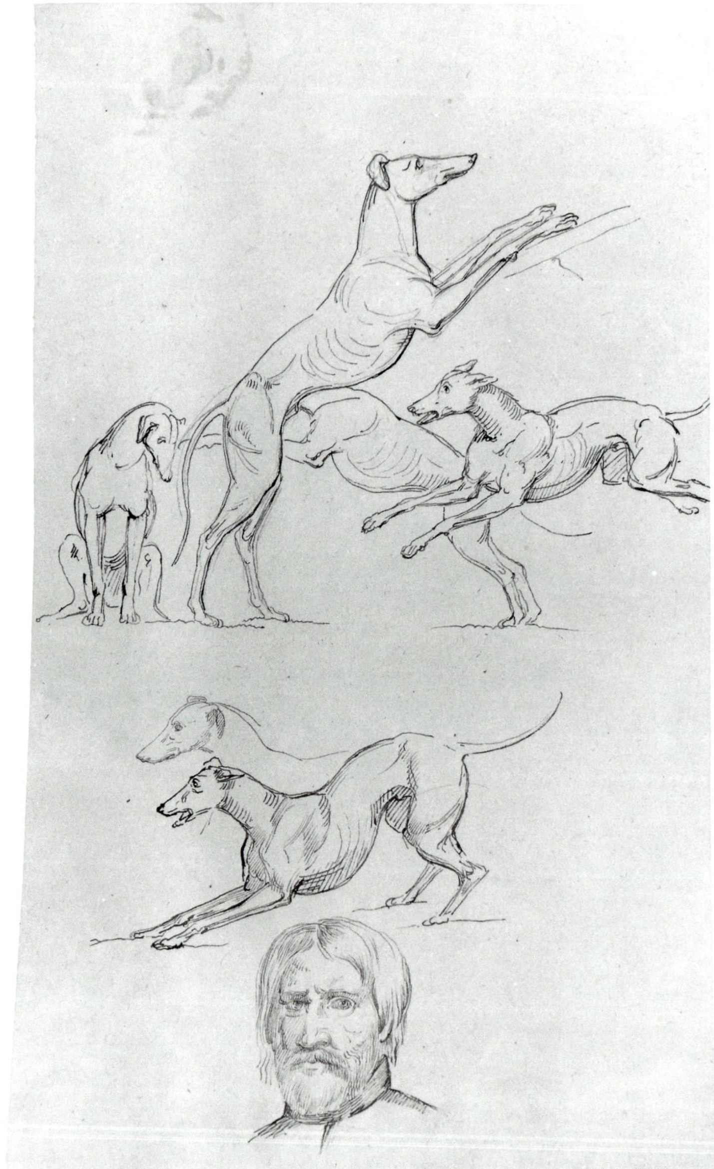

[31]

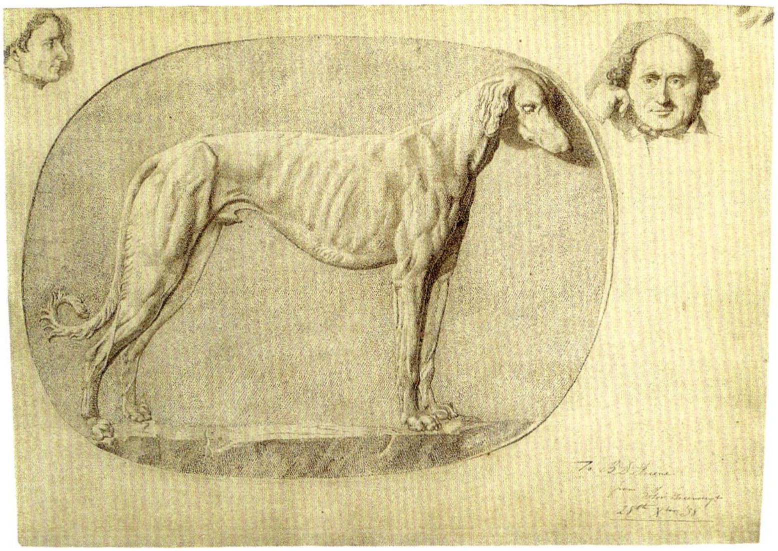

[32]

Arno, his favorite dog. Because of Greenough's increased fascination with bas-reliefs in the late 1830s, it is conceivable that Greenough considered this an alternative format to the full-figure sculpture *Arno* (cat. 28) he produced in 1839.

In any event, on 28 December 1838 Greenough inscribed and presented the drawing to Benjamin Daniel Greene, a fellow Bostonian, whose wife (a daughter of Josiah Quincy) was a childhood friend of Louisa Greenough. Accompanied by his wife and four other family members, Greene visited the sculptor during his four-week stay in Florence between December 1838 and early January 1839.[1]

The night before this drawing was presented to Greene, he and his entourage were dinner guests of the Greenoughs. Mrs. Greene recorded in her diary that the table was set for twelve and the meal was served at the American hour of half-past six:

> entirely in the Italian style, & exactly to my taste. The dessert was on the table . . . presenting flowers, fruit & confectionary. After the soup had been dismissed, olives and butter were handed to each guest—then oyster patties, then fish, & a succession of dishes—pudding, pies, confectionary, wines of every kind, & black coffee—all left the table together.

Afterward, in the billiard room, they had tea, cordials, and heard music.[2]

Greenough may have envisioned this bas-relief drawing as a visual ode to Arno. Certainly, the keenly observed and lovingly detailed drawing recalls his remarks about the relationship between form and function in all things, whether they be animals or architecture: "The horse's shanks are thin, and we admire them; the greyhound's chest is deep, and we cry, beautiful! It is neither the presence nor the absence of this or that part, or shape, or color, that wins our eye in natural objects; it is the consistency and harmony of the parts juxtaposed, the subordination of details to masses, and of masses to the whole."[3]

The portraits of Powers and Persico as adjuncts to the greyhound are not random choices. Powers, who had arrived in Florence only at the end of 1837, was immediately befriended by Greenough, who saw him both as a kindred spirit and, although the same age, as an informal protégé, as well.[4] Persico, too, was very much on his mind while Greenough sought to compose *The Rescue*, a work he hoped would equal the Italian sculptor's design for the Capitol steps. In fact, the two conferred in Florence earlier in the month about the marble to be used for both groups.[5] Two weeks later Greene witnessed Greenough's signing of the government contract for *The Rescue*.[6]

1. Diary of Mrs. Benjamin Daniel Greene. Massachusetts Historical Society. On 30 December she noted, "Mr. Greenough gave Mr. Greene an original drawing." Greene and his wife were traveling with his mother, Elizabeth Clarke Copley Greene; his sisters, Mary Greene Hubbard Sturgis and Mary Copley Greene Amory; and his brother-in-law, James Sullivan Amory. The group visited Florence again 24–28 March 1839. See Wright 1972, pp. 242–243.
2. Diary of Mrs. Benjamin Greene, 27 December 1838, quoted in Wright 1963a, p. 201.
3. Tuckerman 1968, p. 122. Tuckerman quotes from Greenough's essay, "American Architecture," which was first published in 1843 in the *United States Magazine and Democratic Review*. I want to thank Amy F. Ogata, formerly a Ph.D. candidate at Princeton University, for calling this reference to my attention.
4. Wright 1972 includes five letters from Greenough to Powers in 1838 that document the various ways he assisted the new arrival to Florence.
5. Luigi Persico to John Forsyth, 14 December 1838. State Department, Miscellaneous Letters.
6. Wright 1963a, p. 201.

Allegorical, Classical, Biblical, & Literary Subjects

33 *The Ascension of a Child Conducted by an Infant Angel*

1833

Marble, 32⅞ × 23¼ × 13 inches

Signed: *Ho. Greenough Ft. 1832*; inscribed around base: QUAENUNC ABIBIS IN LOCA (To what place will you now go?)

Museum of Fine Arts, Boston. Gift of Laurence Curtis

In the first few years of Greenough's residence in Florence, he desperately sought commissions for idealized works, such as *The Ascension of a Child*.[1] In his mind, the reason was simple: the creation of ideal works, that is, works based on an idea rather than on direct observation, was a far greater test of his skills than the more predictable task of sculpting what was before him. Since Greenough's aspirations were so enormous, he naturally gravitated toward situations that would distinguish him as an artist of great ability.

The Ascension of a Child, which depicts a winged angel escorting to the spiritual realm a recently deceased child, was the direct result of just such an opportunity. In the fall of 1832 Greenough met Samuel Cabot, a Boston merchant, visiting Florence with his wife and two children. After Greenough learned that the Cabots had recently suffered the loss of their third child, at age two, he proposed this sculpture as a memorial.[2] The subject was consistent with changing attitudes toward death which, nationally, precipitated the evolution from graveyards to cemeteries. A more rosy assessment of the afterlife fostered the replacement of ominous, skull-embellished headstones with sculpture gardens, where pleasant memories of the "dearly departed" could be savored.[3]

This subject immediately occurred to Greenough, as it afforded him the opportunity to adapt the subject of *The Chanting Cherubs*, the first idealized work of his career. The latter work, which is now unlocated, depicted two cherubs in song derived from a detail in a painting by Raphael (fig. 29). Even at the time of this earlier commission, Greenough expressed his preference for developing one of his own ideas, rather than copying the work of another artist.[4] Because of these circumstances, *The Ascension of a Child*, which is among the most sentimental of Greenough's surviving works, should be seen as an early, and only partially successful, experiment on his part, whose novelty he abandoned subsequently.

In November 1832 Greenough communicated with Cabot about his price for the work (700 Tuscan crowns, approximately $770) and

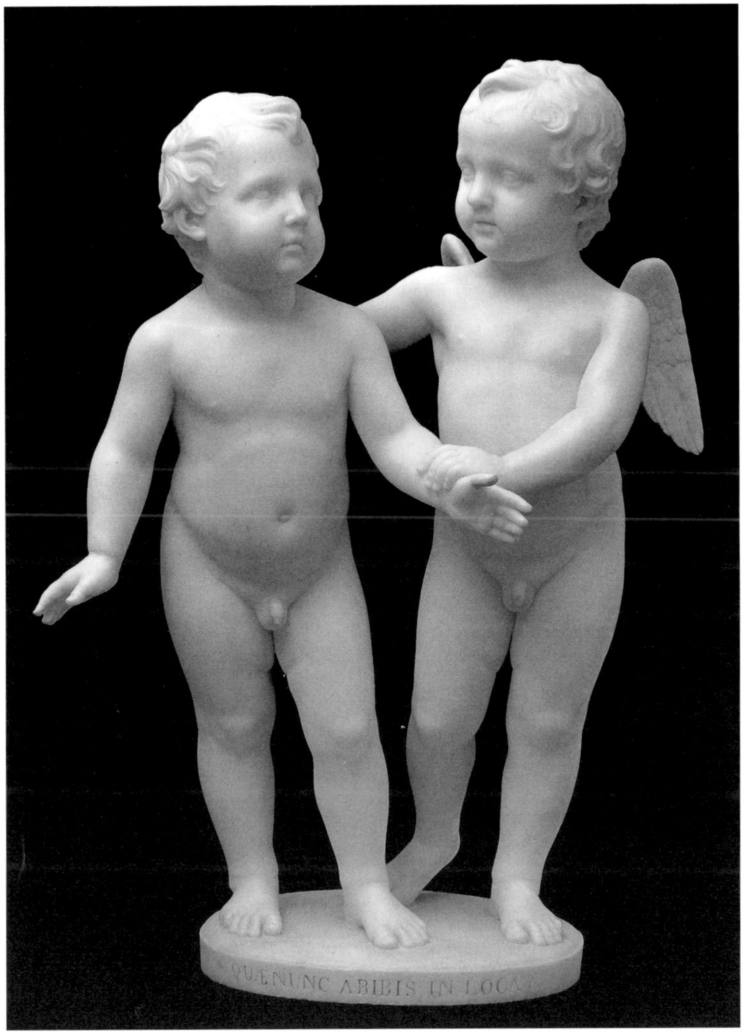

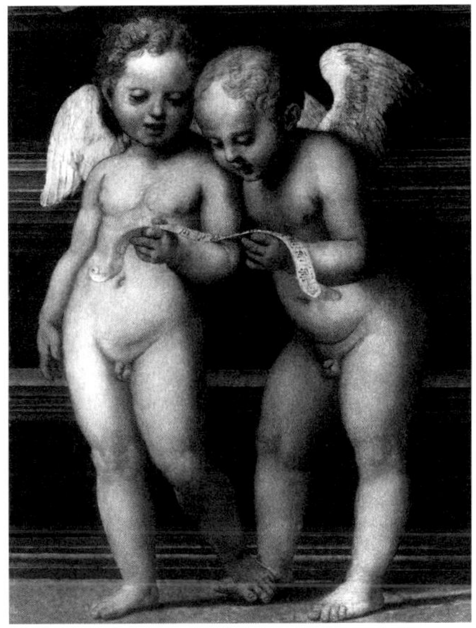

Fig. 29. Raphael, *Madonna of the Baldacchino*, 1507–8. Palazzo Pitti, Florence. Courtesy of Alinari.

the need to receive the customary half-payment in advance. While this was the highest price to date that Greenough had commanded, he reminded his patron that "the production of my statues has more than consumed the prices paid for them" and that all he really hoped to do was avoid debt.[5] Shortly thereafter, Greenough passed along word of the commission to Cooper: "I have received an order for a groupe similar to yours in which I propose to represent a young angelic figure conducting a babe to the other world—The points of expression will be the contrast between the ideal forms and face of the cherub and the milky fatness and shew-baby, half doubting, half pleased look of the child."[6]

As was Cooper's custom, he did not hesitate to make recommendations to Greenough, whom he considered his protégé. While he considered the idea of the work "poetical," Cooper queried, "is it not too much for marble." In sculpting the child, he encouraged Greenough to "veil some part of the chubbiness of the limbs with drapery."[7]

Cabot, too, requested that the figures not be shown completely naked. As a result Greenough outfitted "the little fellows" with alabaster fig leaves, which "shall fall at a tap! of the hammer when the discerning public shall have *digested* the fruit of the knowledge of good and evil."[8] This gesture was also intended to deflect possible objections to the nudity of the figures, which had led to *The Chanting Cherubs* being outfitted with aprons during their exhibition in Boston.[9]

By January 1833 the work was "far advanced" and Greenough had chosen to ignore Cooper's recommendations. In May Greenough was still at work on the piece but was mindful that "Mr. Cabot expected his groupe would be finished as early as possible in which he was perfectly right."[10] Cabot had earlier sent Greenough a plan of his house, which included a wall niche into which the sculpture would be set. This appealed greatly to Greenough, who added, "It is almost necessary indeed, for the protection of the work from accidents—Nothing will be lost—for as you remark the statues should be placed on a turning plinth."[11]

Once in America the work was shown in public at Armory Hall in Boston (4 November 1834–24 February 1835), to which visitors were admitted for a fee of twenty-five cents. A green screen was erected behind the work, and a rose-colored silk hung between it and the sunlight that fell on it. For the most part, the work was highly praised and was the subject of four odes, including one by Allston.[12]

1. This work was also variously called *Ascension of an Infant Spirit, Ascension of a Child Conducted by an Infant Angel*, and (by Greenough) *Journey to Heaven.*
2. Wright 1972, p. 150n. At the same time Greenough was also commissioned to do a bust of the Cabots'eleven-year-old daughter, Elizabeth.
3. Greenthal, Kozol, and Ramirez 1986, p. 16, and Stony Brook 1980, pp. 49–69.
4. Horatio Greenough to Robert Gilmor, Jr., 13 January 1832.
5. Horatio Greenough to Samuel Cabot, 12 November 1832. Greenough later reduced the price by $200 as a gesture to Colonel Thomas Handasyd Perkins, another of the sculptor's patrons, who was also Cabot's father-in-law. See Greenough 1887, Horatio Greenough to Henry Greenough, 17 February 1835.
6. Horatio Greenough to James Fenimore Cooper, 18 December 1832.
7. Beard 1960–68, vol. 2, p. 368, James Fenimore Cooper to Horatio Greenough, 19 January 1833.
8. Horatio Greenough to James Fenimore Cooper, 29 January 1833.
9. Wright 1963a, p. 72.
10. Horatio Greenough to James Fenimore Cooper, 15 May 1833.
11. Horatio Greenough to Samuel Cabot, 17 December 1832.
12. Wright 1963a, pp. 99–100, and Tuckerman 1968, pp. 237–239.

34 Multiple studies for *The Ascension of a Child Conducted by an Infant Angel* and figure of Hebe (?)

verso: Young Hercules Strangling the Serpent; standing full-length figure of Orpheus (?)

c. 1832

Graphite, 16 × 11¾ inches (double sheet)

93.8.047

This drawing, along with a second in the Rinhart collection (93.8.046), depicts early attempts by Greenough to develop a satisfactory compositon for his sculpture *The Ascension of a Child Conducted by an Infant Angel.* Presumably, these drawings were made prior to his effort to sculpt the work, as here the figures are reversed from the final arrangement. Like many Greenough drawings of this type, it shows that the sculptor is primarily concerned with determining the overall composition and draws the figures in a clear, linear fashion.

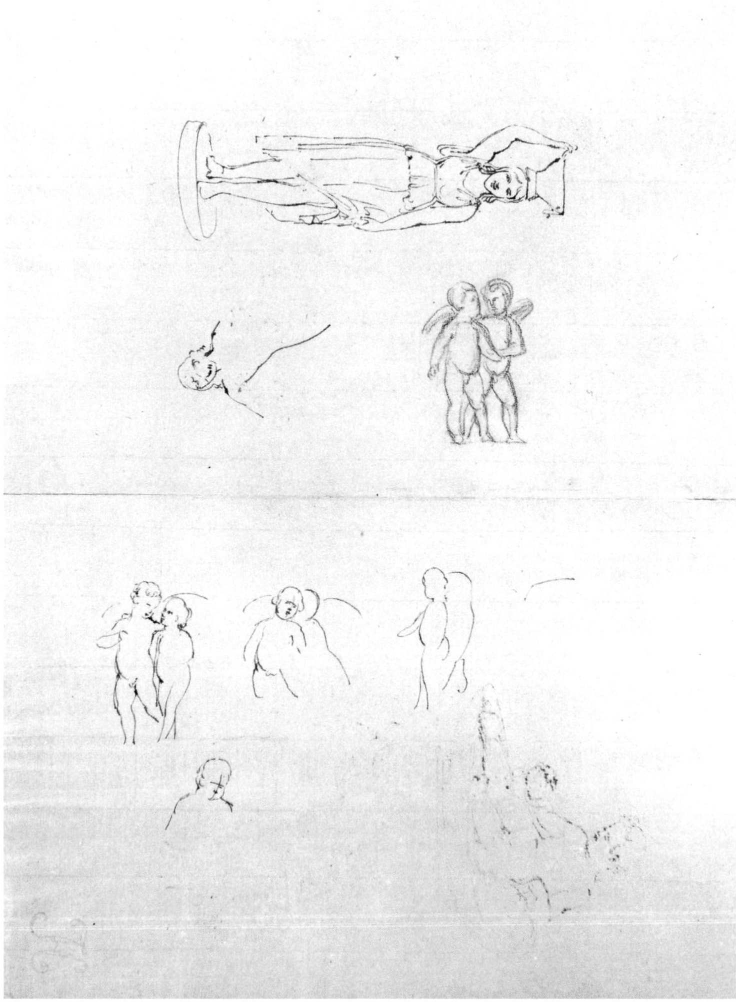

35 Elderly bearded man

c. 1832–36

Charcoal and wash over graphite, 5¼ × 4 inches

93.8.073

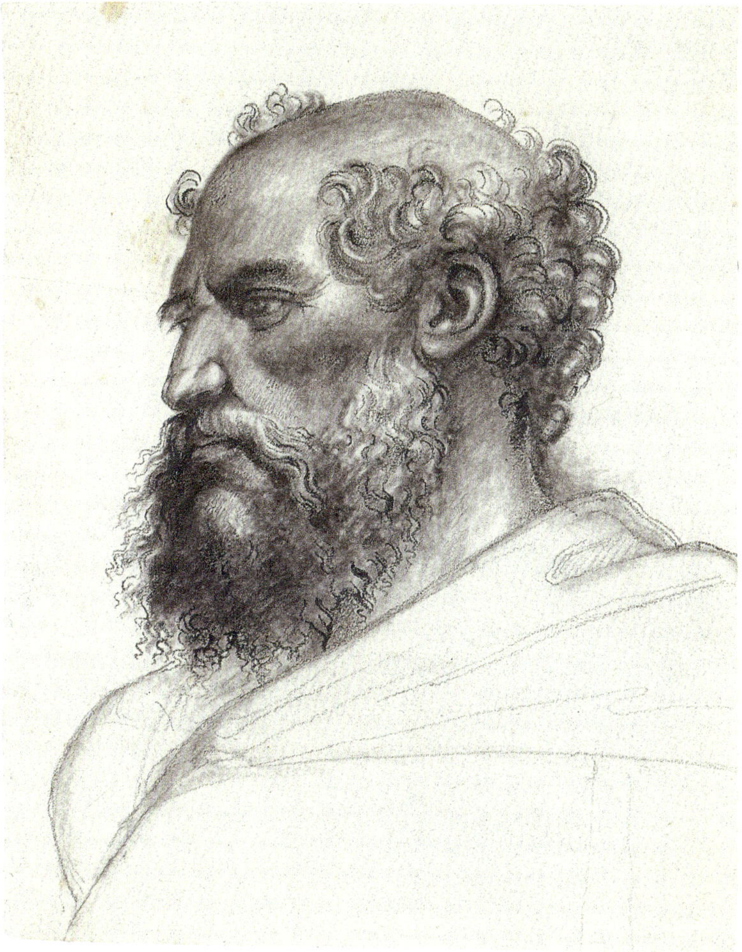

This deceptively small, yet richly detailed drawing has not been related to any specific sculpture by Greenough, yet it is among his most monumental works. It is tempting to believe that this is a life drawing, but more likely it is taken from an unidentified printed or painted source. Nevertheless, it was certainly a figure of importance to Greenough; he took particular care to render precise details of hair and in so doing further demonstrated his skill as a draftsman.

With his luxuriant and untrimmed beard, the figure has the air of a biblical figure, such as St. John (see fig. 18), or perhaps the figure intended to represent the Roman Catholic Church in his bas-relief *The Genius of Italy* (cat. 44).

36 *Lucifer*

c. 1841–42

Marble, 32 × 15¼ × 12½ inches

Courtesy of the Trustees of the Boston Public Library. Gift of Horatio S. Greenough in 1895

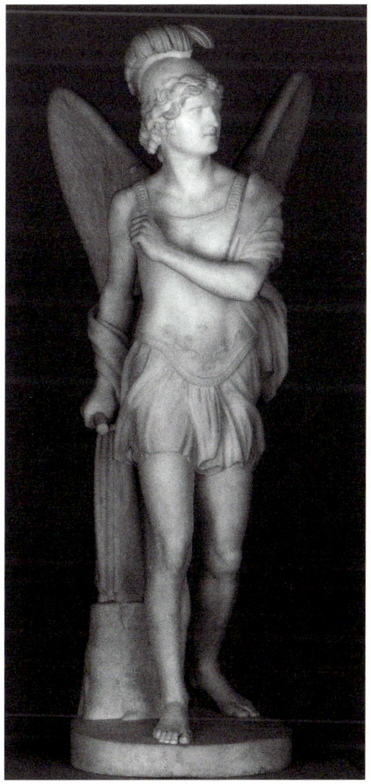

Fig. 30. Horatio Greenough, *The Angel Abdiel*, c. 1838–39. Marble, H. 40¾ inches. Yale University Art Gallery. Bequest of Edward E. Salisbury, B.A. 1832.

This bust, for which there is little precedent in nineteenth-century American sculpture, is astonishing in its power and originality. The subject, inspired by Milton's *Paradise Lost*, depicts Lucifer, the demon of sinful pride. Like other artists before him, Greenough had been drawn to Milton's rich imagery in the late 1830s when he sculpted a figure of Abdiel (fig. 30) and shortly thereafter a bust of him, as well.[1]

Aside from his statue of Washington, this was Greenough's first effort to sculpt a figure of colossal size. The work remained in Greenough's possession, and there is no evidence to suggest it was a commission, so the sculptor presumably made it for his own satisfaction. This seems logical since Greenough acknowledged having "long contemplated modelling for myself" a head of Abdiel. He presumably decided to do a head of Lucifer for himself instead.[2]

Greenough was particularly pleased with *Lucifer*, observing to his brother that he considered it "my highest effort" in the line of ideal works.[3] A number of elements probably led him to this conclusion. Foremost is the figure's monumental size. In addition, the robustness of the carving, particularly the luxuriant hair cascading down the shoulders, sets it apart from other observed and ideal works by the sculptor. Also noteworthy is the inventive use of a coiled viper as the socle. Mouth open, tongue extended, and fangs bared, its menacing potency is made clear.[4] Like the serpent, the matching devil's heads above it are literary clues understood by virtually any nineteenth-century viewer.

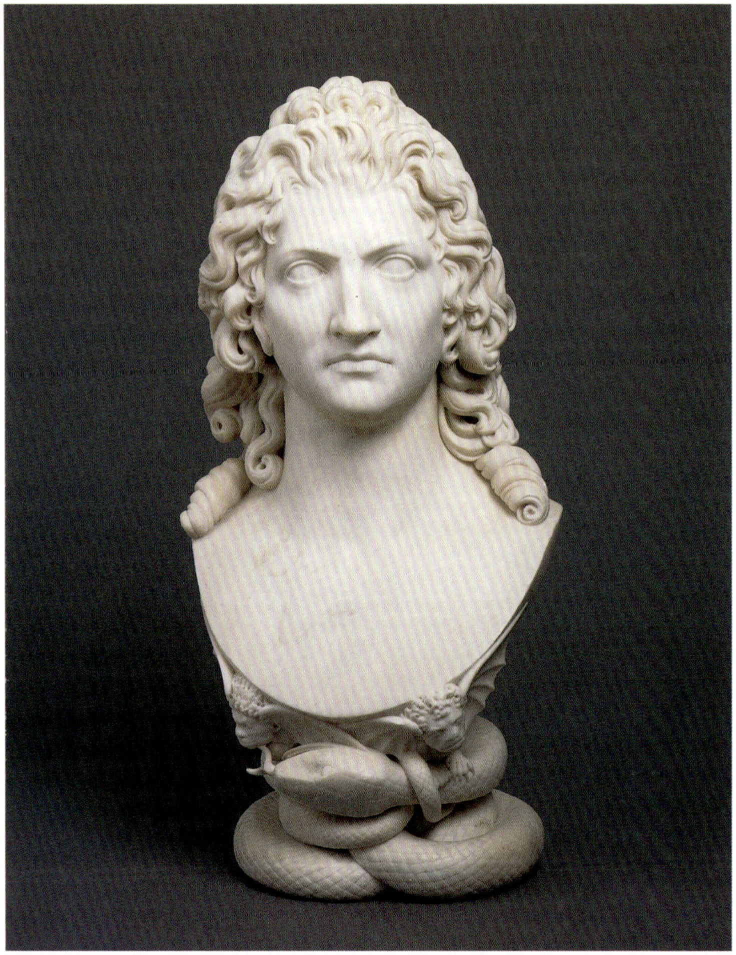

Outwardly, aside from his mildly unruly hair, the figure gives little indication of its diabolical character. Greenough has carefully chosen to depict Lucifer at the time of his expulsion and as a reminder that his transformation and degeneration were gradual. The portrait is that of a fallen angel as defeated hero, rather than distorted fiend. He is an archangel ruined, but still endowed with original brightness. As a result, he still possesses a godlike shape and an exceedingly human form.[5]

It is within, however, that Lucifer is changed, and this fact was noticed by those who saw the work. Tuckerman, for example, observed after visiting Greenough's studio about 1842:

> The countenance has the beauty of an archangel, with the hard uncertain look of an archangel fallen. Here is a noble mould not filled up with the expression commensurate to it. There is no exaggeration to impress the beholder at once with the malevolence of the original which the sculptor had in his imagination. The sinister nature lies concealed, as it were, in the features, and comes out gradually, after they have been some time contemplated. The beauty of the countenance is not yet blasted by the deformity of the mind.[6]

Curiously, no drawings for this work survive.[7]

1. Abdiel was the faithful angel who refuted Satan's claim to divinity. Greenough 1887, Horatio Greenough to Henry Greenough, 18 March 1838; Horatio Greenough to Edward Elbridge Salisbury, 3 January 1838. Greenough credited Allston with suggesting the subject of Abdiel to him. See Horatio Greenough to Washington Allston, 18 February 1838.
2. Horatio Greenough to Edward Elbridge Salsibury, 30 January 1838.
3. Greenough 1887, Horatio Greenough to Henry Greenough, 8 July 1843. In this letter Greenough referred to the head as "Satan," rather than Lucifer. While Lucifer is not synonymous with Satan, the names had been used interchangeably for centuries, and the sculptor apparently made no distinction between them.
4. Hunisak 1994, p. 158.
5. Frye 1978, p. 82.
6. Tuckerman 1968, pp. 227–228. Also, on 3 July 1841 (1841 Travel Diary of Edward Everett, Massachusetts Historical Society) Everett visited Greenough and noted, "called on Mr. and Mrs. Greenough. Mr. G. showed me a head of Satan, as described in Milton, which he is just modeling intending if successful to make on a colossal scale."
7. The robust carving and serpent imagery of Greenough's *Lucifer* vividly recalls *Adam, Eve, and Satan* by Michelangelo Naccherino (1550–1622) in the Boboli Gardens, Florence. It is tempting to think Greenough was familiar with it.

37 Christ

c. 1845

Marble, 32 × 16¾ × 13½ inches

Inscribed on original pedestal: *Christ by Horatio Greenough*

Courtesy of the Trustees of the Boston Public Library. Gift of Horatio S. Greenough in 1895

Greenough's decision, about 1845, to sculpt an over-life-size bust of Christ resulted from a long-standing interest in the subject. It was most likely triggered at this particular moment by a wish to create a pendant to *Lucifer* (cat. 36), which he had sculpted about four years before. Earlier in his career Greenough had made pairs of portrait busts; however, this was the only time he ever paired ideal images.

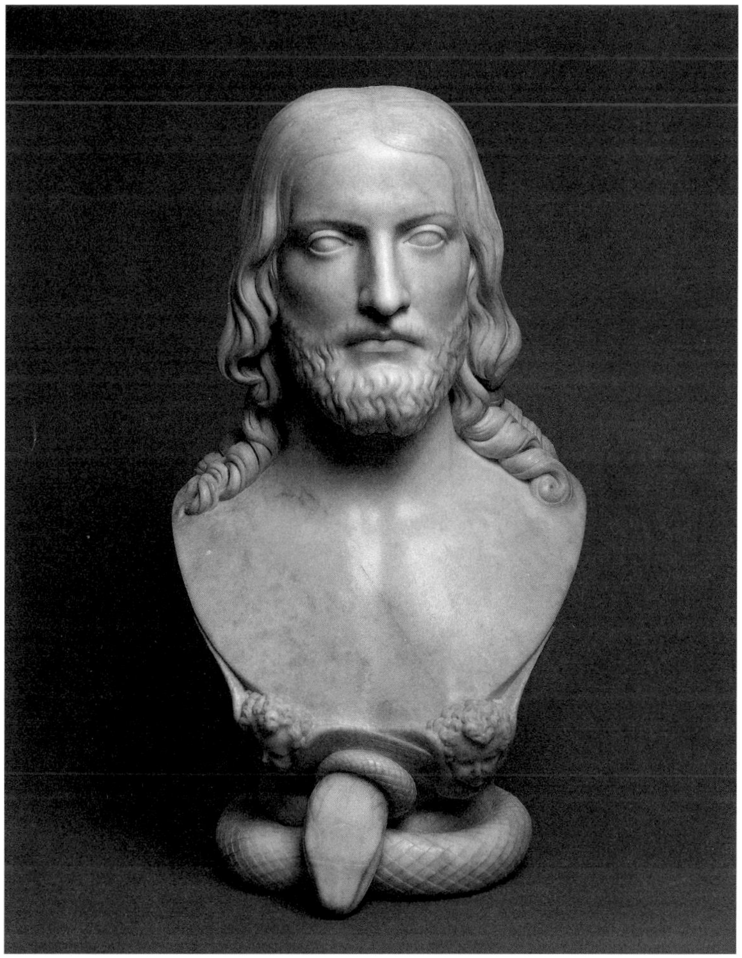

As early as 1828 he had singled out Thorvaldsen's full-length figure of Christ for the church of Our Lady of Copenhagen (see fig. 7, visible to the right of center) as the finest work a sculptor had produced since the Renaissance.[1] It had, in fact, brought tears to his eyes.

Although his enthusiasm for Thorvaldsen tempered with time, in 1839 he wrote his brother Henry, "I have not changed my opinion of the Christ, yet I find it a little hard."[2] By 1845 Greenough decided to sculpt his own bust of Christ. In a letter probably written at the time and later cited by Tuckerman, Greenough surmised that this was very likely the first effort by an American to depict the idealized head of Christ.[3] He readily acknowledged that "the strong prejudice, or rather conviction of the Protestant mind has, perhaps, deterred many." But in defense of his own struggle with the subject he postulated that there was no shame in falling short of the goal. Rather, he felt the effort should be interpreted as the artist's "fervent aspiration after the good and beautiful." He added, "it is a mistake to suppose that the artist, because he stops working, thinks his task perfect, he says only—behold the subject proposed to me as the art which is in me can give it."[4]

By December 1846 Greenough had two copies of the bust cut in marble, and they sold quickly. He admitted to his brother that he could have sold another two copies, if he had them available.[5]

Calm, dignified, and monumental, Greenough's *Christ* is closely modeled on that of Thorvaldsen, which was seen as the archetypal Protestant interpretation of the subject. One departure from Thorvaldsen is that the Savior's head looks straight ahead, rather than down. This adjustment probably resulted from Greenough's awareness that Thorvaldsen's figure is eight feet high and was intended to be seen from below, while his head would sit on a pedestal and be seen at eye level. Another innovation on Greenough's part is the coiled, yet submissive serpent that forms the socle of the bust. Extending downward from the front of the bust, where it joins the serpent, Greenough also introduced two angels' heads.

Various other nineteenth-century American sculptors grappled with the image of Christ, but it never proved particularly popular outside a religious context.[6]

1. Horatio Greenough to Washington Allson, 10, 16, 17 October 1828. Greenough saw it at Carrara.

2. Greenough 1887, Horatio Greenough to Henry Greenough, 25 September 1839.
3. Christ had been depicted in 1843 by Thomas Crawford in his bas-relief *Christ Blessing Little Children.* This he sold to John Parker of Boston, and it appears to have been exhibited in 1844 at the Boston Athenæum, along with a second Crawford loaned by Parker. The relief is presently unlocated, but it can be seen in the foreground of a contemporary photograph of Crawford's studio. See Gale 1964, pl. 8.
4. Tuckerman 1967, p. 260.
5. Greenough 1887, Horatio Greenough to Henry Greenough, 17 December 1846.
6. See Gerdts 1973, pp. 74–75; Wunder 1991, vol. 1, p. 323; and Sotheby's, New York, *American Paintings, Drawings and Sculpture*, 25 March 1997, lot 36, Richard S. Greenough, *Head of Christ*, inscribed and dated, 1852.

38 Multiple drawings, including study for *Christ*

verso: Moses with the Ten Commandments

c. 1845

Pen and ink over graphite, 8⅝ × 7⅜ inches

93.8.100

This drawing was most likely done while Greenough began to determine the general character of his colossal bust of Christ. The profile drawing closely resembles the finished marble (fig. 31), and at this point particular details such as the rhythmic hair curls which fall on the Savior's shoulders have already been worked out.

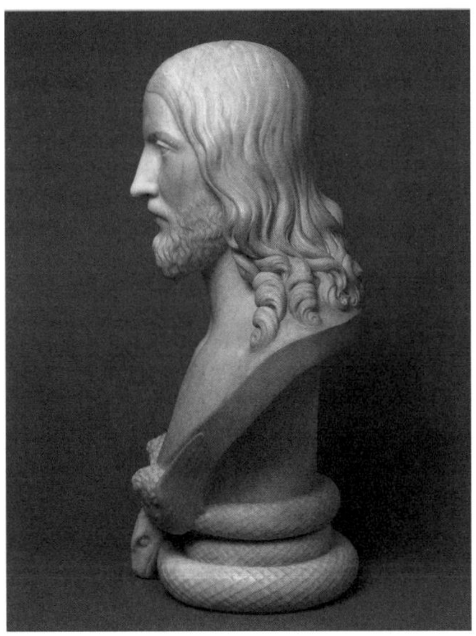

Fig. 31. Horatio Greenough, *Christ.* profile of cat. 37. Courtesy of the Trustees of the Boston Public Library.

Greenough is known to have made only one other drawing devoted to the subject of Christ, although it seems likely that many more originally existed.[1]

1. Brumbaugh 1955, fig. 46, reproduces a full-length drawing he identifies as *Christ at the Column.* It is presently unlocated.

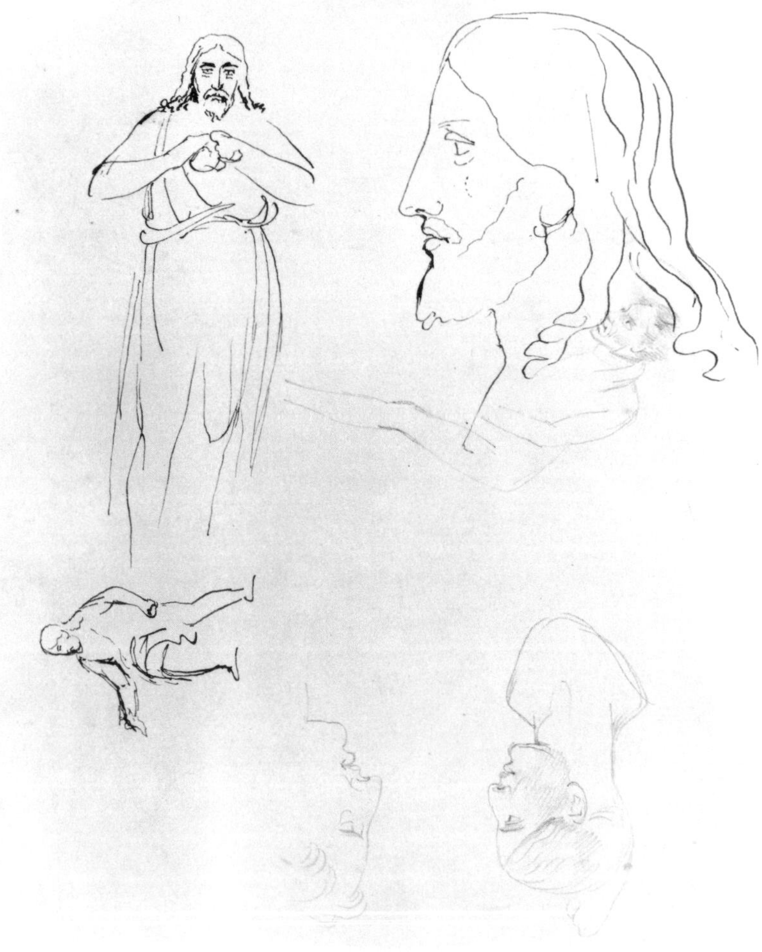

39 *Castor and Pollux*

c. 1847

Marble, 34⅝ × 45³⁄₁₆ × 1¾ inches

Museum of Fine Arts, Boston. Bequest of Mrs. Horatio Greenough

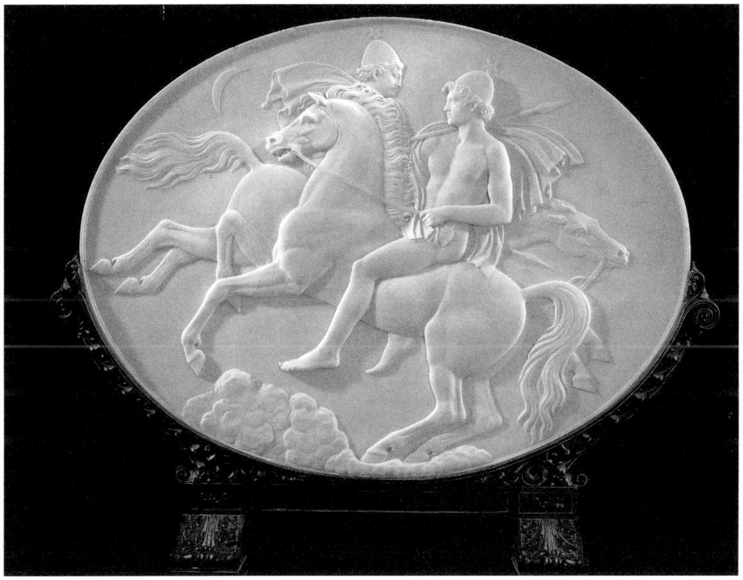

During his career Greenough had a particular fondness for the bas-relief format and utilized it on at least eleven different occasions. By May 1847 he was at work on the first of two reliefs devoted to the subject of Castor and Pollux.[1] The subject, which is taken from ancient myth, depicts the Dioscuri, or sons of Zeus. According to one version of the myth, Pollux was a son of Zeus, while Castor, his brother, was actually the son of a mortal. On the latter's death Pollux appealed to his father to make him immortal. This Zeus did, but with the condition that each spend alternate days among the gods on Mount Olympus, and the other day in Hades. This enabled them to meet only in passing. In another version of the story Zeus rewards Castor and Pollux for their filial love and courage by placing them eternally in the sky as the constellation of the twins, or Gemini. Greenough alludes to both versions of the story in his relief.

Castor and Pollux were worshiped in ancient Rome and as a result were honored with commemorative images on coins, architectural friezes, and sarcophagi reliefs, as well as civil and religious monuments. Greenough's use of an elliptic bas-relief suggests he was aware of this artistic tradition and conceived it in emulation of these neo-Attic effigies and figurative ornaments. The inclusion of the siblings' oval-shaped helmets as well as their horses, Xanthus and Cyllarus, further suggests a familiarity with specific Roman antecedents.[2]

Greenough modeled his composition on a passage from the most famous of all relief sculptures: the Parthenon frieze (fig. 32). Earlier in his career, Greenough made drawings after casts of sections of the frieze (cat. 5), so that it remained a source of inspiration for him is not a surprise. Although he based his relief on ancient models, the satin finish reflects the influence of artists like Thorvaldsen, and the calligraphic clarity recalls the work of John Flaxman whose drawings Greenough also admired.[3]

Silhouetted above the clouds and against the sky, the siblings are depicted on horseback as they move between Mount Olympus and Hades. Behind them is a crescent moon and above each of their heads is a star to signify their identity as the two brightest stars in the constellation Gemini. The relief's elliptical format enhances the composition's sense of motion.

Like Greenough's other reliefs, *Castor and Pollux* was well received. A visitor to Greenough's studio in 1849 lauded it as "Grecian and delicate," while Jarves, writing some years later, was particularly taken with the horses, which he described as "beautiful creations, full of fire and spirit; steeds of eternity, like those of Phidias."[4]

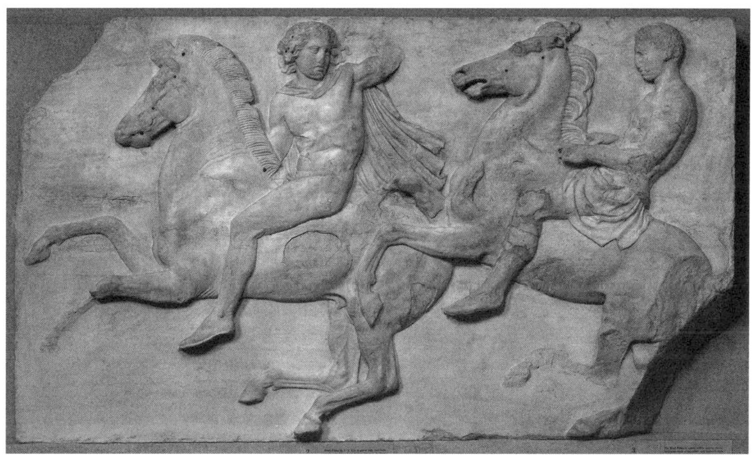

Fig. 32. *Riders.* Slab II 2.3, west frieze of the Parthenon, 438–432 B.C. Marble. © The British Museum, London.

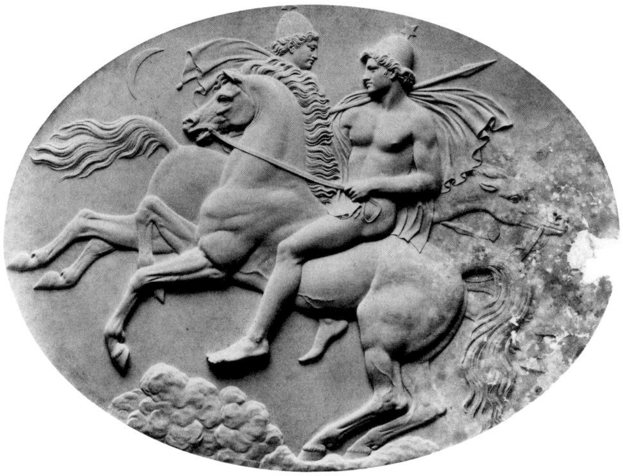

Fig. 33. Horatio Greenough, *Castor and Pollux.*
Albumen photograph of plaster relief. George R. Rinhart Collection.

When Greenough departed Florence in 1851 he left in his studio a number of his plaster models. Among them was the plaster for what appears to be this version of *Castor and Pollux* (fig. 33).

1. Wright 1963a, p. 250, states that in May Greenough was at work on a marble version of the relief for an unnamed Boston client.
2. Greenthal, Kozol, and Ramirez 1986, p. 24.
3. Horatio Greenough to Washington Allston, 19, 20 September 1829. Thorvaldsen's influence on Greenough's *Castor and Pollux* was also noted in Dimmick 1991, p. 177.
4. " A Letter from G. W. C.," *New York Tribune*, 12 October 1849. Jarves 1960, p. 210.

40 Multiple drawings, including study for *Castor and Pollux*

verso: Interlocking circles and ovals drawn with a compass

5 October 1847

Graphite and pen and ink, 8⅞ × 10⅞ inches

Dated on verso: *October 5, 1847*

Inscribed at upper right, in ink: *hand/Each phlange is the diagonal/of the one next it going towards the intersecting* [?]*/Diagonal of the hand is the/length of the ulna—Also the/length of the foot/Diagonal of the breadth of zyogamatic arches equal to/the height from chin to origin of hair—/Diagonal of the distance/from to/cresta* [?] *ilia to the/other equal to breadth/from trochanter to trocher* [?]*/Diagonal of distance from/head of humerus to tother* [?]*/equal to length of torso/from fontanelle to pubis.*

93.8.118

In October Greenough made this faint pencil drawing at the center of this sheet, presumably for his second relief of Castor and Pollux.[1] In this particular drawing, Greenough employed a method of interlocking circles, which he had learned from a book bought the preceding year in Munich. At that time he wrote his brother Henry:

> I have bought a new book here called "The Secret of the Proportions, Attitudes, and Composition of the Ancients." It is geometrical and is curious—highly so. I have made four compositions by it and think there may be much in it. When you have made a free sketch of your designs, take your compasses, making a radius from the centre of the figure. Strike a circle and then follow it out by others, starting from the intersections, till you have covered the whole group, or figure, with a net of circles in faint pencil-marks, and you will see how they guide you for proportion, for lines, for spaces, and for balance.[2]

1. Wright 1963a, p. 250.
2. Greenough 1887, Horatio Greenough to Henry Greenough, 15 October 1846.

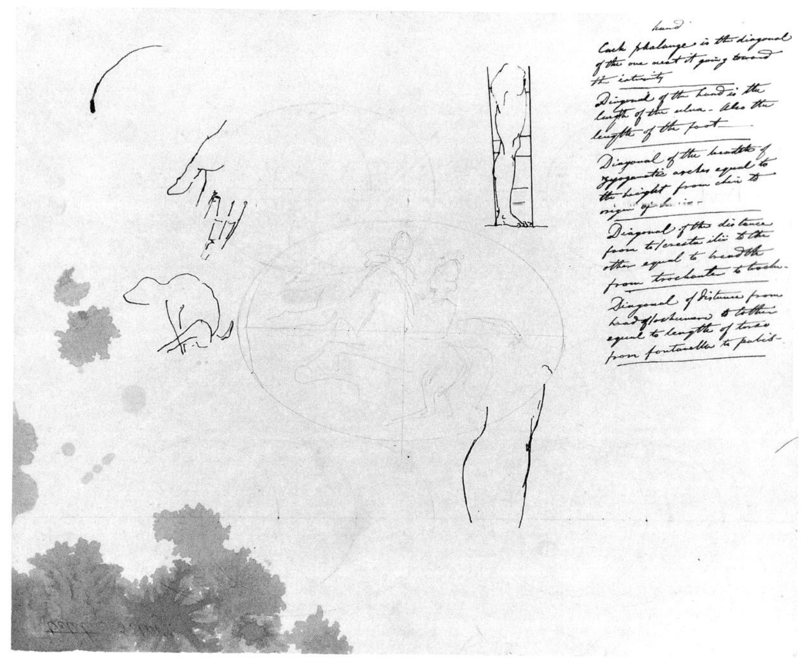

41 *Castor and Pollux*

c. 1851

Pen and brown ink over graphite, 15⅜ × 17⅞ inches

93.8.163

In 1851 an unnamed French draftsman asked Greenough if he might make a lithograph of *Castor and Pollux*. Greenough welcomed the opportunity and reported to his brother that "the group he is now drawing from an invention of my own with which he is much pleased." Greenough went on to describe the process: "The method is this A copy being carefully made out on paper is placed under a square of thin, white ground glass, and the drawing stumped and deepened with lead pencil; the high lights are put in with white gouache. It works evenly, rapidly, and bears any amount of tooling and erasure, of course."[1] This drawing was presumably made after the relief was sculpted, but in preparation for the lithograph.

1. Greenough 1887, Horatio Greenough to Henry Greenough, 30 January 1851.

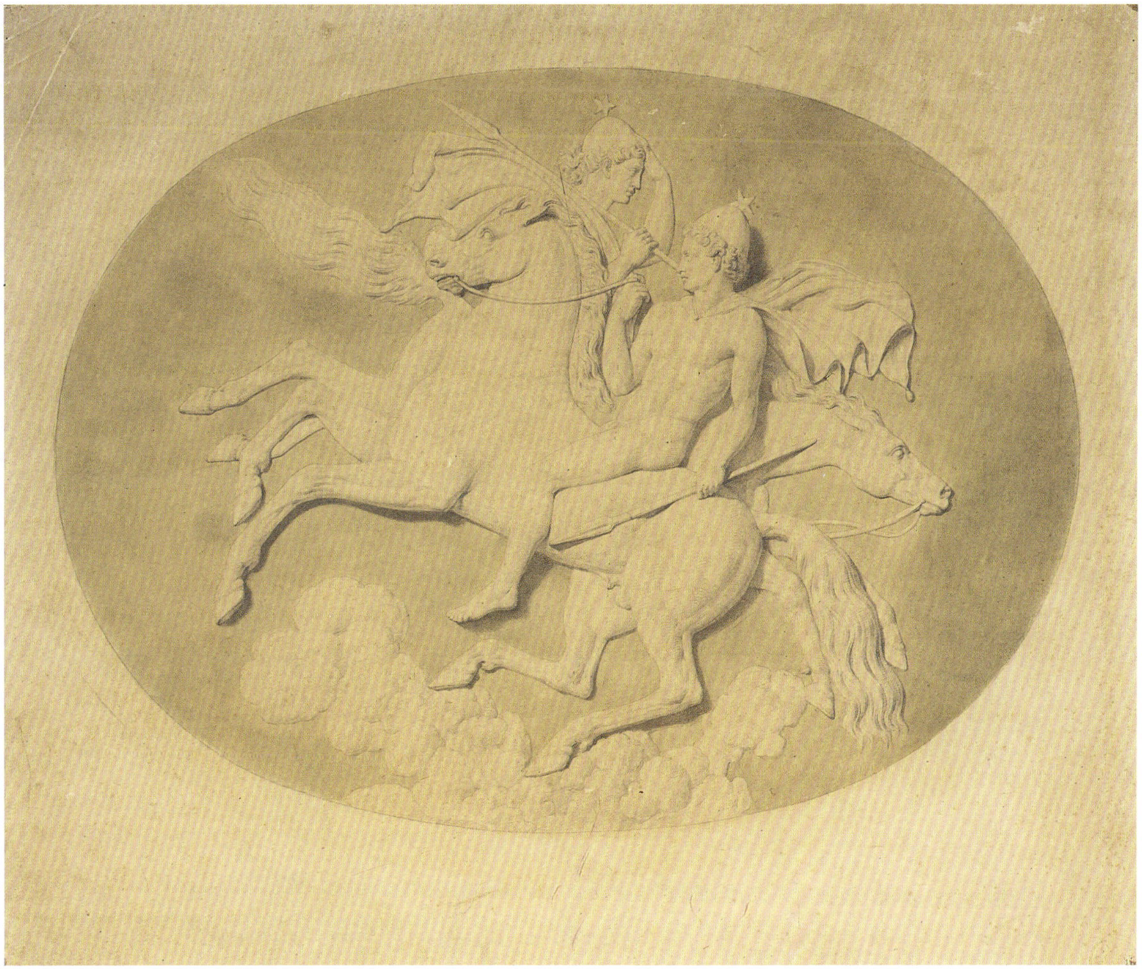

42 *The Discouraged Artist*

c. 1847–49

Pen and ink, 7¼ × 9½ inches (double sheet)

93.8.117

Among those who recognized Greenough's ability from the beginning was George Ticknor, scholar, teacher, and professor of French and Spanish at Harvard when Greenough was a student there. Ticknor was a member of the Board of Artists appointed to review the submissions for the Bunker Hill Monument competition in 1825.

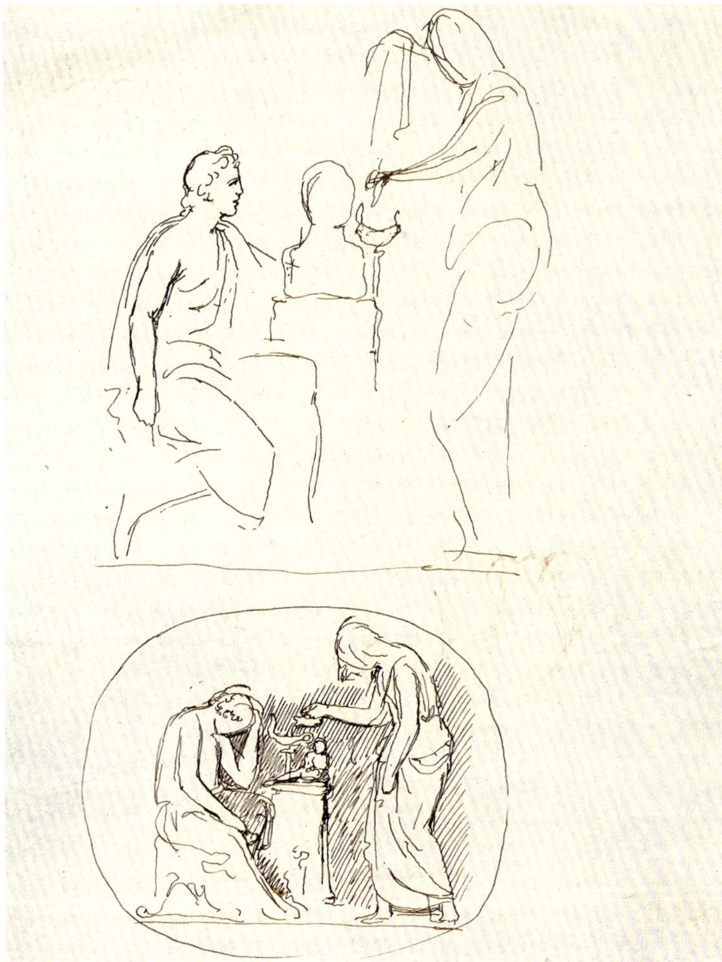

About 1830, before Greenough had firmly established himself in Florence, Ticknor made an anonymous gift of $1,200 to stabilize his finances.

Years later, Greenough discovered that Ticknor was the donor, and in gratitude he created a bas-relief titled *The Discouraged Artist* or *The Artist's Lamp Filled by an Unknown Hand.* Although the relief is unlocated, this sheet of drawings indicates the nature of the composition. A visitor to Greenough's studio in 1849 saw the work in progress, which he described for a New York newspaper:

> Greenough was at work upon a bas-relief. I had the good fortune here of seeing too, a work about to be sent to America, to a friend in Boston. It was also a bas-relief—"The Artist's Lamp filled by an unknown hand"—an incident of personal history. The artist is a young, graceful figure, bent in sleep or sorrow, and on his table before him a statuette of an Anadzomene Venus of exquisite delicacy. Between him and it, a little behind, forming the height and point of the work, is a lamp—a vase upon a long, smooth, slim pedestal, fed by a hand which emerges from a cloud over the artist's hand. It is simple and elegant—a pure little poem.[1]

Greenough drew two versions of the composition on this sheet. In the upper drawing, presumably the earlier of the two, the artist, seated on the left, before a bust, looks toward a figure who refills his lamp of inspiration. In the lower, or second, drawing, the artist's head is bowed so the spirit who replenishes his artistic fuel remains unseen. From contemporary descriptions, it seems likely that the more fully developed drawing is closer to the final composition. Thorvaldsen also experimented with a similar subject he titled *The Genius of Light* (Thorvaldsens Museum, Copenhagen), and the work appears to have influenced Greenough.[2]

Ticknor learned of the relief just prior to its completion. He wrote Greenough on 15 December 1849 to say his assistance was trifling "compared with the acknowledgment you make for it, that I hardly know what I should say." In 1850, after the relief arrived in Boston, it was exhibited at the Boston Athenæum's annual exhibition.[3] Ticknor then had the relief installed in the entrance hall of his house, where Greenough later saw it and "was satisfied with its position."[4]

1. "A Letter from G. W. C.," *New York Tribune*, 12 October 1849.
2. Wright 1963a, p. 250.
3. Perkins and Gavin 1980, pp. 67, 296. It was exhibited with the following description: "The discouraged Artist sitting before his unfinished work with a dying lamp, which a friendly hand replenishes to enable him to continue his labors."
4. Ticknor 1909, vol. 2, p. 241.

43 *The Sculptor's Dream*

c. 1847–51

Pen and ink, 6⅛ × 9¼ inches

93.8.135

During the 1840s Greenough became increasingly reflective about himself and his career. Many of these observations were published in 1852 as *The Travels, Observations, and Experience of a Yankee Stonecutter*. This catalogue of Greenough's insatiable drive for success and recognition was tempered by a realization that his career had failed to achieve universal accolades.

This drawing, presumably made during his last years in Italy, is an allegory about the plight of a sculptor. Barefoot and dressed in his nightshirt, the sculptor has risen and entered his studio. He is seated before a bust of a young woman on which he is at work. Although his eyes are open, he sees only the demons of his imagination. These half-satyr, half-serpent creatures mock him. One demon derisively points with one arm to the artist and with the other to his sculpted bust. Another demon is poised to smash the bust with a mallet.

Behind them is an elephant with a monkey on its back. This is an arcane allusion to Greenough's own parable about Jove and the transformation of a hog into an elephant. The newly endowed hog fails to recognize the importance of his trunk, on which his ability to feed himself now depends. Jove reproaches him: "Know that thy snout is my masterpiece. The rest of thee I made to please thy foolish self: but for this snout thy dignity would soon starve."[1]

Just as the trunk enables the elephant to eat, so the sculpted bust is the vehicle that enables the sculptor to survive. The demons mock the bust because they are the sculptor's alter ego and know that some of his busts are a poor excuse for artistic achievement. The irony is that only through such activity can the artist sustain himself.

The drawing recalls the composition and subject of *The Discouraged Artist* (cat. 42) and was most likely done about the same time.

1. Greenough 1958, pp. 216–217.

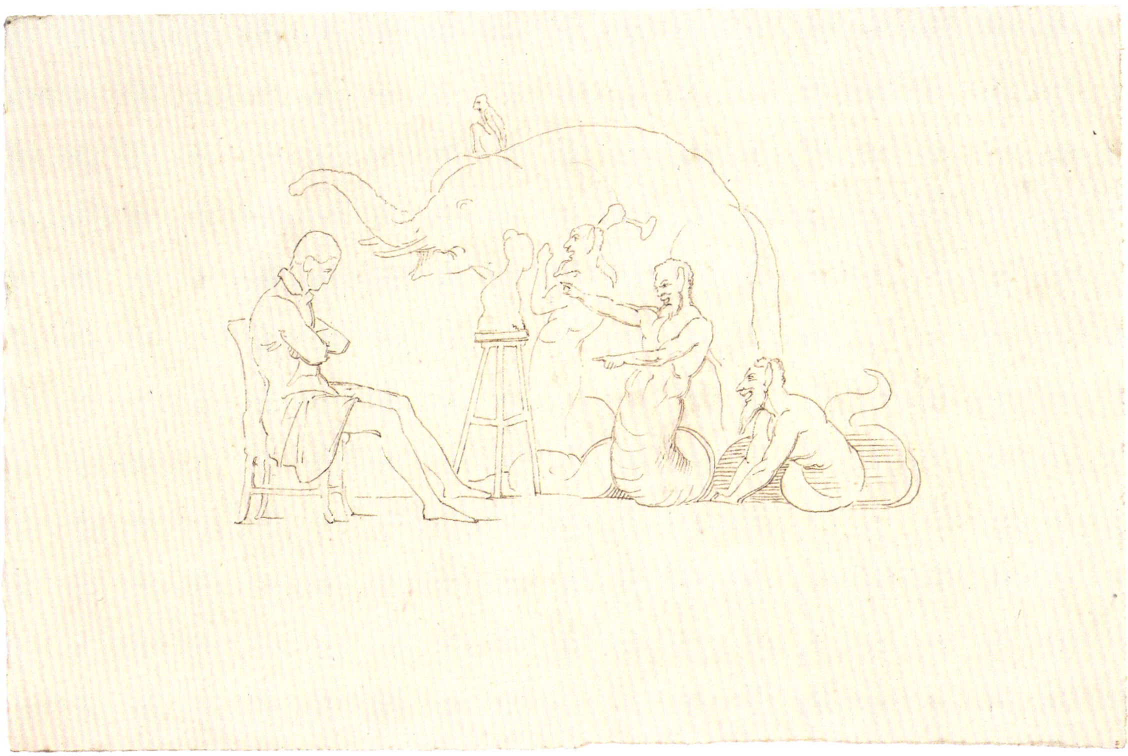

44 *The Genius of Italy*

c. 1847–50

Albumen photograph, 14 × 18¼ inches

93.8.098

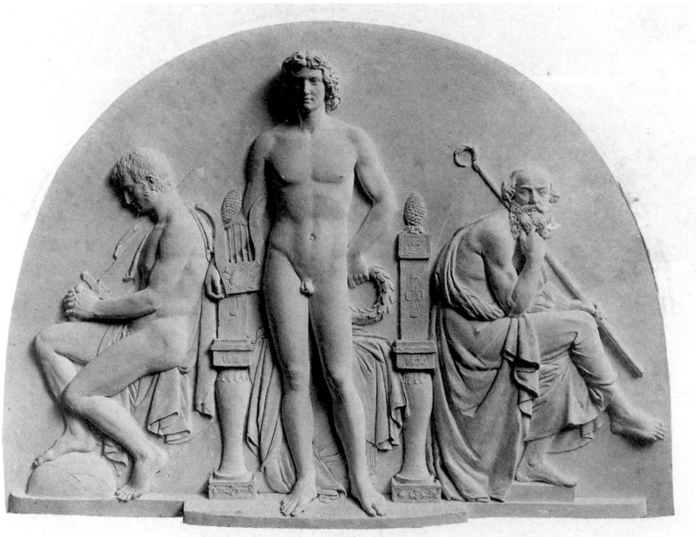

This albumen photograph depicts a lunette bas-relief for a monument to Giuseppi Giusti, the contemporary Italian poet who was a leading figure in the Risorgimento. Greenough was at work on this monument over a four-year period, and it is among the last works he sculpted. As there was no competition for such a monument, it seems likely that Greenough had in mind to develop a design and proposal for which he hoped to find financial support.[1] In June 1847 Greenough wrote his brother that he had "finished the Genius for Giusti's (the poet's) monument."[2] Three years later Greenough reported that he had "modeled the Genius of Italy between the Priest and Soldier, and also a Genius of Poesy."[3] Greenough's plan for the monument apparently included two reliefs, possibly crowned by a figure of Genius. The second relief, called *The Genius of Poesy*, does not survive, nor is there a photograph of it.[4]

This composition consists of three figures. At the center is a nude youth representing Italy, with a lyre in one hand and a wreath in the other. The youth stands between two seated and partially draped figures. On the left, holding a sword, is the figure representing the military. On the right, holding a crook, is an older bearded figure, representing the Church.

Ten months before Greenough left Florence for the last time in July 1851 he wrote a friend, "I have made a Venus which I am anxious to put into marble and I have also 2 or 3 bas reliefs which I intend to get done in the course of a few months."[5] With the monument unfinished and the reliefs of far less value to Greenough outside Italy, he apparently left them behind in his studio. James Jackson Jarves saw them there between 1852 and 1864 and described them as being "replete with the best classical feeling."[6]

1. Crane 1972, pp. 117, 420n.
2. Greenough 1887, Horatio Greenough to Henry Greenough, 23 June 1847.
3. Greenough 1887, Horatio Greenough to Henry Greenough, 22 October 1850.
4. Wright 1963a, p. 253, identified one of the drawings in the Petit Sully collection: "the figure of a nude youth seated with his head resting on one arm and the other holding an object resembling a stylus" (now Rinhart Collection, 93.8.148) as possibly being a preliminary study for this bas-relief.
5. Horatio Greenough to Joseph Cogswell, 28 September 1850.
6. Jarves 1960, p. 210.

45 Study for *The Genius of Italy*

1850

Pen and ink and graphite, 8½ × 13½ inches

93.8.141

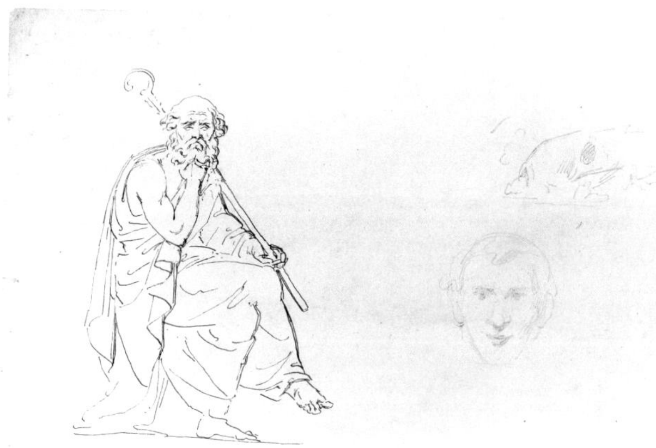

This is a preliminary study for the figure representing the Roman Catholic Church in *The Genius of Italy* (cat. 44). A second preliminary drawing (Department of Drawings, Uffizi Gallery, Florence) for this monument also survives.[1] It depicts all three figures incorporated into the final relief; however, the figure of Italy is blindfolded and manacled.

1. MFF. 109522/SOP 380865. I am grateful to Elizabeth Saunders for calling this drawing to my attention.

46 *Bacchante and Faun*

c. 1847–51

Albumen photograph, 15⅛ × 13¼ inches (oval)

93.8.037

Among the last of Greenough's sculptures is this *Bacchante and Faun.* It is apparently a work done on speculation, and because there was no buyer for it, it never proceeded beyond the plaster stage. The work is a testament to Greenough's lifelong enthusiasm for the bas-relief format; he found it a continuing source of renewal. Here, where he could avoid the restrictions placed on him by the requirements of a commission, he was free to experiment and explore figure combinations he thought particularly suited to the format. It is therefore especially unfortunate that this composition was not put into marble, as it is one of his most delicate and fluid works.

On his departure for America in 1851, Greenough apparently left the plaster in his Florence studio (along with fig. 33).

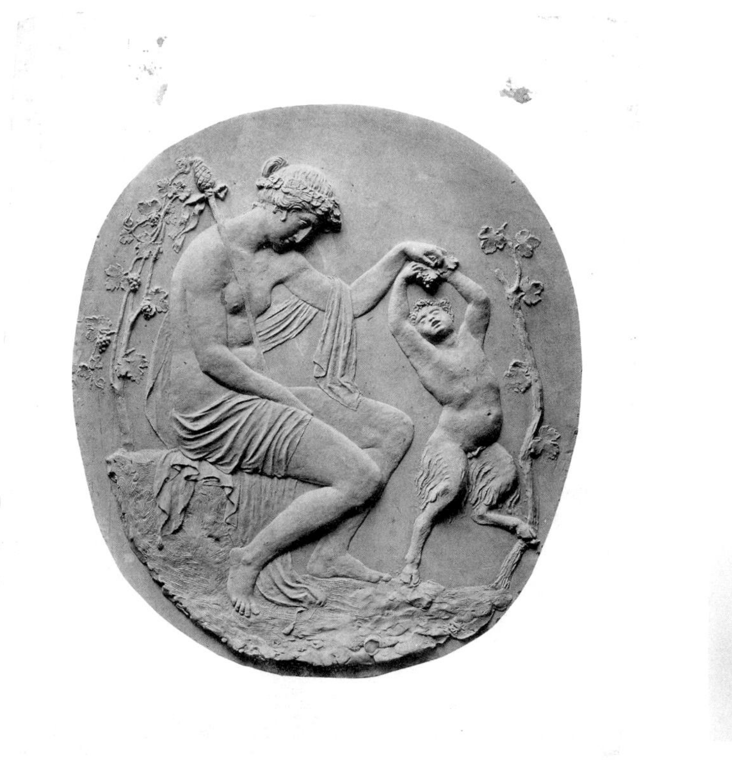

47 *Bacchante and Faun*

c. 1847–51

Graphite, 9⅝ × 15 inches

93.8.149

This drawing, which has the appearance of a tracing, may have been done just prior to Greenough's departure for America. Its purpose may simply have been to provide him with an accurate record of a composition whose plaster relief was remaining behind in Florence.

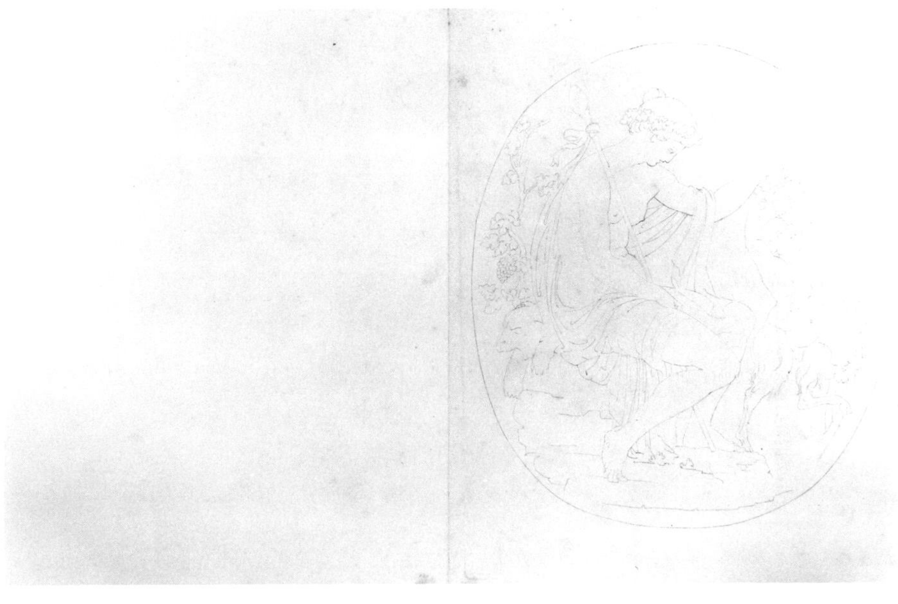

48 *Homer*

c. 1828–51

Marble, 11 × 5½ × 6½ inches

95.58

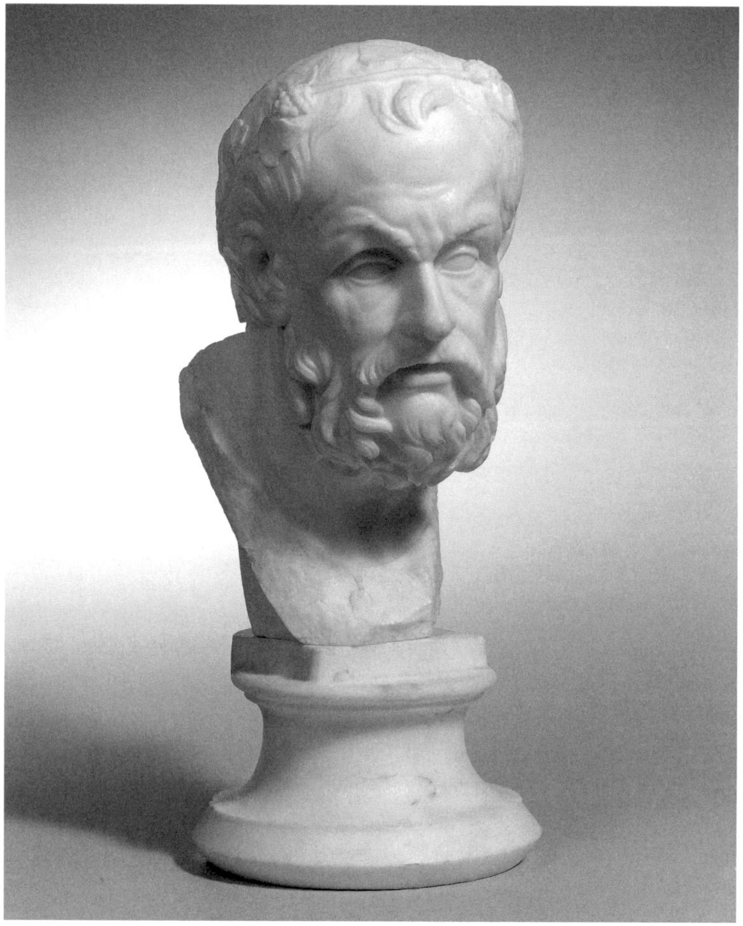

For much of the eighteenth century, busts of Homer, along with such other "ancient worthies" as Seneca, Marcus Aurelius, and Cicero, were frequently copied in marble or cast in bronze as library ornaments.[1] Like many of his generation, Greenough, too, had a lifelong reverence for Homer. Tuckerman noted that Greenough was an enthusiastic reader of the *Iliad* and the *Odyssey* and that "during his early studies in Italy, Homer was frequently in his hands."[2]

This bust, which has never previously been exhibited, was acquired by Nathalia Wright as part of the Petit Sully collection. No drawings for it survive; this would suggest the sculptor modeled it directly from one of the prolific number of ancient models nearby. Further, as there is no mention of it in his correspondence, the bust was most likely done for his own enjoyment.

Thomas Crawford, one of Greenough's fellow American sculptors in Italy, also made a bust of Homer during these years.[3]

1. Haskell and Penny 1981, p. 52.
2. Tuckerman 1968, p. 46.
3. Freedman 1992, p. 50. The bust is dated 1837. At the same time Crawford also made busts of Cicero and Demosthenes.

George Washington

George Washington was a subject to which Greenough returned repeatedly during his career. By the time of the sculptor's death the founding father had inspired some half dozen works or projected works.[1] Charles Sumner, a friend of Greenough's, once remarked that to produce a faithful likeness of Washington was the noblest project an American sculptor could undertake.[2] But the fact of the matter was, that for any American artist of his generation, portraits of Washington were a rite of passage and a possible ticket to fame and fortune.

Washington's portrait had become a national icon. Americans, wrote one Russian visitor in 1811, keep a likeness of Washington in their homes "just as we have images of God's saints."[3] Given the cult of Washington that existed in America, Greenough realized he could quickly establish his reputation if he could sculpt a successful portrait of the *pater patriae.* He also realized that given Washington's popularity, a successful portrait bust by him might be copied and, like Gilbert Stuart's Athenæum portrait of Washington, provide both visibility and income through the opportunities to sculpt replicas. By the 1820s several states already had monuments to Washington, by Antonio Canova, Francis Chantry (1781–1841/42), and Jean-Antoine Houdon (1741–1828), all foreigners. In addition, the desire to see a national monument to Washington was gathering momentum. Greenough hoped, and probably believed, it was his destiny to create it.

As Greenough's career evolved, so did the role that Washington played for him. Despite changes in his professional life, an image of Washington was never very far from Greenough's thoughts. For a number of years it was his colossal Washington that dominated the relationship. But as quickly as Greenough realized this massive figure would not be the vehicle for his commercial and artistic success, he saw a subsequent figure of Washington (cat. 58) as a form of vindication in the public eye.

A Statue for the Capitol

In February 1832 Congress awarded Greenough the commission for a full-length statue of Washington (figs. 34, 35). This was the first major freestanding sculpture commission for the United States Capitol. The resolution authorized the president to employ Greenough "to execute, in marble, a full-length pedestrian statue of Washington, to be placed in the centre of the rotundo of the Capitol; the head to be a

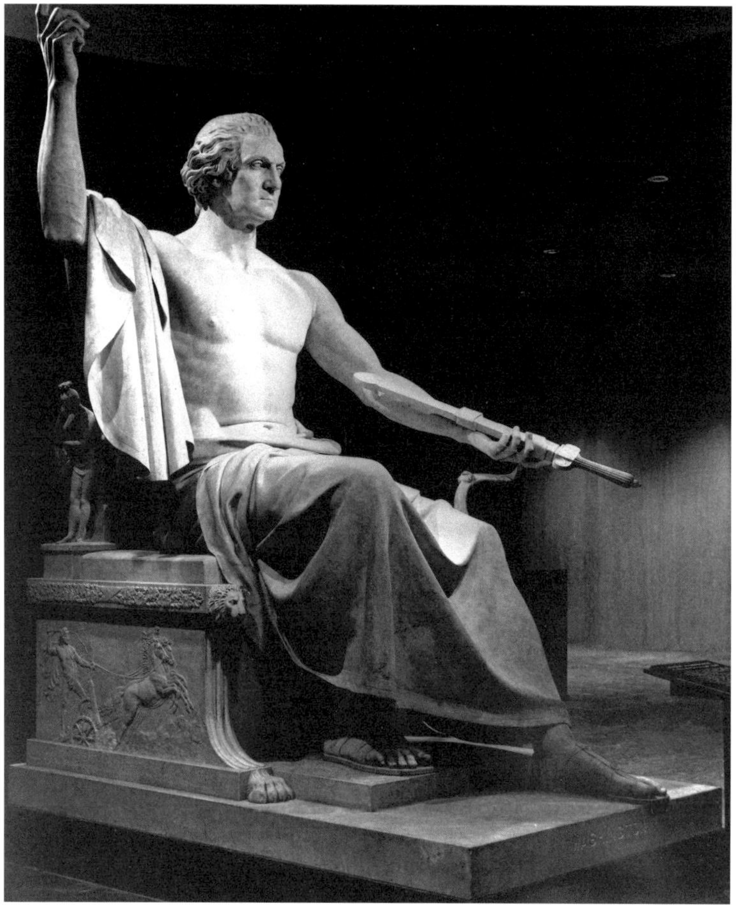

Fig. 34. Horatio Greenough, *George Washington*, 1832–40. Photograph from the right side. Courtesy of the National Museum of American Art, Smithsonian Institution.

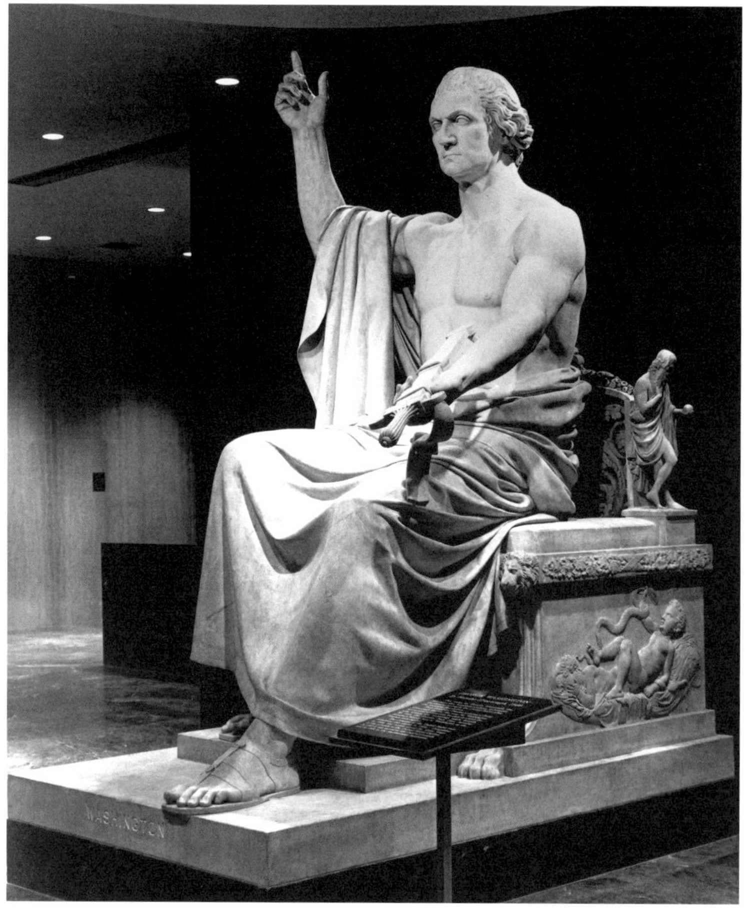

Fig. 35. Horatio Greenough, *George Washington*, 1832–40. Photograph from the left side. Courtesy of the National Museum of American Art, Smithsonian Institution.

copy of Houdon's WASHINGTON, and the accessories to be left to the judgment of the artist."[4]

Greenough formally learned of the commission in July 1832, when he received a letter from Edward Livingston, Secretary of State. Livingston's letter also suggested that the base of the work be rectangular and ornamented with bas-reliefs of Revolutionary scenes. Greenough was to be paid $20,000 in four $5,000 installments. He did not receive this commission by accident. Considerable lobbying efforts by Cooper and Allston, in particular, played a significant role in steering the commission his way.

Greenough devoted over seven years of his career to the completion of this statue. Ultimately, he based his design on a lost antique statue of Zeus at Olympia by Phidias, although a number of contemporary paintings and sculptures have been cited (by Greenough and others) as contributing to his final design. The finished statue weighed twenty tons and was 10½ feet high. It was shipped to Washington in 1841 and installed in the rotunda in November that year.

In fact, in 1783 the Continental Congress had passed a resolution authorizing a bronze equestrian statue of Washington be placed in the future home of the legislature.[5] Although Congress had failed to

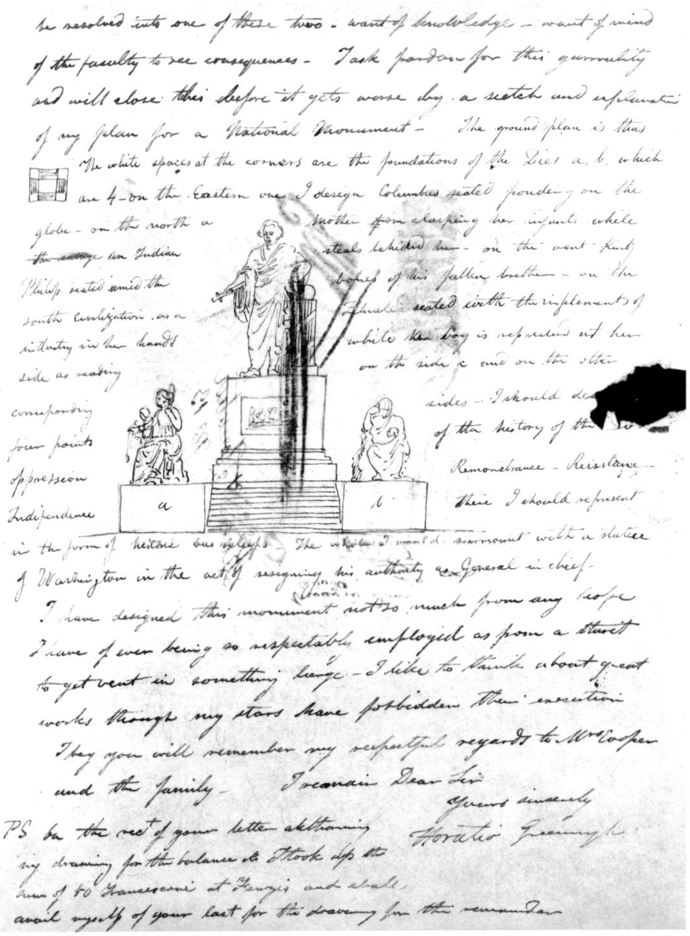

be resolved into one of these two - want of knowledge - want of mind
of the faculty to see consequences - I ask pardon for this garrulity
and will close this before it gets worse by a sketch and explanation
of my plan for a National Monument - The ground plan is thus
The white spaces at the corners are the foundations of the [illegible] a, b which
are 4 - on the Eastern one I design Columbus seated pondering on the
globe - on the north a [illegible] an Indian
Mother [illegible] clasping her infants while
steals behind her - on the west [illegible]
[illegible] seated amid the bones of his fallen brethren - on the
south civilization as a female seated with the implements of
industry in her hands while the boy is represented at her
side as reading on the side c and on the other
corresponding sides - I should de[illegible]
four points of the history of the [illegible]
oppression Remonstrance - Resistance -
Independence these I should represent
in the form of historic bas reliefs - The whole I would surmount with a statue
of Washington in the act of resigning his authority as General in chief -
I have designed this monument not so much from any hope
I have of ever being so respectably employed as from a thirst
to get vent in something large - I like to think about great
works though my stars have forbidden their execution
I beg you will remember my respectful regards to Mrs Cooper
and the family - I remain Dear Sir
Yours sincerely
Horatio Greenough
PS on the rec^t of your letter [illegible]
my drawing for the balance I took up the
sum of 40 Francesconi at [illegible] and shall
avail myself of your last for the drawing for the remainder

Fig. 36. Horatio Greenough, design for a national monument. From Horatio Greenough letter to James Fenimore Cooper, 7 March 1831. Yale Collection of American Literature, Beinecke Rare Book and Manuscripts Library, Yale University.

act on this resolution, Greenough correctly anticipated that the impending centenary of Washington's birth made such a commission more likely. For some time he had imagined what form a national monument might take. In March 1831 he shared with Cooper his current thinking for such a monument (fig. 36). The design consisted of a standing figure of Washington in classical attire. His left hand rested on a podium while his right arm was extended and held a sword—signifying he was resigning his authority as general and chief.[6] Each side of the pedestal's base was embellished with a bas-relief, and the central composition was flanked by four separate figural groups, which recalled his original design for the Bunker Hill Monument (see fig. 6). Greenough's design also bears a striking resemblance to the Demidov Monument (1830–70, Piazza Demidov, Florence), simultaneously designed by Bartolini, his former teacher.[7]

Even before Greenough's statue was unveiled, his design was disparaged. Friends like Cooper urged him to rethink its composition and scale. Others ridiculed his depiction of Washington. Such criticism only served to harden Greenough's resolve. After 1836, by which time the sculpture was cast, retreat was impractical. In the first place, in Greenough's eagerness to accept the commission he failed to anticipate that his expenses would far exceed the $20,000 allocated by Congress, as well as the considerable time lag in being paid by the government. Further delay would mean financial ruin. Second, the loss of face for someone of Greenough's brittle and manic personality was unthinkable.

By 1841, when the work was installed in the rotunda, Greenough had prepared himself for its failure. Correspondence documents his public defense of the aesthetic decisions regarding its design, but in his view little about the sculpture's placement worked. He seemed to have convinced himself that failure resulted more from the rotunda's inadequate lighting and the lack of an appropriate pedestal than from the character of the work.

Almost immediately he petitioned to have the sculpture relocated to the Capitol grounds, where it might be seen to better advantage. The sculpture was subsequently relocated four more times before coming to rest in the National Museum of American History. Greenough would be equally distressed by its present location: confined, dimly lit, it lacks a pedestal of suitable height.

1. Wright 1963a, p. 118.
2. Greenthal, Kozol, and Ramirez 1986, p. 9.
3. Harris 1970, p. 87, quoting from the memoire of Pavel Svinin (1787–1839).
4. *Twenty-second Congress, 1st Session, House Journal* (Washington, D.C., 1832), p. 342.
5. Fryd 1992, p. 62.
6. Horatio Greenough to James Fenimore Cooper, 7 March 1831. A related drawing of this monument was formerly in the John Davis Hatch, Jr., Collection, Albany (Frick Art Reference Library, Greenough File #19580).
7. Hyland 1981, p. 124.

49 *George Washington*

1832

Marble, 32½ × 19 × 12 inches

The Andalusia Foundation, Andalusia, Pennsylvania

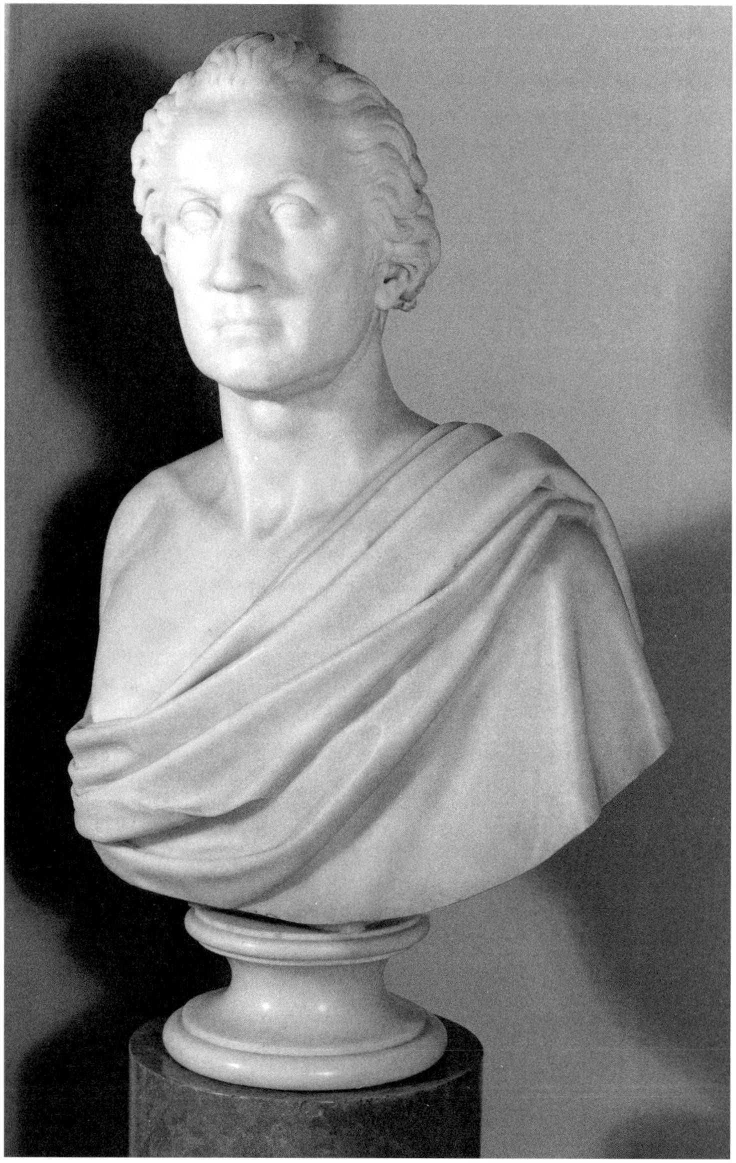

This bust of Washington was commissioned in December 1831 by James Biddle, a United States naval officer who was at the time commodore of the American squadron in the Mediterranean.[1] Earlier in the year, one of Biddle's subordinate officers visited Greenough's studio. There he had admired a bust of Washington that the sculptor was completing for James I. Roosevelt, a New York lawyer, judge, and congressman. On returning to the squadron, he told Biddle about it.

Greenough's sustained interest in sculpting a bust of Washington began during his visit home to Boston in 1826–28. While there, Greenough saw different interpretations of the first president, including Stuart's *Washington at Dorchester Heights* (City of Boston), Raimondo Trentanove's marble bust, both of which were exhibited at the Boston Athenæum in 1827, and Francis Chantry's full-length statue (Massachusetts State House), which was unveiled the same year. Greenough made two quick pencil sketches of Washington's head from the Stuart portrait (fig. 37), as well as a third sketch, thought to be of the Trentanove bust.[2] Two months before he returned to Italy, Greenough also very likely saw a plaster bust of Houdon's life portrait of Washington that Thomas Jefferson placed on deposit at the Boston Athenæum in March 1828.[3]

Greenough's heightened awareness for Washington portraits prepared him to sculpt a clay bust of him that he carried back to Italy.[4]

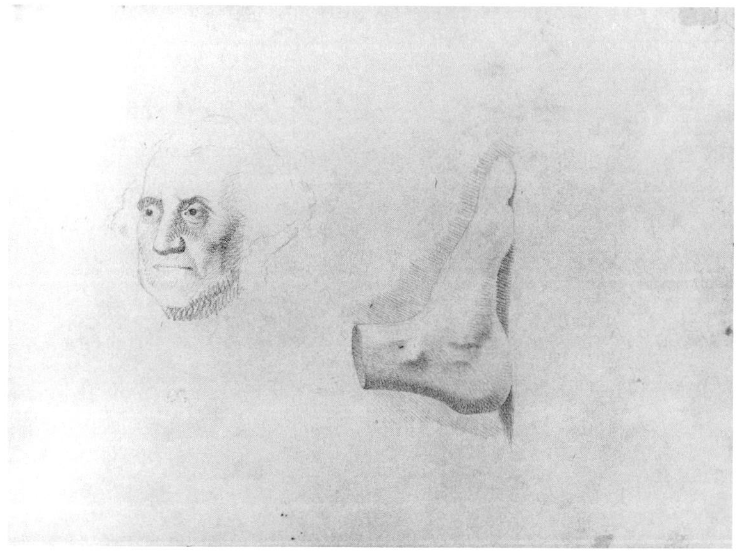

Fig. 37. Horatio Greenough, *George Washington* and cast of a foot. From the Roman sketchbook, 1826–28 (cat. 3). Graphite on paper, 7¼ × 9½ inches. George R. Rinhart Collection.

By April 1830 Greenough reported that he had "succeeded so well in a bust of Washington in pleasing my countrymen."[5] Not until December of the following year was Greenough ready to ship Roosevelt his Washington bust, which he assured his client was "spotless" (i.e., free from any internal discoloration) and was "an improvement on the former one," presumably a reference to a bust of Washington made for an earlier unnamed client.[6] Although the Roosevelt bust of Washington is unlocated, what is most likely a reduced version of it, which Greenough retained, is in the collection of the Museum of Fine Arts, Boston (fig. 38).[7]

Between the time Greenough made the bust for Roosevelt and the one for Biddle, he decided to rework the head, because he felt his skills had improved sufficiently to do so.[8] Another reason for the remodeling was that Greenough wished to make the bust a companion for his *Lafayette* (cat. 20).[9] Greenough undoubtedly hoped such a pairing would improve sales. In addition to giving Washington classical garb to complement Lafayette's, the major changes were a more vigorous treatment of the hair, a slight broadening of the head, and greater definition to the planes of the face, such as the cheekbones. The hair in both busts was treated "au naturel," or without a wig, as was Greenough's preference.[10]

Subsequent correspondence documents that Greenough was unable to complete and ship this bust to Biddle before 1833.[11] By July 1834, however, it reached Philadelphia and was placed on view at the Academy of the Fine Arts alongside Greenough's *Lafayette*.[12]

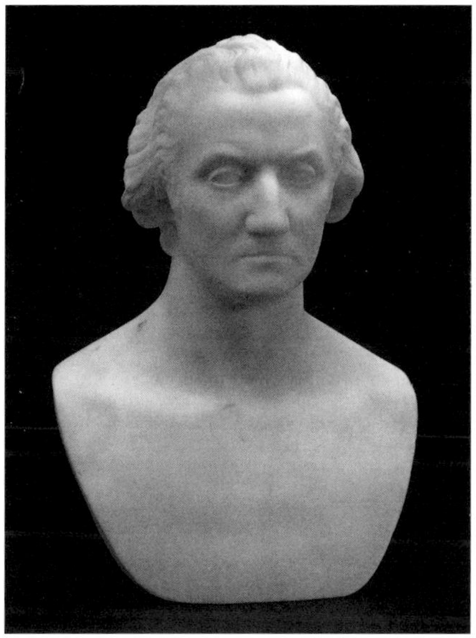

Fig. 38. Horatio Greenough, *George Washington*, c. 1831. Marble, H. 14½ inches. Museum of Fine Arts, Boston. Bequest of Mrs. Horatio Greenough.

1. Horatio Greenough to James Fenimore Cooper, 8 December 1831. Greenough tells Cooper he had received a letter "from Mr. McMurtrie containing an order of a bust of Washington from Com Biddle—Mr McM informs me that the Com intends ordering two other busts, and assures me that he hopes to effect a subscription for a statue among the officers of the squadron at Mahon this winter."
2. See cat. 3, Roman sketchbook, 37r (Stuart), 17v (Trentanove?).
3. Stebbins 1992, p. 333.
4. Wright 1963a, pp. 48 and 317n citing Richard Henry Dana to Gulian Verplanck, 2 April 1830, and Richard Henry Dana to William Cullen Bryant, 15 November 1827, New-York Historical Society.
5. Horatio Greenough to Robert Gilmor, Jr., 25 April 1830.
6. Horatio Greenough to James I. Roosevelt, 8 December 1831.
7. Greenthal, Kozol, and Ramirez 1986, pp. 9–11.
8. Horatio Greenough to Samuel Morse, between 25 March and 23 April 1832: "I'm remodeling Washington the old model was made too long since to repeat any more."
9. Horatio Greenough to Samuel Morse, 23 April 1832: "The 'violent pains in my pocket' have been relieved by the very liberal advancement (voluntarily) on the part of Com' Biddle of the full price of a bust of W[ashingto]n which I am making for him—I have remodelled the bust so as to make it a companion for that of Gen Lafayette—This latter has not only pleased the artists but has drawn many curious and some intelligent people to my study."
10. Greenough 1887, Horatio Greenough to Henry Greenough, 8 March 1828.
11. Horatio Greenough to Thomas Cole, 19 May 1832; Horatio Greenough to James Fenimore Cooper, 18 December 1832: "I have been sadly disappointed in not being able to finish Com Biddl's Washington as soon by 3 months as I had hoped to do—But I hope he will excuse it when he learns the reason." Morse himself had paired Lafayette and Washington, by placing a bust of the president (along with one of Franklin) in his own 1825–26 full-length portrait of the Frenchman (City of New York).
12. *Philadelphia National Gazette and Literary Review*, 24 July 1834.

50 Study for *George Washington* (1832–40), female head profile, and Helios restraining Phaeton from mounting the sun chariot

verso: David playing to Saul; multiple figure studies

c. 1832

Pen and ink, 12⅛ × 15¾ inches (double sheet)

93.8.048

Once Greenough received the commission for a colossal figure of Washington and was aware of the government's specific requirements, he began to derive ideas from his earlier thoughts on a national monument (see fig. 36). His first instinct, as this sheet confirms, was

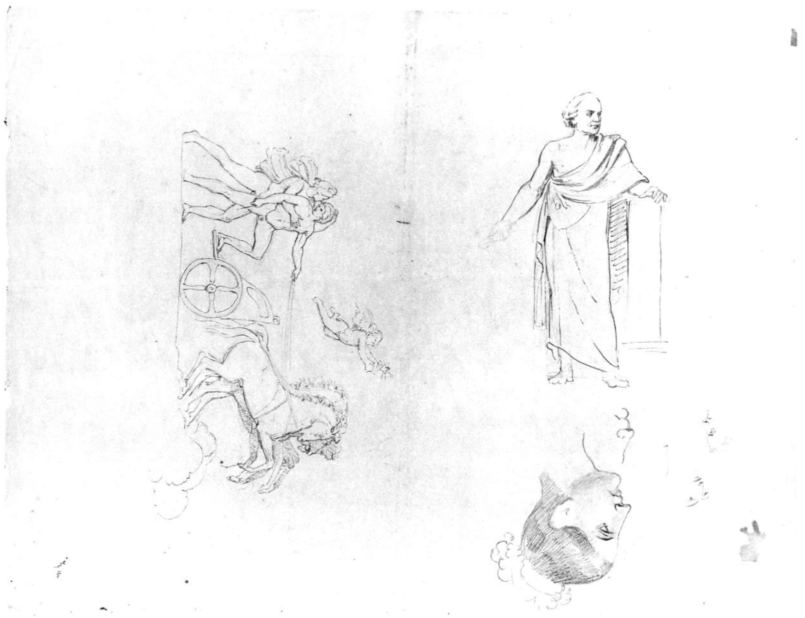

[50]

to depict Washington standing at a podium dressed as an ancient orator, his right arm extended and grasping a rolled decree. The treatment of the head and the toga draped over his left shoulder are clearly borrowed from Greenough's bust for Commander Biddle (cat. 49). The pose mimics Houdon's 1788 full-length figure of Washington in the state capitol at Richmond, Virginia.

This sheet also includes a drawing of Helios restraining Phaeton from mounting the sun chariot. As Greenough's overall design for his statue evolved, this composition became the basis for the relief of Apollo riding a chariot across the sky on Washington's chair (fig. 39),

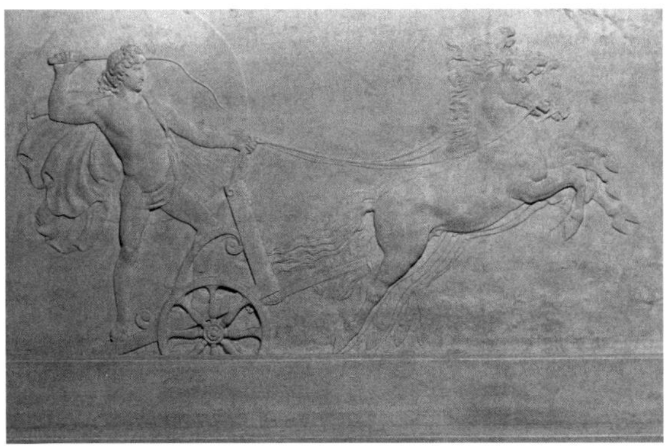

Fig. 39. Horatio Greenough, *George Washington.* Detail of Apollo Riding his Chariot. Courtesy of the National Museum of Art, Smithsonian Institution.

representing the enlightenment that resulted from the North American nation's birth.[1] Greenough later explained that "the bas relief on the right side of the chair represents the Rising Sun which was the first crest of our national arms—under this will be written *Magnus ab integro saeclorum nascitur ordo* (The great sequence of ages is born anew)."[2]

1. Fryd 1992, p. 83.
2. Horatio Greenough to Lady Rosina Wheeler Bulwer-Lytton, before 8 May 1841. The Latin quotation is taken from Virgil's fourth *Eclogue*, as translated by Wright 1972, p. 270n.

51 Multiple figural studies for *George Washington* (1832–40)

verso: Classical figure studies

c. 1832

Pen and ink, 13¼ × 19 inches (double sheet)

93.8.054

The detail of this sheet indicates that in his first phase of thinking Greenough considered various standing poses for Washington. Each of the individual figures here represents Greenough's consideration about such issues as arm gestures and whether or not to have Washington holding a scroll or a sword.

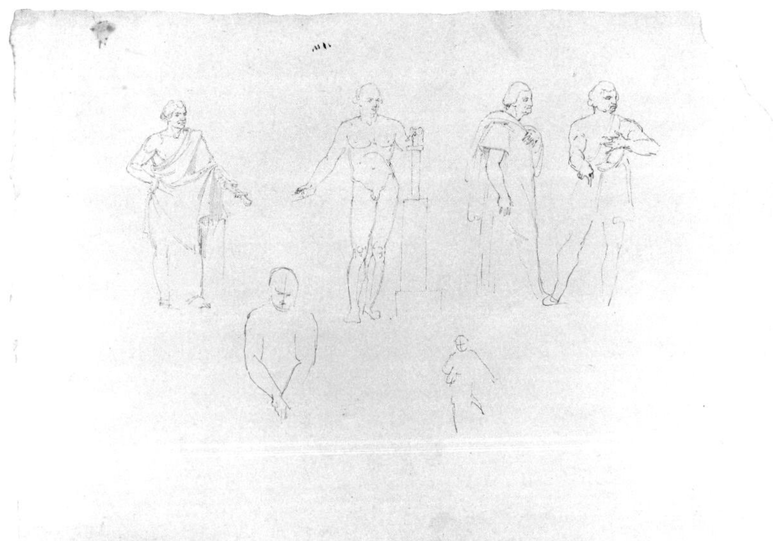

52 Studies for *George Washington* (1832–40)

c. 1832–33

Graphite and pen and ink, 12⅞ × 17⅜ inches (double sheet)

93.8.067

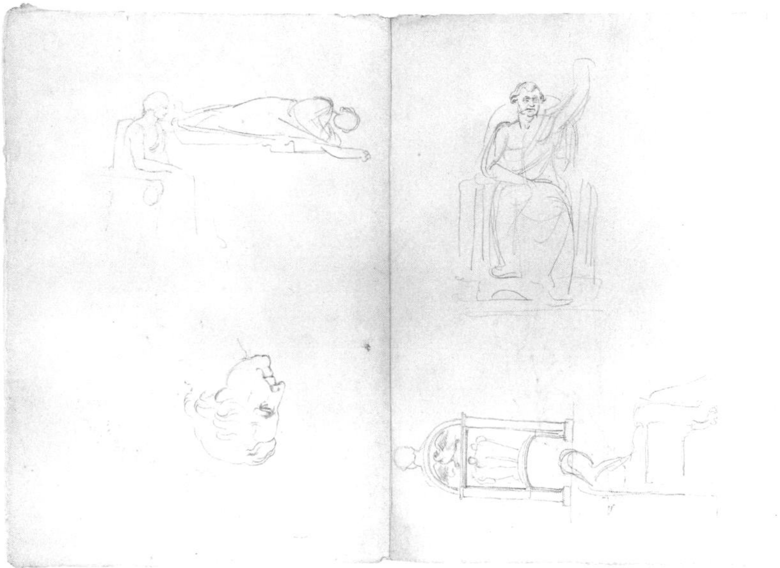

In July 1832 Greenough received a letter from Edward Everett, then congressman from Massachusetts but formerly a professor of Greek literature at Harvard. Everett encouraged Greenough to "elevate [his] imagination by reading the great works of the great masters and particularly the greatest work of the greatest master [of] the Jupiter Olympus of Phidias." By this he meant Quatremère de Quincy's *Jupiter olympien* (1815), in which the archaeologist reconstructed the fifth-century B.C. statue of Zeus at Olympia (fig. 40), generally regarded as the most important ancient statue of the Greek god. Everett observed that the Capitol rotunda was as spacious as the ancient temple of Jupiter. Most important, he implored Greenough to keep "that immortal work ever before your mind" and to depict Washington "seated like the Jupiter and as near the colossal as modern taste permits."[1]

This double sheet of drawings documents the point at which Greenough began to incorporate Everett's ideas about the Phidian model into his design. On the reverse of the sheet Greenough shows Washington with his left arm raised in emulation of the ancient *adlocutio* gesture to suggest a statesman addressing his citizens (fig. 41).[2] Here Washington retains the *adlocutio* gesture, yet is now depicted seated. Even the chair, with an arched back, is clearly derived from the Quatremère de Quincy throne. Subsequently Greenough modified this chair significantly to make it a more subsidiary element in the composition.

Simultaneously, Greenough must have looked at the edition of the *Iliad* that Flaxman illustrated—a copy of which he owned—as a number of elements of that sculptor's *Jupiter* are incorporated into the pose for Washington.[3]

1. Edward Everett to Horatio Greenough, 29 July 1832. Edward Evertt Papers, Massachusetts Historical Society, as quoted in Fryd 1992, p. 72.
2. Fryd 1992, p. 67.
3. This relationship was first pointed out in Craven 1963, pp. 436–438. The fact that Greenough owned a copy of the Flaxman edition of the *Iliad*, however, has been overlooked. Greenough's copy was included in C. F. Libbie and Co. Auctioneers and Appraisers, Boston, *Auction Sale, Tuesday and Wednesday, May 7th, 8th, 1895 . . . Catalogue of Miscellaneous Books, . . . Together with the Remaining Portion of the Library of the Late Horatio Greenough, Sculptor of Boston and Florence, Italy*, lot 487.

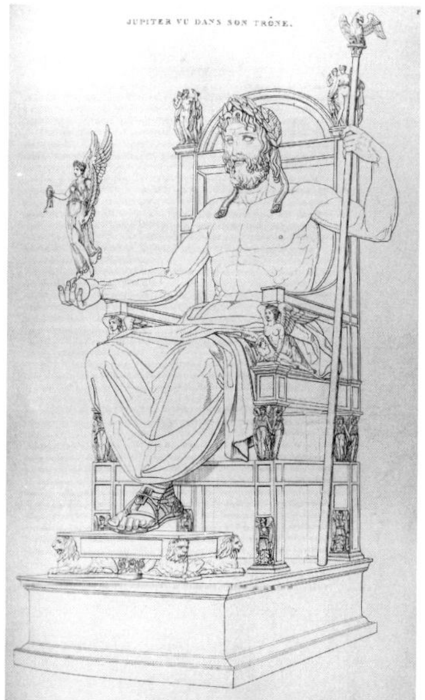

Fig. 40. Antoine-Chrysostome Quatremère de Quincy, *Jupiter vu dans son thrône*, 1815. Engraving. Courtesy of the Trustees of the Boston Public Library.

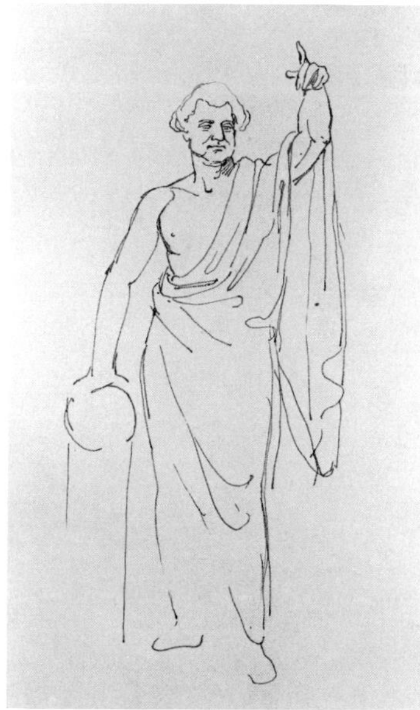

Fig. 41. Horatio Greenough, *George Washington*. Detail, recto of cat. 52. George R. Rinhart Collection.

53 Study for *George Washington* (1832–40)

c. 1832–34

Pen and ink on paper mounted on cardboard, 11¼ × 9¼ inches

National Archives and Records Administration, Washington, D.C.

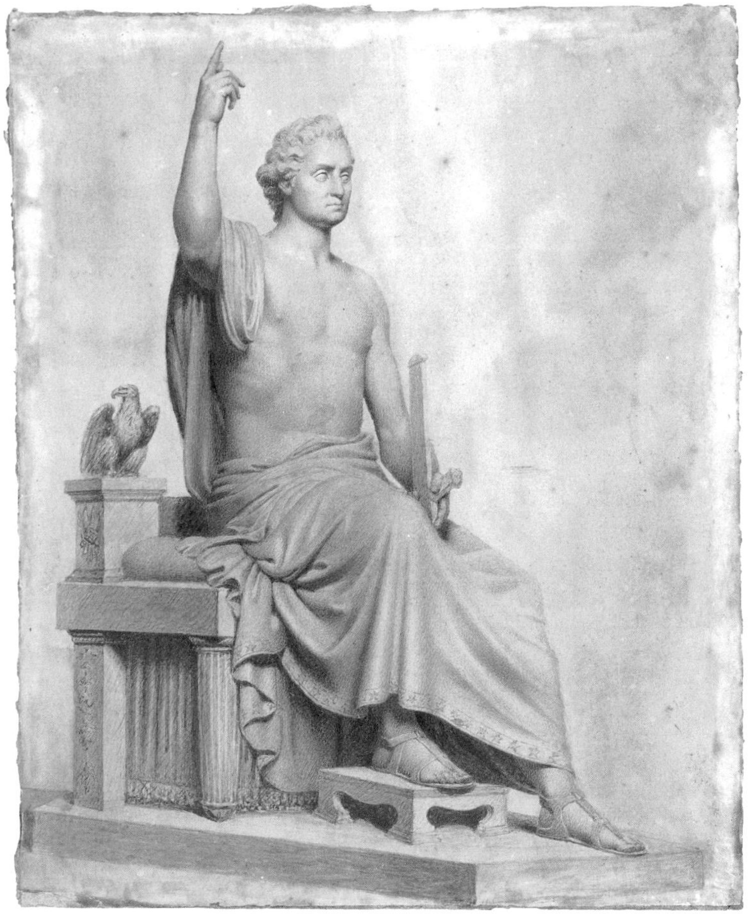

In January 1834 Greenough submitted this presentation drawing to Edward Livingston to apprise the government of the "general idea of the position, action and sentiment of the figure, its dress and the nature of its accessories." Greenough also noted that it was "a drawing from the small sketch in clay of the Statue of Washington on which I am employed." Greenough went to considerable length to explain that he intends to depict, not a specific moment, but rather movement, which is "characteristic of his whole life," and that he is not in contemporary dress because it would call "attention to trifles." He goes on to alert Livingston that the footstool shown in the drawing is to be replaced by a step and that he plans on "changing the position of the left arm for a more extended one." In addition, he emphasized that "in the head you will not look for a portrait as the drawing is made from a rapid sketch."[1]

This is among the most finished of Greenough's surviving drawings and indicates a type to which he alluded on numerous occasions in his correspondence. In November 1833 he sent a rough version of this drawing to Morse, noting that "the drawing will in a few days be ready to send to Washington." His primary purpose was to elicit Morse's opinion, but he alluded to his uncertainty over the government's reaction when he observed, "We shall see how it pleases at headquarters."[2]

In 1841, when Greenough computed his "account of expenses" for this project, he valued the cost of this drawing at $42.00.[3]

1. Horatio Greenough to Edward Livingston, 28 January 1834.
2. Horatio Greenough to Samuel F. B. Morse, 18 November 1833.
3. Horatio Greenough to Daniel Webster, 12 March 1841.

54 Study for *George Washington* (1832–40)

c. 1834–35

Graphite and pen and ink, 11⅛ × 14 inches

93.8.76

Greenough's instructions from the government required that he model his head of Washington on that of Houdon. The reason was simple. Houdon was the only sculptor of note to have had the opportunity to sculpt Washington's portrait from life. Greenough concurred with this decision, noting to Livingston that "I am much pleased that Houdon's bust was mentioned in the Resolution as my authority for the features of Washington—I have always used it from choice."[1] In his search for a copy of the Houdon, Greenough wrote Cooper to see if he might help him acquire "a cast of the model of Washington which is in Gen Lafayette's possession."[2]

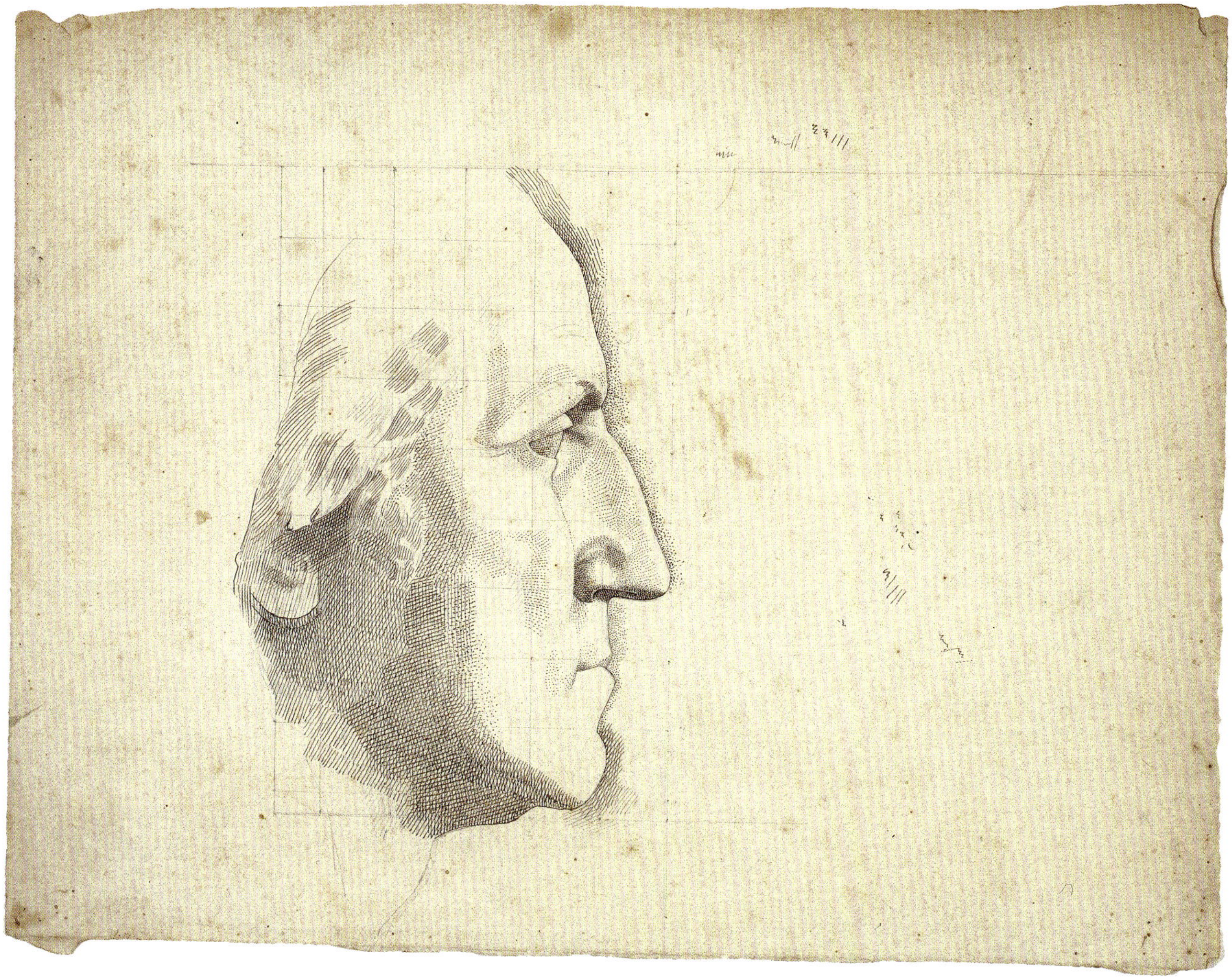

In 1834, by which time Greenough had resolved the general nature of his composition, he turned his attention to the modeling of the head. As yet unable to acquire a cast of the Houdon head, he traveled to Paris in August to obtain casts of the one at Fontainebleau. The preceding year he had also commissioned Francis Alexander to copy for him Gilbert Stuart's Athenæum portrait of Washington.[3]

This profile drawing was presumably made during the period Greenough closely studied the Houdon cast in preparation for sculpting his colossal Washington. With this in mind, he used a painstaking stippled technique, markedly different from his normal mode of sketching. Such effort is a clear indication of Greenough's willingness to adapt his drawing style to the task at hand. Over the drawing he has superimposed a grid pattern, which would allow him to make the scale adjustment necessary to transfer a design from life-size to colossal.

1. Horatio Greenough to Edward Livingston, 8 July 1832.
2. Horatio Greenough to James Fenimore Cooper, 18 December 1832.
3. Wright 1963a, p. 123.

55 Study for *George Washington* (1832–40), standing figures of Columbus holding the globe and an Indian chief

c. 1839

Graphite, 11¼ × 8¼ inches

Inscribed at top: *There seems to be an analogy between the advantage taken by governments of the need we have of them and* [unfinished sentence from a letter]

93.8.102

This delicate pencil drawing is the only surviving preparatory sketch for the figures of Columbus and an Indian chief who flank Washington's chair. Greenough's statue was designed to place Washington, both literally and figuratively, as the centerpiece of a complex allegory that showed him to be the crucial figure in the creation of the United States. As such, Columbus (fig. 42) and an American Indian chief (fig. 43) are diminutive subsidiary figures who stand to the rear of Washington's chair. In describing his intention Greenough wrote in 1841: "By the figure of Columbus who leans against the back of the chair on the left side I wished to connect our history with that of Europe—By that of the Indian chief on the right to shew what state our country was in when civilization first raised her standard there."[1]

Greenough recognized that his figures of Columbus and the American Indian would complement the larger program of Capitol ornament already in place, or commissioned. Reliefs by Antonio Capellano (active in America 1815–27), Enrico Causici (active in America 1822–32), and Nicholas Grevelot (active in America 1826–27) and a rotunda painting by John Gadsby Chapman had already featured the Indian, while in 1837 John Vanderlyn chose to depict Columbus's landing in the New World for a painting commissioned for the rotunda.

Columbus is depicted as an ancient philosopher contemplating the significance of his hypothesis of a globular Earth. Columbus symbolizes the process of discovery and the beginning of America as a place where Washington helped form a nation.[2] As a counterpoint, Greenough employs the figure of a meditative Indian who has begun to comprehend the inevitable subjugation of his race. He leans against a tree stump, a frequent symbol in nineteenth-century American painting for the progress of European civilization.

Greenough further reinforces these themes with the bas-reliefs

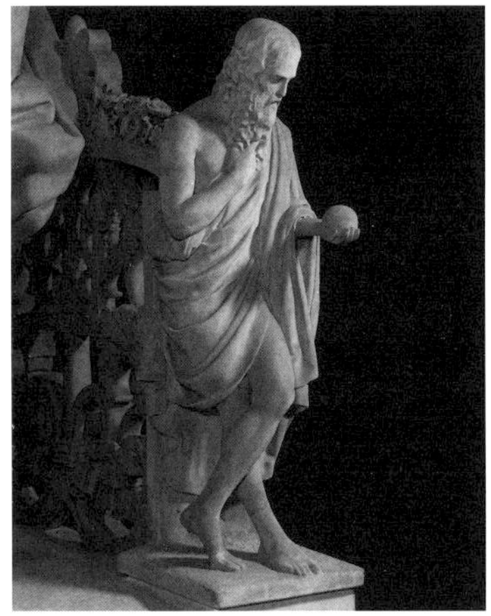

Fig. 42. Horatio Greenough, *George Washington*. Detail of Columbus. Courtesy of the National Museum of American Art, Smithsonian Institution.

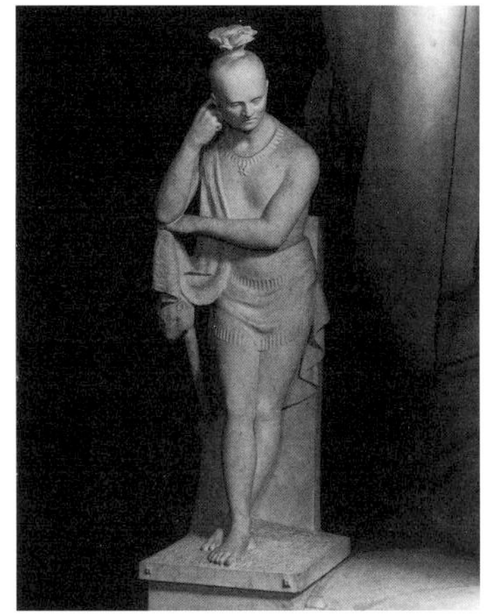

Fig. 43. Horatio Greenough, *George Washington*. Detail of Indian. Courtesy of the National Museum of American Art, Smithsonian Institution.

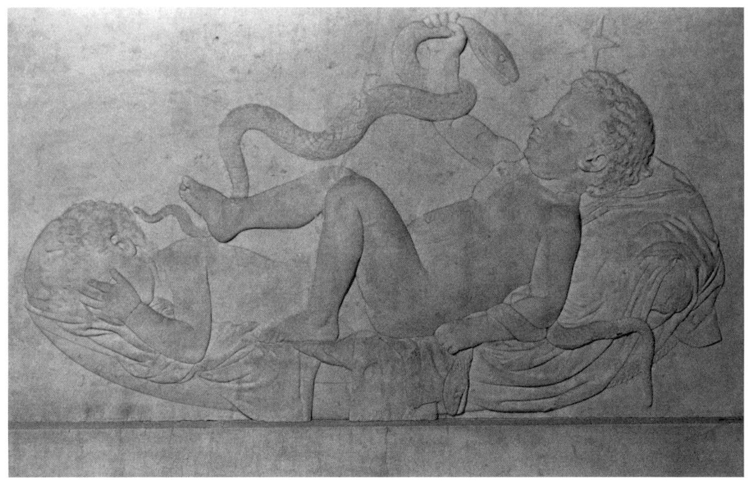

Fig. 44. Horatio Greenough, *George Washington*. Detail of Hercules and Iphikles. Courtesy of the National Museum of American Art, Smithsonian Institution.

that are incorporated into either side of Washington's chair. His composition of the rising sun on the right (see cat. 50) is flanked by the infant Hercules strangling a serpent, while his brother Iphikles cowers beside him (fig. 44). The subject of the infant Hercules was one that had appealed to Greenough for years. Here he sought to contrast

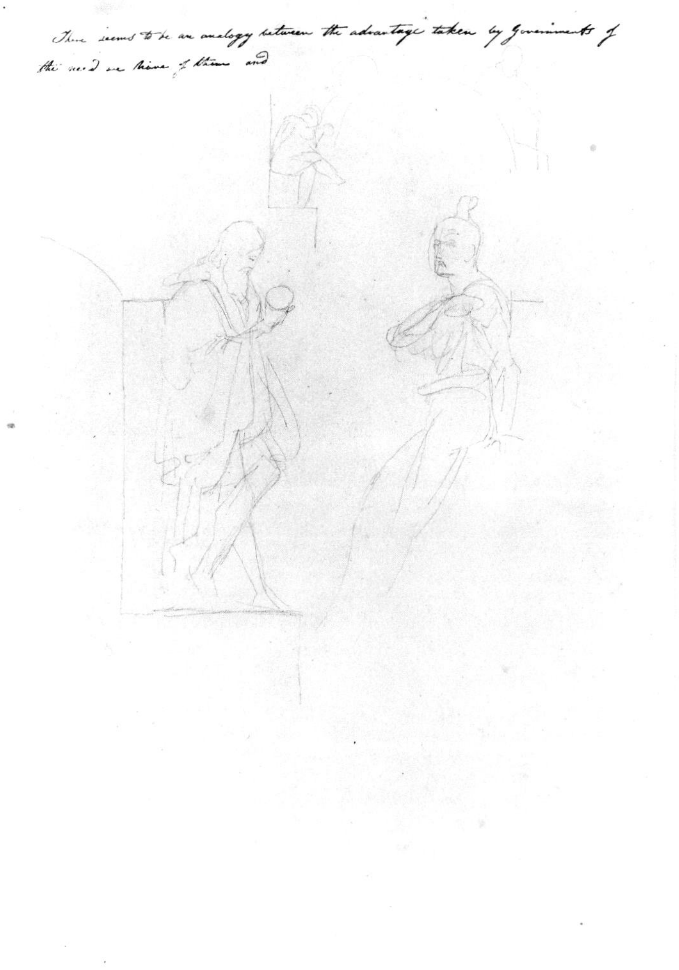

the "Genii of North and South America" with "the latter shrinking in dread while the former struggles successfully with the obstacles and dangers of an incipient political existence."[3] As early as 1828 he had copied it in his sketchbook (cat. 3), and later it provided the inspiration for the pose of Ada Reviczky (cat. 26).[4]

1. Horatio Greenough to Lady Rosina Wheeler Bulwer-Lytton, before 8 May 1841.
2. Fryd 1992, p. 80.
3. Horatio Greenough to Lady Rosina Wheeler Bulwer-Lytton, before 8 May 1841.
4. A graphite drawing in the Baltimore Museum of Art also depicts the infant Hercules strangling the serpent (36.147.26).

56 Studies for the chair for *George Washington* and figure studies

verso: Studies for chair for *Washington*, female figure studies, male profile, and snake swallowing a rabbit

c. 1832–33

Graphite and pen and ink, 16¼ × 11¾ inches (double sheet)

93.8.068

An element integral to Greenough's statue was Washington's chair. Over time Greenough's thinking about the suitable design for it evolved. This drawing depicts early attempts (which he described as

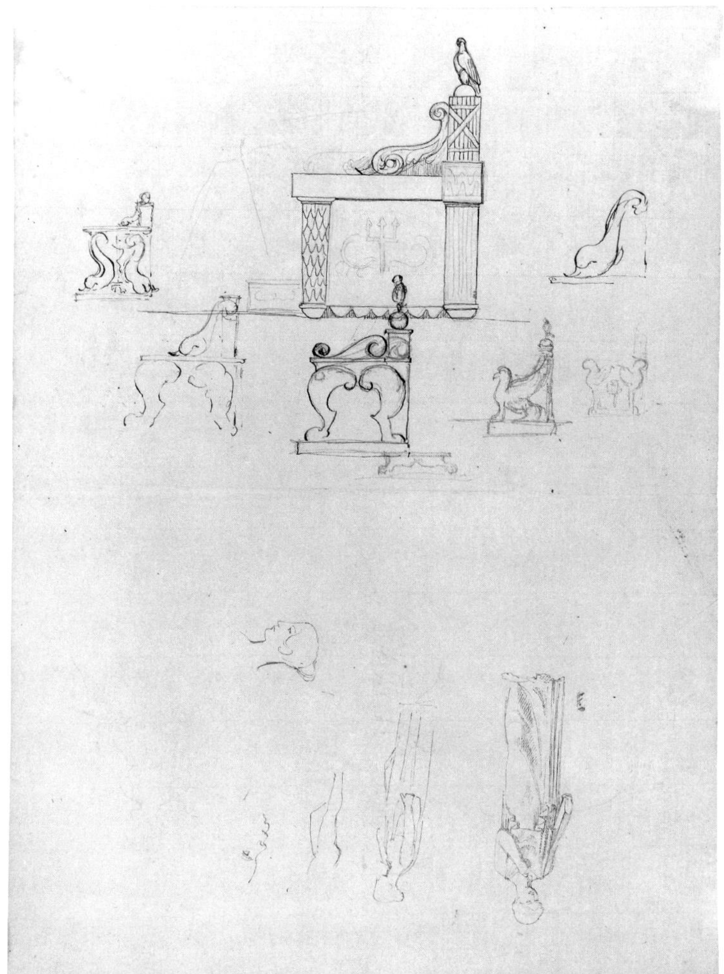

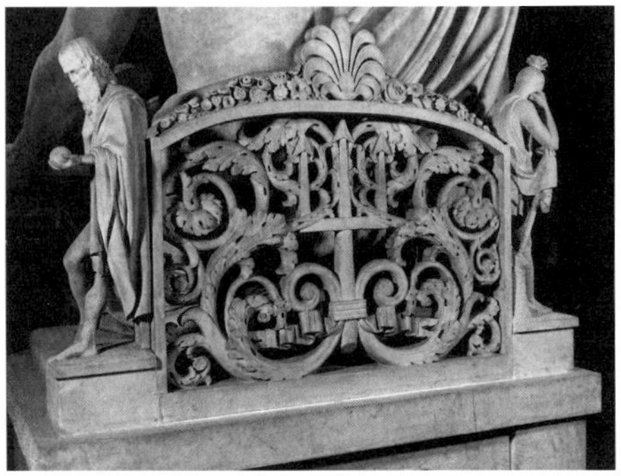

Fig. 45. Horatio Greenough, *George Washington*. Detail of back of chair. Courtesy of the National Museum of American Art, Smithsonian Institution.

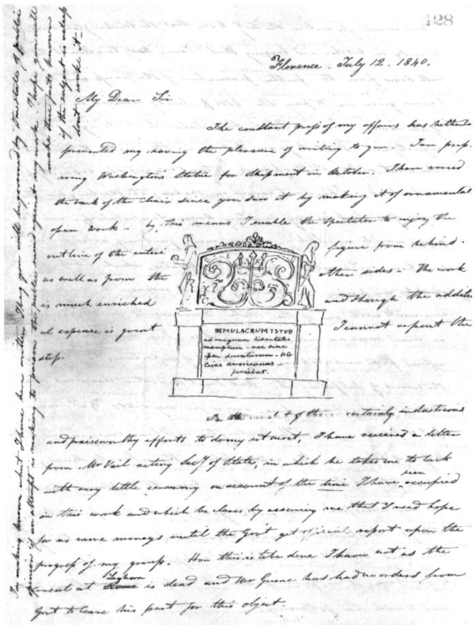

Fig. 46. Drawing of the chair for George Washington. From Horatio Greenough letter to Charles Sumner, 12 July 1840. Sumner Correspondence, MS Am 1. By permission of the Houghton Library, Harvard University.

"French") to determine an appropriate design for the chair, before he departed from more literal adaptations of classical prototypes. Eventually he settled on what he described as a "curule" chair, loosely modeled on Roman models.[1]

In February 1835 Greenough wrote his brother asking, "Have I told you of the immense difficulty I have had in composing a suitable chair for the figure? I have drawn and modelled quantities of *roba* [stuff], but the instant I saw my Colossus on his block the chair came to me. It is thus: you will see by this sketch that the form gives breadth and grandeur of masses, and has none of that French air which sinned in my first drawing."[2]

While an early design for the chair's back (cat. 52) suggests that Greenough envisioned it as a figural bas-relief, he eventually abandoned this for an elaborate and costly openwork figural design (fig. 45). It uses a triton motif, which appears in this drawing on the side of one chair design. He described and sketched (fig. 46) the transformation in a letter to Charles Sumner: "I have varied the back of the chair since you saw it by making it of ornamental open work—by this means I enable the spectator to enjoy the outline of the entire figure from behind as well as from the other sides—The work is much enriched and though the additional expense is great I cannot repent the step."[3]

1. Horatio Greenough to James Fenimore Cooper, 28 September 1839. Another drawing in the Rinhart Collection (93.8.069) includes a study of an eagle for the chair back.
2. Greenough 1887, Horatio Greenough to Henry Greenough, 17 February 1835.
3. Horatio Greenough to Charles Sumner, 12 July 1840.

57 Pedestal for *George Washington*

1841–43

Pen and ink, 9⅞ × 15½ inches

Inscribed, in block letters: IN THE HEARTS OF HIS/COUNTRYMEN

93.8.157

The resolution commissioning Greenough's statue of Washington made provision for a pedestal. But the lack of specificity eventually led to disagreement between the sculptor and the government regarding both the choice of material and its cost. In 1841, as plans to transport the statue to Washington were being made, Greenough balked at having to include a marble pedestal, which he estimated would cost $10,000. Since his entire contract for the statue only paid him $20,000 and expenses already far exceeded this amount, he suggested a granite pedestal be acquired in the United States at a fraction of the cost.[1] When the issue was not resolved, an agreement was reached to install the statue on a temporary wooden pedestal, which would be replaced once the final height of the statue was determined.

Greenough had anticipated being invited to the United States to supervise the installation of the statue. But the fact that this did not happen, combined with the government's delay in paying him the last

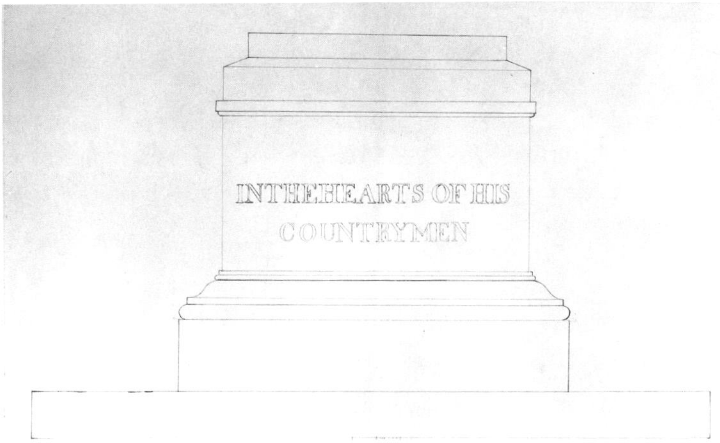

two $5,000 installments for his work, prevented him from making the trip. In November 1842, when he finally saw the sculpture in the rotunda, it was 13 feet off the ground, which one visitor commented made Washington look as though he were sitting in a tree. Although the figure was later lowered to 8½ feet, Greenough felt the lack of sufficient light would prevent the sculpture from ever being seen to advantage.

By January 1843 Greenough requested that the sculpture be removed to the Capitol grounds and installed on a pedestal of his design. This drawing is Greenough's preliminary design for the granite pedestal that was eventually cut from a quarry in Quincy, Massachusetts.[2] Around three sides of the pedestal were the raised letters *First in War, First in Peace, First in the Hearts of His Countrymen.* By August the pedestal was in place on the northeast Capitol grounds, opposite the east entrance to the Capitol and the following month the statue was relocated there (see fig. 1). At first it was covered by a temporary wooden structure, but this fell into disrepair and was later removed. In 1876 the statue was relocated to the East Plaza and in 1908 transferred to the Smithsonian Institution and placed indoors.[3] At that time the granite pedestal was used as a foundation block for the Capitol heating plant, where it remains today.

1. Wright 1963a, p. 136.
2. In March he wrote his brother Henry that he planned to "make a drawing for the pedestal, to be forwarded to Quincy." Greenough 1887, Horatio Greenough to Henry Greenough, 3 March 1843.
3. Office of the Curator of the Capitol, Art and Reference Files, "Washington" (General).

58 Study for *Equestrian Statue of Washington*

c. 1851–52

Pen and ink on blue paper, 7 × 8⅞ inches

93.8.134

This drawing, along with two others in the Rinhart Collection,[1] stems from Greenough's efforts during the last decade of his career to create a publicly acceptable statue of Washington. Here Greenough has drawn Washington on a rearing horse, most likely influenced by Clark Mills's bronze statue of Andrew Jackson (1848–53, Lafayette Square, Washington, D.C.).

Immediately on his return to Italy in 1842, Greenough began to design an equestrian statue of Washington, clad in a uniform of the Revolution, which he hoped to execute in Boston or New York.[2] Some years later Everett recalled that Greenough's motivation resulted from "the bitterness of his heart, saying that he intended to make an equestrian statue of Washington in small-clothes and Hussar boots, to show his loving countrymen that he was a tolerable tailor and bootmaker, which they seemed to think was the main thing in a sculptor."[3]

It was not for another decade, however, until Greenough had the

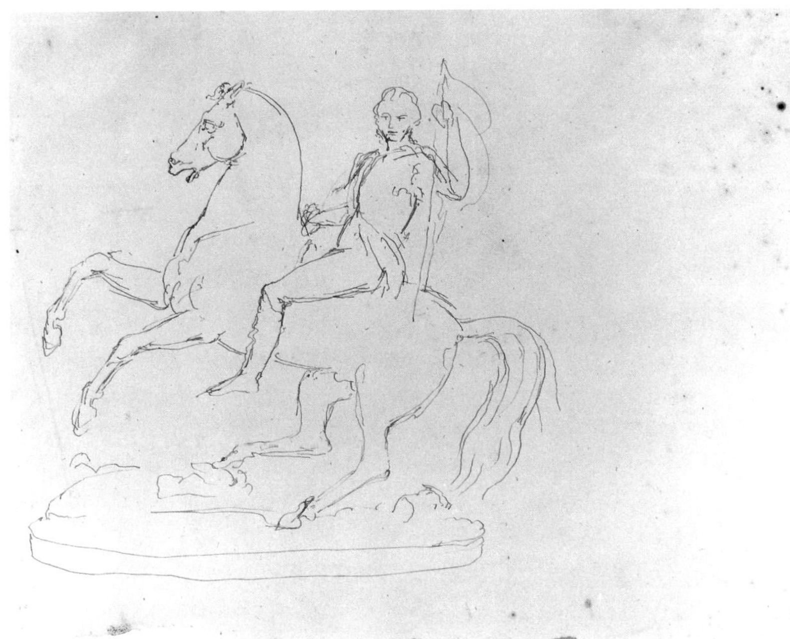

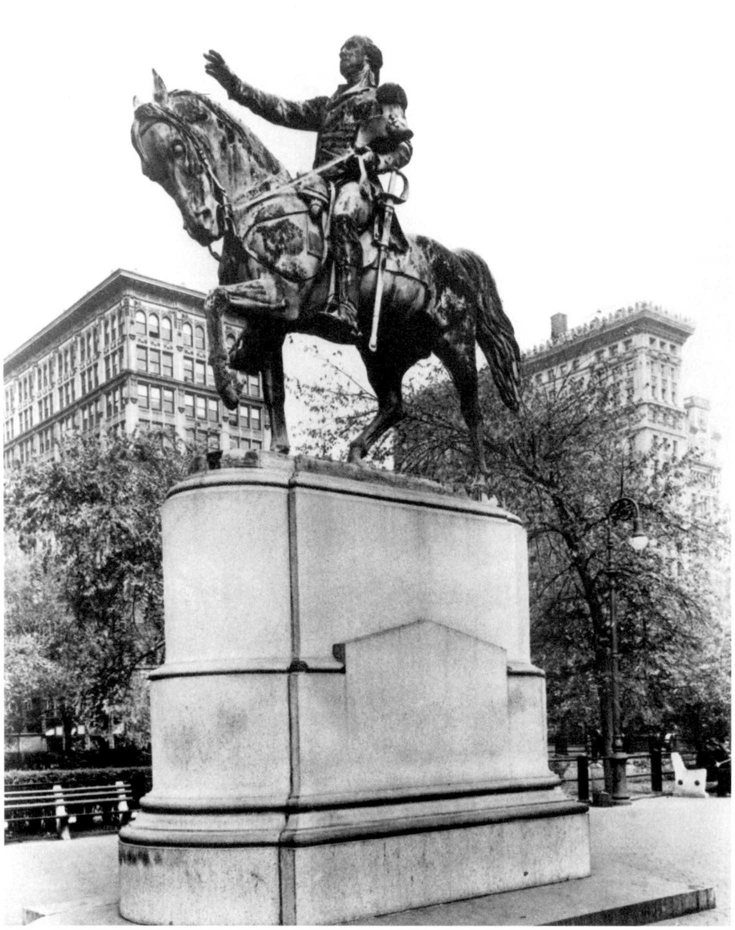

Fig. 47. Henry Kirke Brown, *George Washington*, 1853–56. Bronze. Collection of the City of New York.

opportunity to act on such wishes. In the spring of 1852 Greenough and a second sculptor, Henry Kirke Brown, were jointly commissioned by a group of New Yorkers to create a bronze equestrian monument of Washington. While Greenough brought an international reputation to the project, Brown, who then had a studio in Brooklyn, contributed experience at casting bronze. Despite this presumably awkward relationship with a second sculptor, Greenough was particularly intrigued by the prospect of this commission, which specified that Washington be shown in contemporary military attire and on horseback. By April Greenough had determined that the sculpture would be fourteen feet high exclusive of the pedestal. He also embarked on a more ambitious design, which would entail figures of subordinate generals at the base of each corner and the figure of Benedict Arnold in the rear, veiled to the waist.[4] Before the end of the summer, however, Greenough's role in the project ended. Greenough had a falling-out with James Lee, a merchant who was the leader of the subscribers to the sculpture. When their disagreement over how the work was to be funded could not be resolved, the contract for the sculpture was transferred to Brown, who completed it by 1856 (fig. 47).[5]

1. 98.8.132 and 98.8.040.
2. Wright 1963a, p. 154.
3. Everett 1868, vol. 4, p. 156.
4. Horatio Greenough to George Bancroft, 7 May 1852.
5. Wright 1963a, p. 277, and Horatio Greenough to Samuel F. B. Morse, August 1852. Morse Papers, Library of Congress.

THE RESCUE

After his colossal figure of George Washington, *The Rescue* (see fig. 2)[1] is Greenough's most important work and, like it, was commissioned by the federal government to adorn the Capitol. His contract, signed in 1839, like that for Luigi Persico, provided for a statue nine feet high with a six-foot base to be completed in four years. Greenough was to be paid $21,000 in five installments. He started immediately, and John Gadsby Chapman, a fellow American artist, provided him with casts and drawings of Indian objects to assist him with accuracy. Because the work would be exposed to the elements, Greenough wanted the work to be in bronze.[2] But presumably because of the extra cost, he was unable to convince the government to do so. By late 1840 or early 1841 the first of Greenough's blocks of marble for the sculpture was quarried at Serravezza.

The theme of contact between Native Americans and European settlers was already part of the vocabulary of ornament for the Capitol by the time Greenough chose it for *The Rescue*. While many of these depictions are peaceful in nature, reliefs by Antonio Capellano and Enrico Causici (see fig. 9) had depicted combat. With *The Rescue* Greenough picked up where he had left off with his figure of a contemplative Indian on the chair of his colossal *Washington* (see fig. 43). Here, however, he sought to balance Persico's figure of Columbus and simultaneously depict the theme of the Indian's inevitable

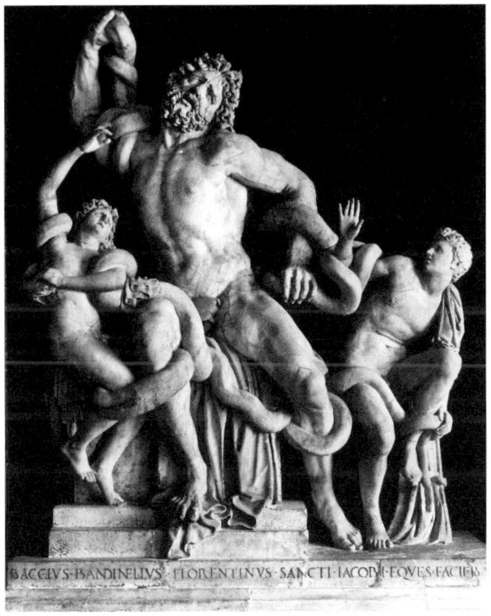

Fig. 48. *Laocoön*, A.D. 1st century. Marble, H. 95¼ inches. Rome, Musei Vaticani (Belvedere Courtyard). Courtesy of Alinari.

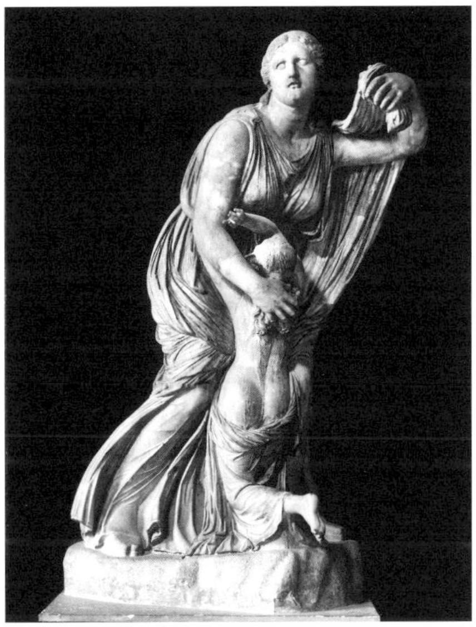

Fig. 49 . *Niobid Group*. Marble, H. 89¾ inches. Florence, Uffizi. Courtesy of Alinari.

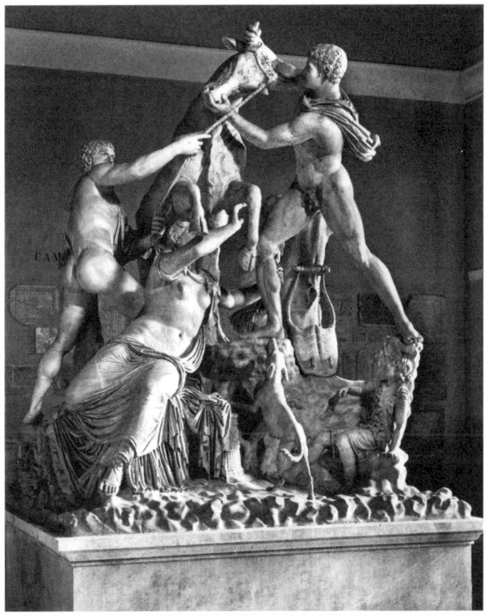

Fig. 50. *Farnese Bull*, A.D. 3rd century. Marble, H. 145⅝ inches. Naples, Museo Nazionale. Courtesy of Alinari.

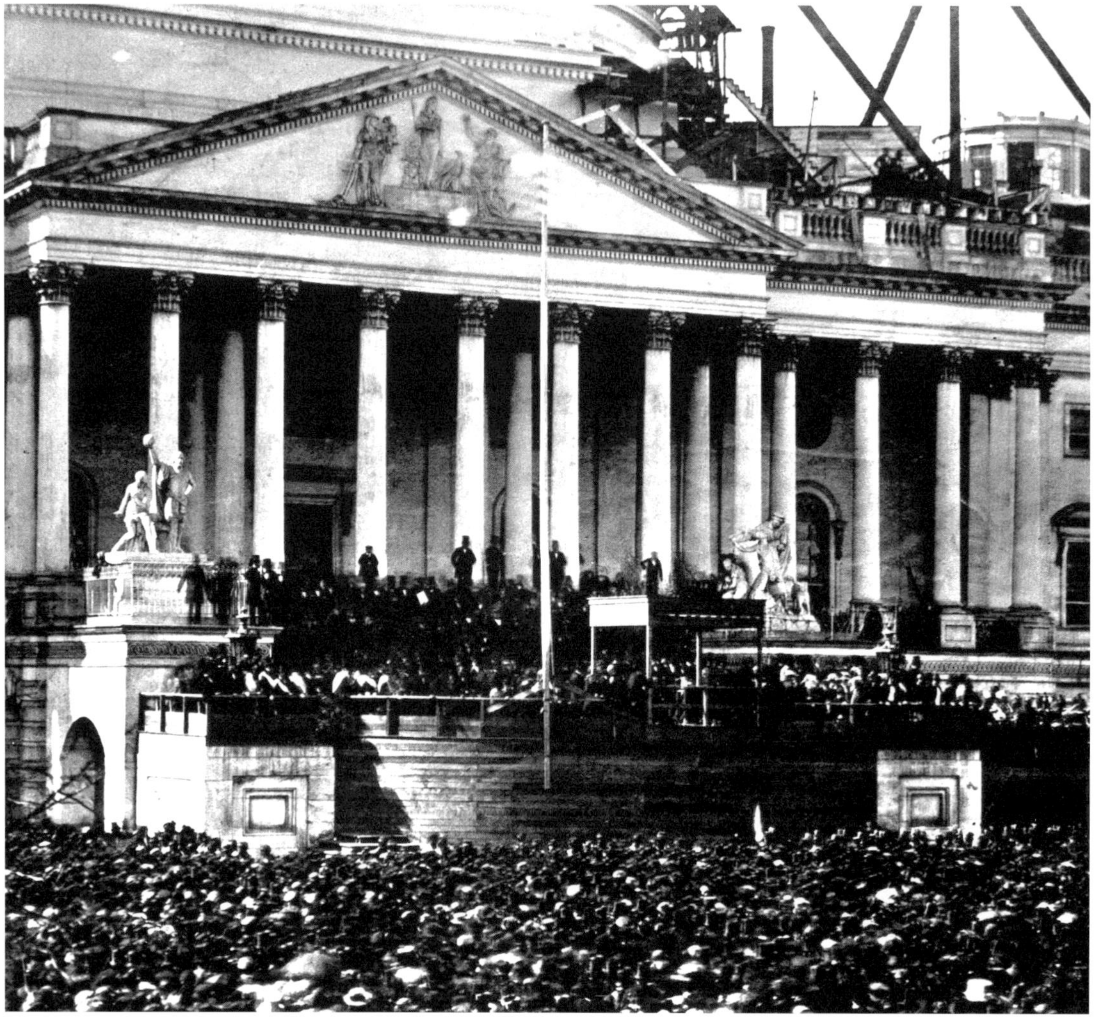

Fig. 51. Mathew Brady, *Inauguration of Abraham Lincoln, March 4, 1861.* Greenough's sculpture *The Rescue*, visible in right background. Courtesy Meserve-Kunhardt Collection.

subjugation. While many in government would have preferred a more sanitized image of this unavoidable conflict, they nevertheless agreed with its message of Manifest Destiny. It was a subject that occupied Congress repeatedly in the 1840s and 1850s.[3]

Greenough's composition for *The Rescue* was inspired by a variety of sources, but of particular importance were two well-known classical models. Given Greenough's great enthusiasm for the antique, it was natural for him to turn to the *Laocoön* (fig. 48) for the pose of the Indian, a figure locked in mortal combat, as well as the *Niobid Group* (fig. 49) for the mother and child. His decision to take the general pyramidal shape of the composition from the *Farnese Bull* (fig. 50), however, is more adventuresome, given the difference of opinion about the original's aesthetic importance by 1800.[4]

The Rescue's route to completion was tortuous and filled with numerous stops and starts. Some were the fault of the government, as when they failed to pay Greenough on a reasonable schedule. Others were the result of family distractions, such as the declining state of Louisa Greenough's health. Still others were beyond anyone's control, as when Czar Nicholas I of Russia reserved all the marble at the Serravezza quarries until his project for a church in St. Petersburg was complete.[5] This delay lasted four years.

By the fall of 1850 Greenough began to make arrangements to have *The Rescue* transported to America. In the subsequent months, however, confusion over its size and weight resulted in additional shipping delays. Ultimately, Greenough departed Italy before *The Rescue* did, and despite efforts on his part to be in Washington to supervise its installation, the work arrived and was installed after his death.

Unlike his statue of Washington, *The Rescue* was greeted with greater applause, and for the next 106 years it was visible behind each president as he took the oath of office (fig. 51). By the second quarter of the twentieth century, however, there began to be a call for the sculpture's removal. Although there had been the occasional objection to its theme in the nineteenth century, after territories with large Native American populations became states, more and more congressmen saw this sculpture as particularly insulting. Beginning in 1939 resolutions were introduced for both the Greenough and Persico statues to be removed. This act was eventually accomplished in 1958, and they were removed in preparation for the Capitol expansion.

Once they were removed, no one called for the sculptures' return. For the past forty years *The Rescue* has remained in storage. In 1976, when it was being transported from one storage area to another, it was accidentally dropped. The only piece left intact was that of the dog (cat. 63). Since that time it has remained in pieces at the government storage facility at Suitland, Maryland.

1. His first title for this work was *The Indian and the Backwoodsman*. See Horatio Greenough to Edward Everett, 1 September 1853. National Archives, Letters Received, vol. 33, Numbers 3233–3306, 6 January 1852 to 23 December 1853.
2. Horatio Greenough to Daniel Webster, 16 March 1841.
3. Fryd 1992, p. 98.
4. Haskell and Penny 1981, pp. 165–167, 243–247.
5. Horatio Greenough to Joseph Green Cogswell, 26 September 1850.

59 *Washington Raising from the Ground the Figure of America*

c. 1837

Graphite and pen and ink, 11¾ × 8⅛ inches

93.8.146

This drawing is one of the two designs Greenough submitted in 1837 as possible choices for a sculptural group to serve as a pendant to that being sculpted by Luigi Persico to flank the east steps to the Capitol. Persico chose to sculpt *The Discovery of America*. In addition to the subject that became known as *The Rescue*, Greenough offered as an

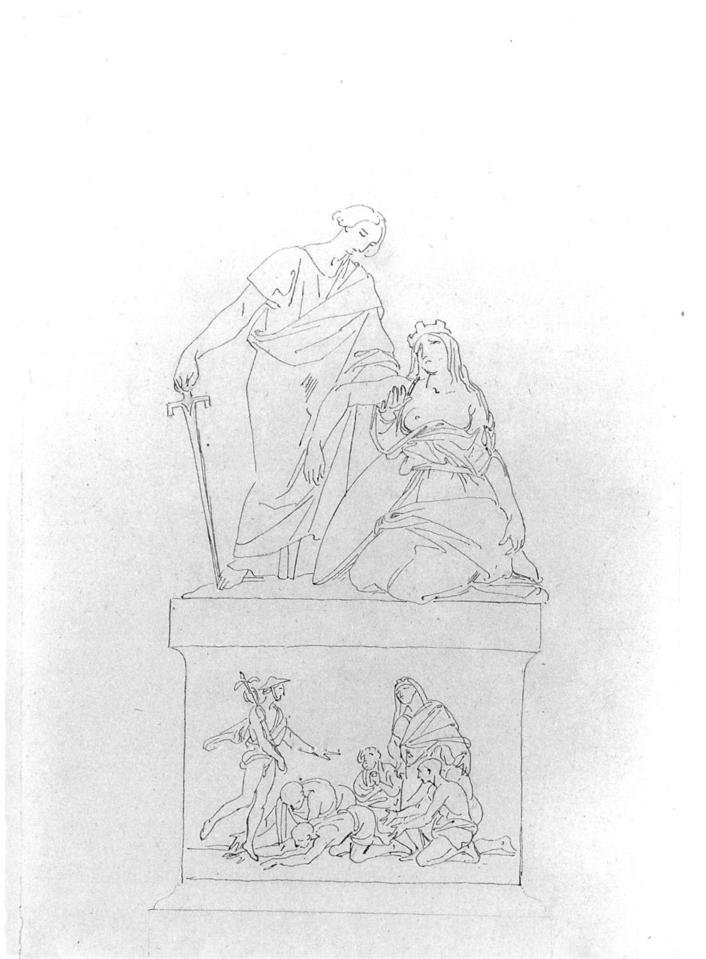

alternative this subject: "Washington raising from the ground the figure of America." While he admitted that such a subject would balance Persico's composition "figure for figure," he suggested that some observers might criticize its lack of specificity to a particular historical event. So as to leave no confusion that his real choice was for the subject seen in *The Rescue*, he described this alternative as bordering on the commonplace and "superfluous, since Washington's agency in achieving our liberties, is more distinctly told elsewhere in the same edifice."[1]

On 16 October he sent Secretary of State Forsyth a letter, presumably accompanied by a design for this group.[2] Although neither document survives, the drawing was probably similar to this one. Greenough has depicted a youthful Washington extending his hand to a sorrowful America kneeling before him. Below these figures is a bas-relief that depicts the somewhat obscure classical myth of Perseus coming to the rescue of Andromeda and the Ethiopians. The subject is actually one that had been part of Greenough's pictorial subject file for many years. As early as 1825 he had proposed a related subject as one of the four sculptural groups for his Bunker Hill Monument (cat. 2). Given the two options, it probably came as little surprise to Greenough when the government endorsed the theme of *The Rescue*.

1. Horatio Greenough to John Forsyth, 1 July 1837.
2. State Department, Index of Letters Received by the Secretary of State.

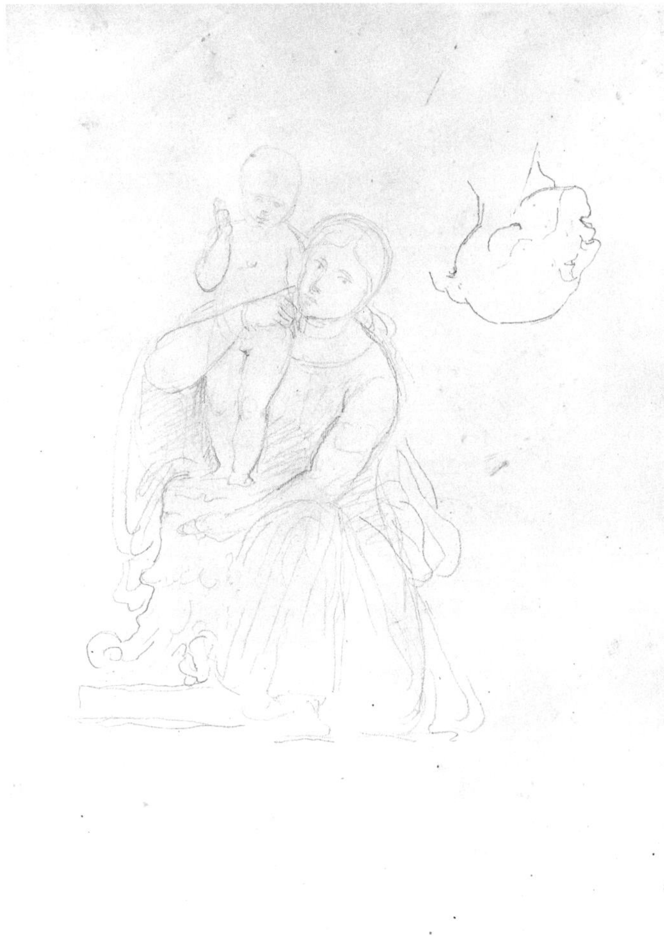

60 Study for *The Rescue*

c. 1839–41

Graphite, 11¾ × 8 inches

93.8.103

This is the earliest of the three surviving drawings for *The Rescue*. It shows a kneeling mother and her nude child standing on a tree stump. It is readily apparent that Greenough's immediate model was a Renaissance Madonna, but in subsequent drawings he abandoned the static and awkward elements of this figural arrangement to make his composition more active. The drawing was most likely made between signing the contract for *The Rescue* and October 1841, by which time the figures were cast.

The theme of *The Rescue* had been part of Greenough's thinking for some time. For example, in his 1831 design for a national monument to Washington he had included "a Mother clasping her infants while an Indian steals behind her."[1] In fact, as early as 1828 he had also made sketches of Indian visitors to Charles Bird King's studio and admitted to his brother, "I should like much to model an Indian skulking."[2]

1. Horatio Greenough to James Fenimore Cooper, 7 March 1831.
2. Greenough 1887, Horatio Greenough to Henry Greenough, 8 March 1828. Several other sketches in the Rinhart Collection also depict Indian subjects. The most notable is an Indian on horseback (93.8.156).

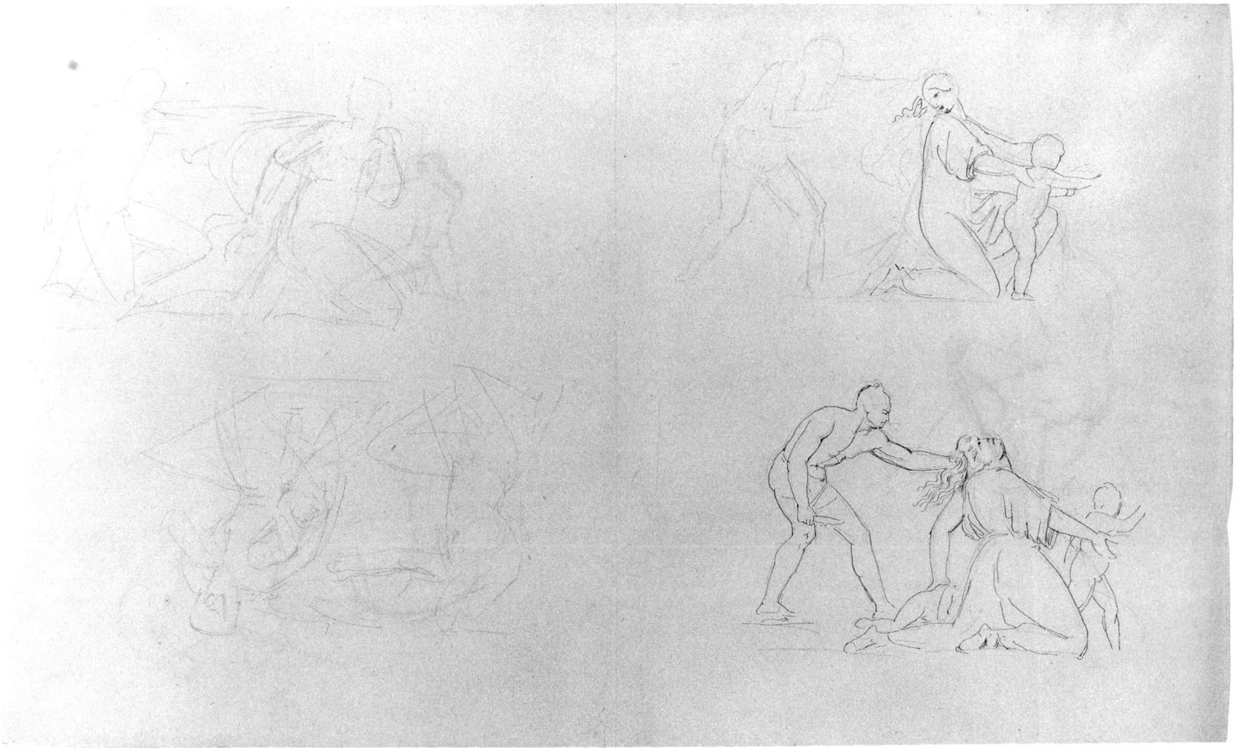

61 Studies for *The Rescue*

verso: Studies for the Indian in *The Rescue*

c. 1839–41

Graphite, 10⅛ × 16¾ inches (double sheet)

93.8.99

Greenough's thinking evolved from depicting a static image of the mother and child to the sequence seen on the right side of this sheet in which the Indian grasps the woman's hair to pull her backward. Greenough very likely recalled John Vanderlyn's painting, *The Death of Jane McCrea* (1804, Wadsworth Atheneum), which depicts virtually the same arrangement of Indian and pioneer woman.

He later abandoned the idea of direct physical contact when he decided these two particular figures needed to be carved from separate blocks of marble.

62 Study for *The Rescue*

verso: Study for *Castor and Pollux* and figure of a young man

1846–47

Graphite, 9⅞ × 15¾ inches (double sheet)

93.8.127

Of the three surviving drawings for *The Rescue*, this is the last and most important, as it depicts Greenough's final configuration for the group. Greenough's working method was to cast in plaster from the clay model and carve the sculpture from independent marble blocks: the mother and child from one, the Indian and pioneer from a second, the dog from a third. As a result he seems to have considered alternative configurations for the relationship between the two larger blocks. Although the figures of the mother, child, pioneer, and Indian were cast in October 1841, the delays Greenough experienced in

getting the marble blocks from the quarry meant the figures were not carved until late in 1849.

By 1850 the sculpture was transported from Florence to Leghorn in five boxes. Greenough's agents, however, had underestimated both the crate sizes and weight of the sculpture (the largest case weighed 32 tons), and the ship expected to transport it could not handle this weight nor was it possible to get the crate into the hold. As a result, it was not until December 1852, shortly after Greenough's death, that final shipping arrangements were made for the sculpture. When it actually arrived in Washington, Clark Mills was appointed to supervise its installation.

Commentary about the work after its installation was generally favorable, although about six years later Judge Edward G. Loring, brother-in-law to Frances Greenough, complained that Mills had misinterpreted the arrangement of the figures.[1] He argued that the figures of the mother and child should have been placed immediately in front of the Indian and pioneer. This drawing, however, confirms that the sculpture was installed as Greenough drew it. The mother and child are clearly to the side of the pioneer and Indian.[2]

The confusion resulted from a combination of factors. Greenough's death deprived those involved with the installation of his supervision. And just as he made adjustments to the height of his colossal *Washington* after its installation in the rotunda, one can imagine he may have wished to make similar adjustments to *The Rescue*, once he saw it in place. Further, it is not unreasonable to assume that he mentioned to his brother Henry that he was not entirely satisfied with *The Rescue* and anticipated such modifications once he got to Washington.

This sheet provides additional information that reinforces such speculation. The verso of this drawing depicts a study for Greenough's *Castor and Pollux*, which was sculpted in 1847. The presence of a work from this later period suggests that the study for *The Rescue* on the opposite side was, not a preliminary figure study prepared prior to casting (i.e., 1839–41), but rather a drawing done later when Greenough was still undecided about the relationship between the subgroups of the mother and child and the Indian and pioneer. That he continued to puzzle over the sculpture after the figures were cast in 1841 is confirmed by a reviewer who noted that "the figures of the mother and child were entirely remodeled in the year 1846 and '47."[3]

1. Judge Edward C. Loring to Senator James Pearce, chairman of the Joint Committee on the Library, 14 March 1859. Office of the Architect of the Capitol.

2. In September 1853 Henry Greenough wrote Edward Everett in response to a query about the configuration of *The Rescue*. He replied: "The group of the mother and child joins that of the male group, being placed on the *left* of that group as in this sketch: [sketch] The position of the dog (which was added to the composition after my leaving Florence) must, I fancy, be evident from an inspection of the sketch. It is scarcely necessary to say that when these pieces are properly put together, the spectator has a front view of the Indians and backwoodsmen facing the center of the composition, and a front view of the mother and child which are on the left of the spectator, although on the right of the principle figures." National Archives, Letters Received, vol. 33, numbers 3233–3306, 6 January 1852 to 23 December 1853.

3. Calvert 1853, p. 320.

63 Dog, from *The Rescue*

1837–51

Marble, 55⅛ × 60¼ × 28¾ inches

The United States Capitol, Washington, D.C.

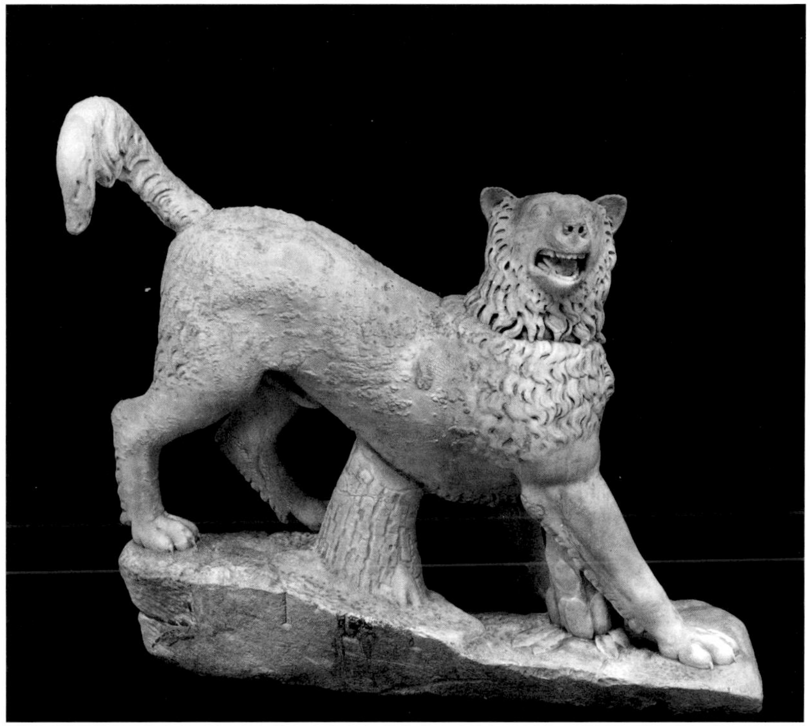

As Greenough developed this composition he never was able to overcome the fact that mentally and physically he composed it of separate elements: the Indian and pioneer for one; the mother and child for the other. Not only were these figures to be cut from separate blocks of stone, but when finished they had to be physically interlocked to create the larger sculpture. As a result, the figures are particularly stiff and disconnected.

In addition, Greenough realized that to achieve compositional balance he needed to add another component. It was primarily for this reason that he chose to add the figure of a dog, which he may have loosely based on a Newfoundland he owned during the 1830s.[1] In April 1851 he sent his brother a sketch of *The Rescue* and noted, "you will see by the enclosed sketch that I have introduced the household dog, but you do not see with what excellent effect. Take my word for it that it is a note wanting in the tune."[2] Inspiration for this element may also have come from the dog that plays a minor role in the *Farnese Bull* (see fig. 50). In so doing, however, Greenough failed to connect his dog fully to the larger composition. Its lack of alarm troubled some viewers, while others wondered about its breed.

1. Greenough 1887, Alfred Greenough to Horatio Greenough, 30 August 1830. The dog also resembles the Cerberus in Thomas Crawford's *Orpheus*, which was sculpted during a period when the two artists had recently become friends. See Dimmick 1987.
2. Greenough 1887, Horatio Greenough to Henry Greenough, 14 April 1851.

Portraits of Greenough

64 Hiram Powers (1805–1873)

Horatio Greenough

1838–54

Marble, 26½ × 14 × 9¼ inches

Signed on back: *H. Powers/ Sculp*

Museum of Fine Arts, Boston. Bequest of Charlotte Gore Greenough Hervosches du Quilliou

This bust is the one surviving sculpture to result from the cordial but uneasy relationship that existed between Greenough and Powers.[1] The two artists met in Washington during the summer of 1836 on one of Greenough's infrequent trips to the United States. By the following year Powers and his wife took up residence in Florence. There, over the next fourteen years, the two sculptors saw each other frequently.

Although the two artists were the same age, Powers lacked Greenough's education, knowledge of Italian, and cosmopolitan flair. Greenough relished the opportunity to nurture Powers and was magnanimous toward him. While certainly not Greenough's protégé, Powers, at least in the first years of their relationship, turned to the more established artist for advice and assistance. Greenough, for example, lent Powers workmen and marble, introduced him to the chief artists of Florence at a dinner (at which Greenough had sculptures by Powers displayed), purchased his bust of John Quincy Adams for $1,000, recommended him for government employment, and praised him in print. The two artists also jointly imported clay for modeling and in the fall of 1838, together with three other artists, formed a club that met weekly.[2]

In 1838 Greenough wrote his brother Henry that Powers "is making an admirable bust of me. I like him very much, and esteem his talent as highly as ever."[3] This bust is the only sculpture of Greenough to survive and depicts a mature young man wearing fashionable muttonchop whiskers. His head is cocked to his left, and his firm expression suggests a confident air entirely consistent with Greenough's status: recently married to a Boston heiress and at work on two commissions for the United States Capitol.

The bust is one of Powers's finest early works and was done at his request, in one sense a form of flattery by the less-established sculptor. A plaster was cast during the year it was sculpted, yet Powers's attempt to have the work carved in marble was halted when a work-

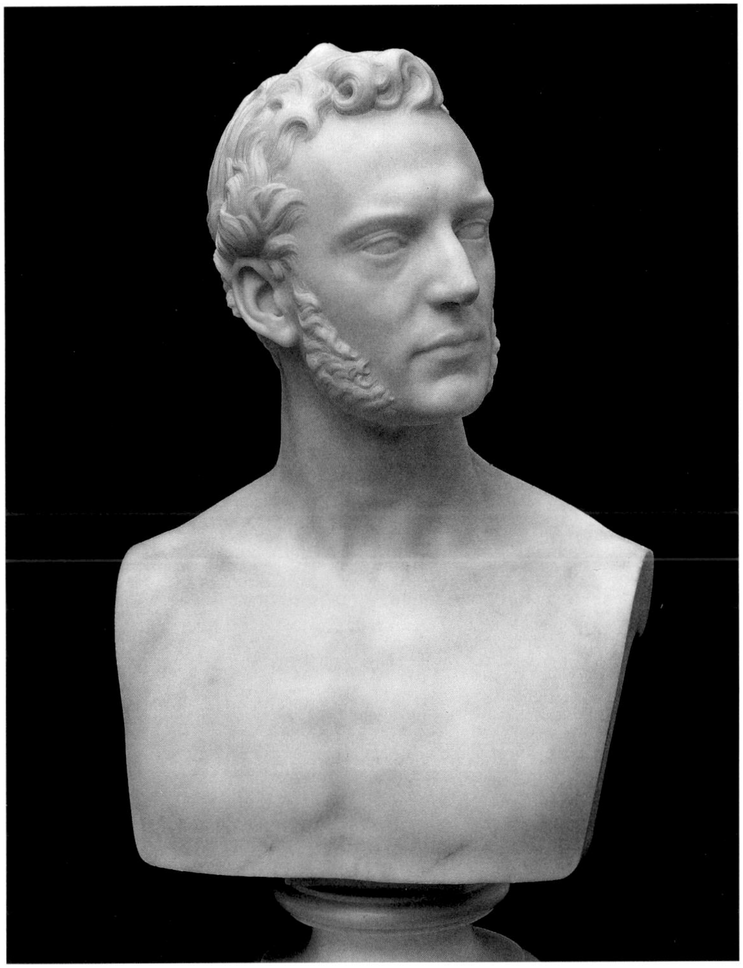

man blundered in carving the hair.[4] For this replica, which was commissioned by Louisa Greenough after her husband's death, Powers only charged for the cost of the marble.[5]

Unlike the urbane Greenoughs who in the late 1830s entertained lavishly, the Powerses came from a far more modest background and, to some degree, envied the more established couple. Mrs. Powers admitted to feeling patronized by the Greenoughs when she observed, "Being possessed of an ample fortune they live in a palace & she has her carriage, servants, etc. . . . of course has little time or inclination to visit me in a social manner. She is amiable & friendly and I have stated the above not as a complaint, but merely as a matter of fact."[6] Despite such social inequities, Greenough's physician cared for the Powerses' son during his fatal illness, and Greenough's sister Louisa attended Mrs. Powers at the birth of their first daughter, who was named Louisa Greenough Powers in her honor.[7]

As the careers of the two sculptors took different paths, Powers developed a degree of conceit. In a letter to his wife he noted that he did not think that Greenough "has an eye for likenesses. I should not have known his bust of Mr. [John Quincy] Adams [cat. 16]. I should be loath to say these things publicly, although I hear others say so frequently. They say his ideal works are much better."[8] After Greenough's death he remarked to Nathaniel Hawthorne that he thought Greenough was unable to make a good bust.[9]

By the time Greenough left Italy in 1851 he publicly would admit to no bitterness in their relationship. He must have found it very difficult, however, to read of Powers's enormous success with *The Greek Slave*, when it was exhibited at the Crystal Palace Exhibition in London that year. On Greenough's death Powers observed that "it shocked me a good deal, but it did not surprise me so much. His mind had been affected more or less for years. I have often heard him make strange remarks. . . . We were once together on the bank of the Arno at the Cascine, talking pleasantly, when suddenly he stared at something apparently before him, and exclaimed: 'Did *you* see that?' 'What? Where?' 'Why just there before us.' He rushed across our path and leapt into the river. At this he rubbed his forehead, and presently became as calm and sensible in his conversation as before."[10]

1. Wunder 1991, vol. 2, p. 48, notes that in 1839 Powers sculpted a bust of Greenough's younger sister, Louisa Greenough (1809–1892). It is presently unlocated.
2. Wright 1963a, p. 210.
3. Greenough 1887, Horatio Greenough to Henry Greenough, 27 April 1838.
4. Wright 1963a, p. 210.
5. Hiram Powers to Louisa Gore Greenough, 19 May 1853. Hiram Powers Papers, Archives of American Art, Smithsonian Institution. An entry in Powers's ledger for 1859 again mentions Greenough's bust being carved. This may be a reference to a second, unlocated marble.
6. Elizabeth G. Powers to her mother, 3 March 1842. Quoted in Wright 1963a, p. 211.
7. Greenthal, Kozol, and Ramirez 1986, p. 32.
8. Hiram Powers to Elizabeth Gibson Powers, 2 July 1837. Hiram Powers Papers, Archives of American Art, Smithsonian Institution.
9. Wright 1963a, p. 212.
10. Hiram Powers to Edward Everett, 12 January 1853. Hiram Powers Papers, Archives of American Art, Smithsonian Institution.

65 William J. Hubard (1809–1862)

Horatio Greenough

c. 1838–39

Oil on canvas, 36 × 29⅛ inches

Valentine Museum, Richmond, Virginia

During the winter of 1838–39 Greenough was visited by William Hubard, an English-born silhouettist, portrait painter, and sculptor. Hubard had arrived in America in 1824 and exhibited his silhouettes in an installation he called the Hubard Gallery. After a dispute with his manager, which left him penniless, he was variously encouraged by Gilbert Stuart, Robert W. Weir, and Thomas Sully to give up silhouettes for oil painting. Following a return trip to England (1826–28), Hubard painted in Philadelphia and Baltimore before settling in Gloucester County, Virginia.[1]

The occasion for this portrait was Hubard's second trip to Europe, at which time he was newly married and traveling with his wife, Maria Mason Tabb. He may have arrived with a letter of introduction from Greenough's patron Robert Gilmor, Jr., whose portrait Hubard had painted a few years before.[2]

Greenough appears to have endured rather than enjoyed the opportunity to sit for Hubard. It is the most ambitious portrait made of the sculptor and depicts him in his studio, nattily attired in a dressing gown. The darkened interior setting was favored by Hubard; however, in this instance it seems to accentuate Greenough's discomfort at being the sitter rather than the artist. The grim but debonair Greenough is accompanied by two greyhounds, presumably Arno (cat. 28) and a mate. Hubard has placed the sculptor in the room he used for modeling busts. In a pictorial conceit, Greenough is shown in the chair reserved for his own clients. Visible on the adjoining sculpture stand is a bust of Heloise, the ill-fated lover of Peter Abelard, the twelfth-century philosopher and theologian. Beside him on the floor are sketchbooks and an unidentified bust, possibly Venus. Behind him in the adjoining room is an unidentified ideal bust and a full-length figure of one of the Thomson boys playing badminton.

This canvas is a copy of the original. The first painting was unfortunately damaged in transport, as Hubard wrote Powers: "All my pictures that came by Italy were so injured as to be worth nothing. I shall be obliged to copy Greenough's again."[3] This painting was later acquired by Mann S. Valentine II, author and art enthusiast, whom Greenough met in New York in 1852.[4]

1. Caldwell and Rodriguez Roque 1994, pp. 531–532.
2. Hubard's portrait of Gilmor is in the Baltimore Museum of Art.
3. William J. Hubard to Hiram Powers, 20 January 1839. From the Papers of Mann S. Valentine II, Valentine Museum, Richmond, Virginia, quoted in Cooper 1993, p. 63.
4. Wright 1963a, pp. 272–273.

66 Unknown, possibly John Adams Whipple (1823–1891)

Horatio Greenough

1852

Daguerreotype, 2⅝ × 2⅛ inches, sixth plate

93.9.001

It is probably fitting that the last surviving portrait of Greenough is neither a sculpture nor a painting, but this daguerreotype. As it was Greenough's good friend Samuel F. B. Morse (cat. 22) who introduced the medium to America, Greenough was undoubtedly well familiar with its revolutionary qualities.

This portrait, a sixth plate, most likely was taken in Boston during the fall of 1852. It may be this daguerreotype that Louisa Greenough later described as "speaking" and made "a few weeks" before the sculptor's death.[1]

Set in a gilt oval window mat and silhouetted against a dark background, this daguerreotype is a remarkably poignant image. Here Greenough's head is turned in profile, like so many of the portrait sketches he made of friends. The format, with the head shown close to the picture plane, as well as the case, recall other works by Whipple.[2]

Lacking any accessories, the format focuses the viewer's attention on the sitter's somber expression. This image confirms that the events of recent years had aged Greenough considerably beyond his forty-seven years. Appearing weary and tense, it is not hard to believe that Greenough's fragile state of mind would be easily fractured by the series of professional disappointments and financial setbacks that emerged in the last months of 1852.[3]

Earlier in 1852, while in New York, Greenough manifested a growing interest in the daguerreotype medium. He was there primarily to create an equestrian monument to Washington but also in hopes that

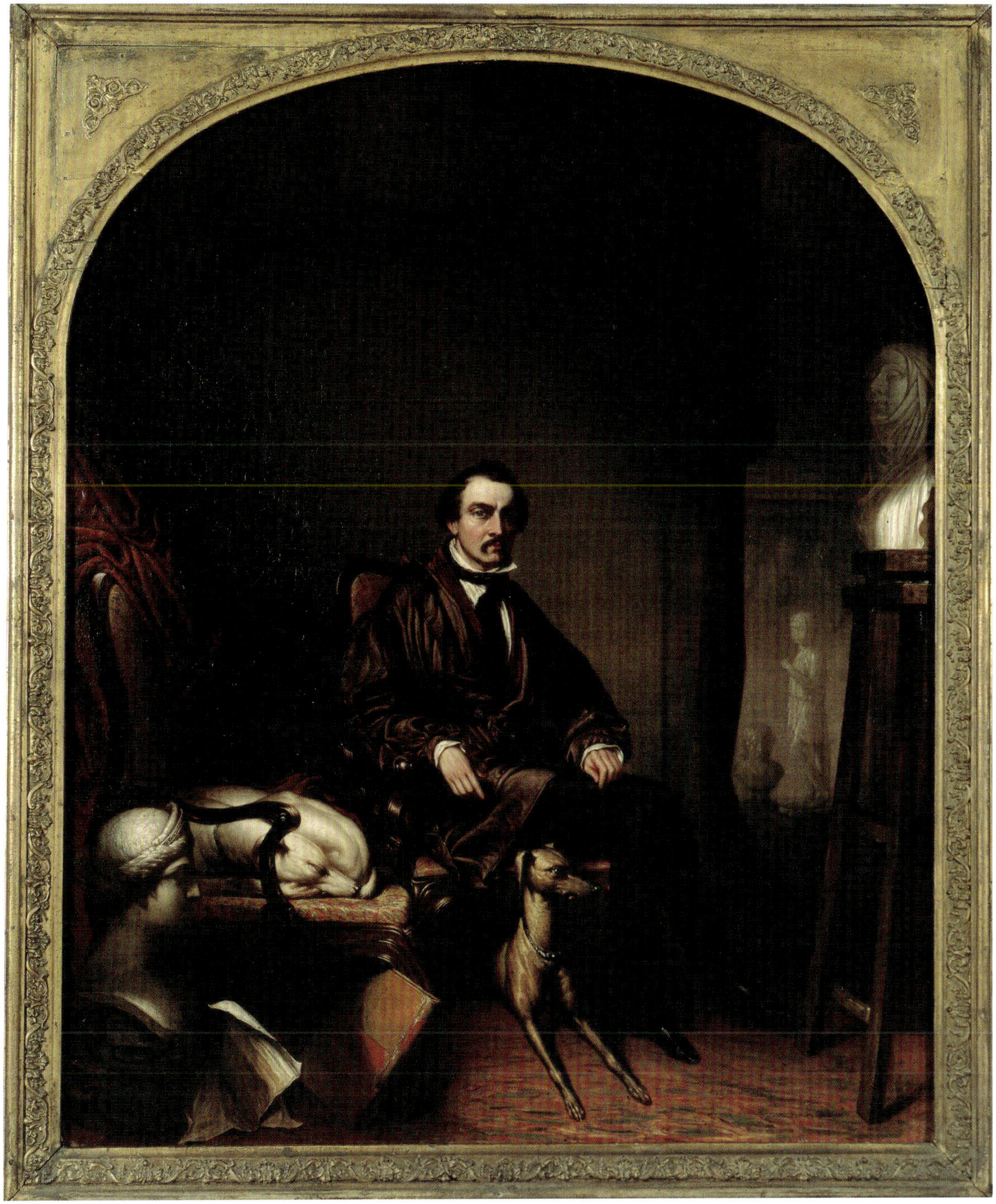

[65]

he might generate sufficient interest in a monument to Cooper, who had recently died. In April he wrote Henry that he had visited Mathew Brady, among the most prominent daguerreotypists of the period: "I have a superb daguerreotype of Cooper which Brady furnished, seeing 'I was one of the brotherhood.' He wanted to add my phiz to his collection; but I escaped by asking him to wait till I shaved, which he said he would do gladly, as he thought I should be much improved!"[4] On 4 May he was back at Brady's studio to meet Fitz-Greene Halleck, the poet and editor, whose profile he planned to engrave from a daguerreotype they had arranged to have taken.[5]

1. Louisa Gore Greenough to Hiram Powers, 2 April 1863, cited in Wright 1963a, pp. 280, 356n.
2. Pierce 1987, pp. 5, 7, 10.
3. This daguerreotype, as well as a second, was acquired by Nathalia Wright as part of the Petit Sully Collection.
4. Greenough 1887, Horatio Greenough to Henry Greenough, 12 April 1852. The date of this letter is a puzzle, as on 22 April 1852 Brady and his wife are reported in the *New York Daily Times* as being passengers on the ship *Gallia*, which just arrived in New York. See Panzer 1997, p. xvi.
5. Horatio Greenough to Fitz-Greene Halleck, 4 May 1852.

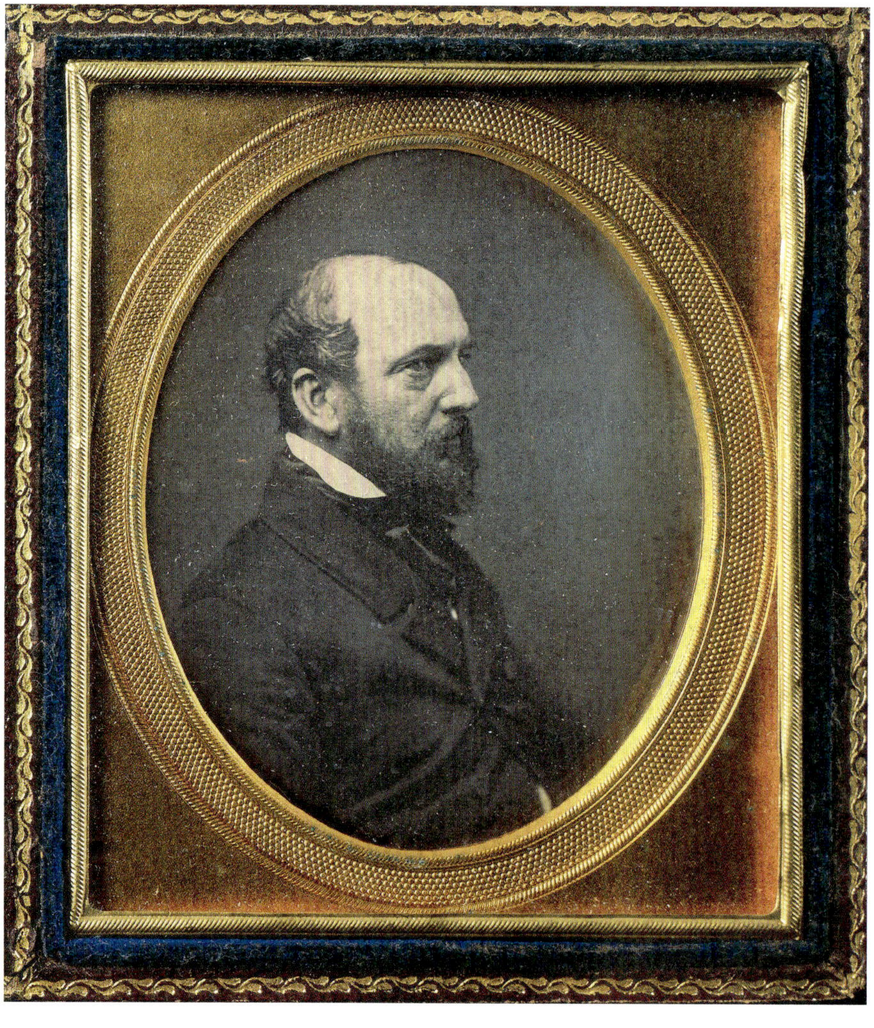

[66]

Works Cited

Beard 1960–68
Beard, James Franklin, ed. *The Letters and Journals of James Fenimore Cooper.* 6 vols. Cambridge, Mass.

Bronson 1928
Bronson, Charlotte Brinckerhoff. *The Letters of Charlotte Brinckerhoff Bronson.* Cambridge, Mass.

Brumbaugh 1955
Brumbaugh, Thomas B. "Horatio and Richard Greenough: A Critical Study with a Catalogue of Their Sculpture." Ph.D. diss., Ohio State University.

Brumbaugh 1971
———. "Horatio Greenough in the Classic Mold." *Antiques* 99, no. 2: 252–256.

Bryant 1850
Bryant, William Cullen. *Letters of a Traveller.* New York.

Caldwell and Rodriguez Roque 1994
Caldwell, John, and Oswald Rodriguez Roque. *American Paintings in the Metropolitan Museum of Art.* Volume 1. New York.

Calvert 1853
Calvert, George. "Greenough, the Sculptor." *Putnam's Magazine* 1, no. 3: 317–320.

Campbell and Carlson 1993
Campbell, Richard J., and Victor Carlson. *Visions of Antiquity: Neoclassical Figure Drawings.* Los Angeles.

Chamberlain 1959
Chamberlain, Georgia S. "Horatio Greenough's Proposed Designs for the United States Coinage." *Art Quarterly* 22, no. 3: 257–271.

Cooper 1993
Cooper, Wendy. *Classical Taste in America.* New York.

Cowdrey 1943
Cowdrey, Mary Bartlett. *National Academy of Design Exhibition Record, 1826–1860.* New York.

Crane 1972
Crane, Sylvia. *White Silence: Greenough, Powers, and Crawford, American Sculptors in Nineteenth-Century Italy.* Coral Gables, Fla.

Craven 1963
Craven, Wayne. "Horatio Greenough's Statue of Washington and Phidias' Olympian Zeus." *Art Quarterly* 26: 429–440.

Craven 1984
———. *Sculpture in America.* Newark, Del.

***DAB* 1964**
Dictionary of American Biography. Edited by Dumas Malone, under the auspices of the American Council of Learned Societies. 22 vols. New York. Reprint. Edited by Allen Johnson and Dumas Malone. 11 vols. New York.

Dimmick 1987
Dimmick, Lauretta. "Thomas Crawford's *Orpheus*: The American *Apollo Belevedere.*" *American Art Journal* 19, no. 4: 47–85.

Dimmick 1991
———. "Mythic Proportion: Bertel Thorvaldsen's Influence in America." In *Thorvaldsen: l'ambiente, l'influsso, il mito,* edited by Patrick Kragelund and Mogen Nykjaer. Analecta Romana Instituti Danici, Supplement 18: 169–191.

Dunlap 1918
Dunlap, William. *A History of the Rise and Progress of the Arts of Design in the United States.* 1834. New ed., edited by Frank W. Bayley and Charles E. Goodspeed. 3 vols. Boston.

Emerson 1909–14
Emerson, Ralph Waldo. *Journals of Ralph Waldo Emerson.* 10 vols. Boston.

Everett 1842
Everett, Edward. "American Sculptors in Italy." *Boston Miscellany of Literature* 1: 4–9.

Everett 1868
———. *Orations and Speeches on Various Occasions.* 4 vols. Boston.

Freedman 1992
Freedman, Paula B. *A Checklist of American Sculpture at Yale University.* New Haven.

Fryd 1992
Fryd, Vivien Green. *Art and Empire: The Politics of Ethnicity in the United States Capitol, 1815–1860.* New Haven.

Frye 1978
Frye, Roland Mushat. *Milton's Imagery and the Visual Arts.* Princeton, N.J.

Gale 1964
Gale, Robert L. *Thomas Crawford: American Sculptor.* Pittsburgh.

Gerdts 1973
Gerdts, William H. *American Neo-Classic Sculpture.* New York.

Gerdts and Stebbins 1979
Gerdts, William H., and Theodore E. Stebbins, Jr. *"A Man of Genius": The Art of Washington Allston (1779–1843).* Boston.

Greenough 1887
Greenough, Frances Bott, ed. *Letters of Horatio Greenough to His Brother, Henry Greenough.* Boston.

Greenough 1958
Greenough, Horatio. *The Travels, Observations, and Experience of a Yankee Stonecutter.* 1852. Gainesville, Fla.

Greenthal, Kozol, and Ramirez 1986
Greenthal, Kathryn, Paula M. Kozol, and Jan Seidler Ramirez. *American Figurative Sculpture in the Museum of Fine Arts, Boston.* Boston.

Harris 1970
Harris, Neil. *The Artist in American Society: The Formative Years, 1790–1860.* New York.

Haskell and Penny 1981
Haskell, Francis, and Nicholas Penny. *Taste and the Antique.* New Haven.

Headley 1991
Headley, Janet A. "Horatio Greenough's Heroic Subjects: *Abdiel* and *David*." *Yale University Art Gallery Bulletin,* 32–47.

Hunisak 1994
Hunisak, John M. *Carvings, Casts, and Replicas.* Middlebury, Vt.

Hyland 1981
Hyland, Douglas K. S. "Lorenzo Bartolini and the Italian Influences on American Sculptors in Florence, 1825–50." Ph.D. diss., University of Delaware.

James-Gadzinski and Cunningham 1997
James-Gadzinski, Susan, and Mary Mullen Cunningham. *American Sculpture in the Museum of American Art of the Pennsylvania Academy of the Fine Arts.* Philadelphia.

Jarves 1960
Jarves, James Jackson. *The Art-Idea.* 1864. Cambridge, Mass.

Lawrence 1855
Lawrence, Amos. *Extracts from the Diary and Correspondence of the Late Amos Lawrence.* Boston.

Metzger 1954
Metzger, Charles R. *Emerson and Greenough.* Berkeley, Calif.

Murray and Murray 1963
Murray, Peter, and Linda Murray. *Dictionary of Art and Artists.* Baltimore.

Neal 1943
Neal, John. *Observations on American Art: Selections from the Writings of John Neal (1793–1876).* State College, Pa.

New Haven 1977
English Landscape 1630–1850: Drawings, Prints, and Books from the Paul Mellon Collection. Yale Center for British Art. New Haven.

Oliver 1970
Oliver, Andrew. *Portraits of John Quincy Adams and His Wife.* Cambridge, Mass.

Panzer 1997
Panzer, Mary. *Mathew Brady and the Image of History.* Washington, D.C.

Perkins and Gavin 1980
Perkins, Robert F., Jr., and William J. Gavin III, eds. *The Boston Athenæum Art Exhibition Index, 1827–1874.* Boston.

Pierce 1987
Pierce, Sally. *Whipple and Black: Commercial Photographers in Boston.* Boston.

Sadik and Pfister 1980
Sadik, Marvin, and Harold Francis Pfister. *American Portrait Drawings.* Washington, D.C.

Staiti 1989
Staiti, Paul J. *Samuel F. B. Morse.* Cambridge.

Stebbins 1976
Stebbins, Theodore E., Jr. *American Master Drawings and Watercolors.* New York.

Stebbins 1992
———. *The Lure of Italy: American Artists and the Italian Experience, 1760–1914.* Boston.

Stony Brook 1980
A Time to Mourn: Expressions of Grief in the Nineteenth Century. The Museums at Stony Brook, N.Y.

Swett 1864
Swett, Samuel. "Horatio Greenough, the Designer of the Bunker Hill Monument." *New England Historical and Genealogical Register* 18: 60–65.

Ticknor 1909
Ticknor, George. *Life, Letters, and Journals of George Ticknor.* 2 vols. Boston.

Tuckerman 1967
Tuckerman, Henry T. *Book of the Artists: American Artist Life Comprising Biographical and Critical Sketches of American Artists: Preceded by an Historical Account of the Rise and Progress of Art in America.* 1867. New York.

Tuckerman 1968
———. *A Memorial of Horatio Greenough.* 1853. New York.

Vermeule 1975
Vermeule, Cornelius C. "Neoclassic Sculpture in America: Greco-Roman Sources and Their Results." *Antiques* 108, no. 5: 972–981.

Voss 1986
Voss, Frederick S. *John Frazee, 1790–1852, Sculptor.* Washington, D.C.

Wadlin 1911
Wadlin, Horace G. *The Public Library of the City of Boston.* Boston.

Warren 1877
Warren, George Washington. *The History of the Bunker Hill Monument Association.* Boston.

Wright 1955
Wright, Nathalia. "Horatio Greenough's Borrowings from the Harvard College Library." *Harvard Library Bulletin* 9: 405–410.

Wright 1960
———. "Francis Kinloch: A South Carolina Artist." *South Carolina Historical Magazine* 41: 99–100.

Wright 1963a
———. *Horatio Greenough: The First American Sculptor.* Philadelphia.

Wright 1963b
———. "Horatio Greenough's Roman Sketchbook." *Art Quarterly* 26, no. 3: 323–332.

Wright 1972
———, ed., *Letters of Horatio Greenough American Sculptor.* Madison, Wis.

Wunder 1991
Wunder, Richard P. *Hiram Powers, Vermont Sculptor, 1805–1873.* 2 vols. Newark, Del.

Index

Numerals in **bold type** indicate illustrations of works in the exhibition.